Image Processing

ESSEX SERIES IN TELECOMMUNICATION AND INFORMATION SYSTEMS

Series editors
Andy Downton
Ed Jones

Forthcoming titles
Computer Communication Networks
Speech Processing
Engineering the Human–Computer Interface
Satellite and Mobile Radio Systems

IMAGE PROCESSING

Edited by

Don Pearson

Department of Electronic Systems Engineering
University of Essex

McGRAW-HILL BOOK COMPANY

London · New York · St Louis · San Francisco · Auckland
Bogotá · Caracas · Hamburg · Lisbon · Madrid · Mexico · Milan
Montreal · New Delhi · Panama · Paris · San Juan · São Paulo
Singapore · Sydney · Tokyo · Toronto

Published by
McGRAW-HILL Book Company (UK) Limited
SHOPPENHANGERS ROAD · MAIDENHEAD · BERKSHIRE · ENGLAND
TELEPHONE: 0628 23432
FAX: 0628 770224

British Library Cataloguing in Publication Data

Image processing
  1. Image processing
  I. Pearson, Don   II. Series
  621.3827

  ISBN 0-07-707323-1

Library of Congress Cataloging-in-Publication Data

Image processing
  editor Don Pearson.
    p.   cm.—(Essex series in telecommunications and information systems)
  Includes bibliographical references and index.
  ISBN 0-07-707323-1
  1. Image processing.   I. Pearson, D. E. (Donald Edwin)
  II. Series.
  TA1632.I4718   1991
  621.36'7—dc20   90-48420 CIP

1234 CUP 94321

Typeset by Computape (Pickering) Ltd, North Yorkshire
and printed and bound in Great Britain
at the University Press, Cambridge

Contents

Part 2   Implementation

Part 3   Coding

Notes on the contributors

Don Pearson studied for his PhD at Imperial College, London, which he received in 1965. Thereafter he spent a period at Bell Laboratories in the USA, returning to England in 1969 to take up an appointment at the University of Essex. He founded the Visual Systems Research Laboratory at the University, which is now active in a number of areas of digital image processing. In 1986 he was appointed Professor of Telecommunication and Information Systems in the Department of Electronic Systems Engineering. He has helped to organize over twenty conferences connected with image processing, including the 1979 Picture Coding Symposium, held at Ipswich, England, for which he was Program Chairman. From 1980 he has been a member of Professional Group E4 Committee (Image Processing and Vision) of the IEE, serving as Chairman from 1987 to 1989.

Adrian Clark is a lecturer in the Department of Electronic Systems Engineering at Essex, following periods with British Aerospace and King's College London. His main research interests are in software techniques and parallel algorithms for image processing and computer graphics, especially for restoration and remote-sensing applications. He is chairman of the BSI panel concerned with developing a standard application programmer interface for image processing.

Tim Dennis is a senior lecturer in the Department of Electronic Systems Engineering at the University of Essex. He obtained his PhD in 1977 from the same department for work on real-time digital interframe coding techniques for video. His teaching and research interests remain in applications of digital picture processing, for image coding and industrial uses. He holds patents on implementations of real-time colour video inspection systems.

Mohammed Ghanbari was born in Saveh, Iran, in 1948. He received his BSc in electrical engineering from Aryamehr University of Technology, Tehran, in 1970 and both his MSc in telecommunications and PhD from the University of Essex in 1976 and 1979, respectively. He was appointed a research officer in 1986 and later a lecturer in the

Department of Electronic Systems Engineering at the same university. His research work is connected with the data compression of television signals and the coding of video signals for packet-switched networks.

Graham Leedham obtained his BSc in electronic engineering from Leeds University in 1979. After a period in industry he returned to university, being awarded an MSc in 1981 and a PhD (for work on the automatic transcription of Pitman's shorthand) in 1985, both from Southampton University. Since 1984 he has been a lecturer in the Department of Electronic Systems Engineering of the University of Essex. His research interests are in the man–machine interface and the automatic recognition of handwriting.

Kirk Martinez studied physics at Reading University, then went on to obtain his PhD in parallel processing architectures for image processing at the University of Essex, where he was also a temporary lecturer for a year. He is currently Arts Computing lecturer in the History of Art Departments of University College and Birkbeck College, London. There he is researching into high-resolution colorimetric imaging of paintings as part of a European project (VASARI). His research interests include image-processing systems, parallelism, image coding, and analysis.

Charles Nightingale was born in South London in 1933. After four years' RAF service he took a mathematics degree at Woolwich Polytechnic. He worked at Standard Telephone and Cables designing filters before obtaining a PhD in 1971. He then joined British Telecom Research Laboratories, where he is now senior engineering advisor on neural nets and visual processing. He is the author of about forty papers and several books—both technical and non-technical.

Graham Thomas is a senior research engineer with the BBC Research Department, where he has worked since graduating in 1983 with an honours degree in physics. Much of his work has been in the field of digital image processing and has been concerned with motion compensation and its applications to broadcast television. He has been actively involved with the work of the Eureka HDTV project.

Gary Tonge joined the Independent Broadcasting Authority in 1980 after completing postgraduate research in applied mathematics at Southampton University. He was involved in the image-processing activities and HDTV work of the Authority's Experimental and Development Department until he took up his present post as head of the Engineering Secretariat in 1987. He has written over thirty papers in the fields of sampling, motion, and HDTV, and holds patents covering various picture quality-enhancement techniques applied to MAC transmission.

Bill Welsh graduated from Liverpool University in 1980 with a degree in electronics. In 1984, he joined the Visual Telecommunications Division of British Telecom Research Laboratories to work on image-coding algorithms. He began work on model-based coding in 1985 and has recently been involved in research into neural networks and computer vision. He is an external PhD student of Essex University.

Series preface

This book is part of a series, the *Essex Series in Telecommunication and Information Systems*, which has developed from a set of short courses run by the Department of Electronic Systems Engineering at the University of Essex since 1987. The courses are presented as one-week modules on the Department's MSc in Telecommunication and Information Systems, and are offered simultaneously as industry short courses. To date, a total of over 600 industrial personnel have attended the courses, in addition to the 70 or so postgraduate students registered each year for the MSc. The flexibility of the short course format means that the contents both of individual courses and of the courses offered from year to year have been able to develop to reflect current industrial and academic demand.

The aim of the book series is to provide readable yet authoritative coverage of key topics within the field of telecommunication and information systems. Being derived from a highly regarded university postgraduate course, the books are well suited to use in advanced taught courses at universities and polytechnics, and as a starting point and background reference for researchers. Equally, the industrial orientation of the courses ensures that both the content and the presentation style are suited to the needs of the professional engineer in mid-career.

The books in the series are based largely on the course notes circulated to students, and so have been 'class-tested' several times before publication. Though primarily authored and edited by academic staff at Essex, where appropriate each book includes chapters contributed by acknowledged experts from other universities, research establishments and industry (originally presented as seminars on the courses). Our colleagues at British Telecom Research Laboratories, Martlesham, have also provided advice and assistance in developing course syllabuses and ensuring that the material included correctly reflects industry practice as well as academic principles.

As series editors we would like to acknowledge the tremendous support we have had in developing the concept of the series from the original idea through to the publication of the first group of books. The successful completion of this project would not have been possible without the substantial commitment shown not only by individual authors but by the Department of Electronic Systems Engineering as a whole to this project. Particular thanks go to the editors of the individual books, each of whom, in addition to authoring several chapters, was responsible for integrating the various contributors' chapters of his or her book into a coherent whole.

July 1990   Andy Downton
                                                                       Ed Jones

Preface

Like others in the series, this book evolved from a set of notes for a one-week short course. The aim of the course was to bring together both academic and industrial viewpoints on the principles and practice of image processing in the field of telecommunication and computer communication systems. In drawing up a syllabus for the course, it proved to be difficult to place a boundary around the subject, since in recent times there has been much of relevance and interest going on in neighbouring areas such as computer vision and computer graphics. The presentations ended up featuring not only classical techniques such as filtering, sampling, and coding, but also some of the interdisciplinary areas concerned with image understanding.

The course itself has been a great success in terms of attendance, with students being drawn from a wide cross-section of industry as well as from other universities. There have also been MSc students, for whom it constituted an optional module. All the contributors to the book wish to express their thanks to the many students who, through their enthusiasm and questioning, helped to mould the content of the course (and the book) into its present form.

During the development of the course content, a constructive dialogue developed between those in academia and those outside it. This blend of theory and practice distinguishes the book from some of the more mathematical treatises on the subject. The reader may find that the mathematics is somewhat attenuated and the hardware and software aspects somewhat amplified in comparison with other academic offerings in the field. In practice, however, successful image-processing systems result from a judicious fusion of concepts, software, and hardware.

The book begins with an introductory chapter by Don Pearson which aims both to acquaint the non-specialist reader with some of the basic concepts and to provide a structural setting for some of the more specialist material in later chapters. The remaining chapters are divided into four sections, each with its own brief preface, which the reader may tackle with whatever degree of selectivity suits his or her preference.

1 Introduction

DON PEARSON

1.1 Scope of the book

Images are two-dimensional representations of the visual world. They are encountered in a wide variety of disciplines including art, human vision, astronomy, and engineering. *Image processing* is a term used to describe operations carried out on images, with the aim of accomplishing some purpose. This might be, for example, to convert the image into a form where it can be more easily transmitted over a telecommunication link or stored in computer memory; it might also be to reduce noise or to extract information of particular interest to a human observer. Common image-processing operations include filtering, sampling, scaling, coding, feature extraction, pattern recognition, and motion estimation (Pratt, 1978).

Several methods, including optical ones, can be used to process images, but most image processing is accomplished electronically, where it is possible to use the power and sophistication of modern computing hardware and software. As computers become faster, cheaper and smaller, with larger memories, so the opportunities for image processing become ever more interesting.

This book forms part of a series concerned with telecommunication and information systems. Particular emphasis therefore is given to those processing techniques that are found in telecommunications, computer communications, and broadcasting. Recent advances in broadband communication, particularly in the areas of optical-fibre networks and optical storage methods, are likely to result in many new services that use images. These include high-definition television, low bit rate video, and a variety of interactive systems. Reference is also made in the book to some of the ideas that have arisen, in recent years, in computer graphics and in machine and human vision. These ideas are currently interacting with the more classical concepts in image processing to produce some profoundly novel developments.

This chapter provides an introduction, for the non-specialist reader, to some of the ideas pursued by other contributors to the book.

1.2 Images and objects

The formation of an image using a lens is a fundamental and familiar operation in both photography and television. In electronic imaging

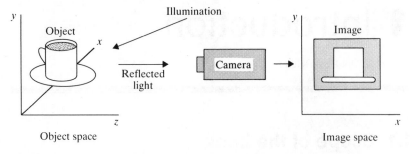

Figure 1.1 The formation of images using an electronic camera.

(Fig. 1.1), light falling on an object is reflected towards the camera and is imaged onto a photosensitive surface; this is then scanned to produce an electrical representation.

The image obtained from an object depends fundamentally on two factors, namely the nature of the illumination and the way in which the surfaces of the object reflect that illumination towards the camera. There is considerable complexity and fascination in considering how light with different spatial and wavelength distributions of energy, reflected from surfaces of different material at various orientations, gives rise to form, shading and colour in images. This subject has received particular attention in recent years from those concerned with computer vision (Horn, 1986).

Certain concepts and units are commonly used in describing images. As light is a form of electromagnetic radiation, it is possible to express its power in *radiometric units*, for example in watts or watts per square metre. More frequently we take account of the fact that the human eye's sensitivity to light depends on the wavelength, with a peak in the yellow–green around 555 nm. By applying a weighting curve (the so-called V_λ function) to the distribution of electromagnetic power over the visible region, we obtain *photometric units*. The common photometric unit for the illumination in Fig. 1.1 is the *lux*, while that for reflected light from a small patch on an object in a particular direction is the *candela per square metre* (cd/m^2). The cd/m^2 is a measure of *luminance*, which is related to the perceived brightness of the patch as we humans see it. Self-luminous areas in displays are also typically described by their luminance.

Mathematically, image formation can be represented as a mapping process from three-dimensional *object space* into two-dimensional *image space*. When the object is distant from the camera, this mapping is an orthographic projection of the visible surfaces of the object onto the image plane. For close objects, however, we need to use a perspective projection. In the mapping certain information is lost, as for example the handle of the cup in Fig. 1.1.

When considering operations on images, it is often instructive to

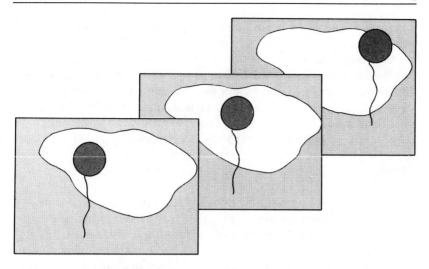

Figure 1.2 An image sequence.

imagine the equivalent effect on the object. This inverse mapping seeks to discover, for a particular patch of shading or colour in the image, what surface with what orientation under what illumination could have produced it. In general it is not possible to obtain an exact answer, but partial answers can be useful!

1.3 Mathematical representation

In the camera the image is converted into a video signal by scanning. The scanning process in television typically produces 25 or 30 new images every second, each being called a *frame* or *picture*. A succession of these frames, representing the movement of some object, is termed an *image sequence*. Figure 1.2 illustrates an image sequence of a balloon drifting across a background of a cloud in the sky.

How can we describe such a sequence mathematically? We note that the scanning process not only divides up time into frames, it also divides up the space within the image into lines. Most cameras produce their video output in analogue form, complete with blanking intervals when the scanning spot retraces at the end of a line or frame. In digital image processing there is a further sampling operation on the video signal that divides each scanning line into points, termed *picture elements* (usually abbreviated to *pels* or *pixels*). The end product is a three-dimensional array of numbers derived from the continuous, moving image on the photosensitive surface of the camera. Neglecting colour for a moment, we see therefore that an image sequence can be expressed as a function

$$g(\mathbf{n}) \equiv g(n_1, n_2, n_3)$$

where n_1, n_2 and n_3 are horizontal spatial, vertical spatial, and temporal dimensions.

Describing a point in space-time as a vector $\mathbf{n} = (n_1, n_2, n_3)$ is convenient in considering mathematical operations on images (Dubois, 1985). We could also use x, y and t to represent the independent variables, particularly before the image is scanned; however, the use of n_1, n_2, and n_3 is a reminder that an image sequence, for processing purposes, is a three-dimensional array. Two types of lattice structure are commonly encountered in image arrays and these are treated in Chap. 2. Chapters 7–10 give descriptions of the hardware and software used to store and access such arrays.

If the images are in colour, with red, green, and blue components, three functions could be used: $r(\mathbf{n})$, $g(\mathbf{n})$, and $b(\mathbf{n})$. It is more usual, however, to perform a colour transformation on the red, green, and blue camera signals and convert them (reversibly) into a luminance and two chrominance images (Pearson, 1975), which in sampled form give the arrays $l(\mathbf{n})$, $c_1(\mathbf{n})$, and $c_2(\mathbf{n})$. An advantage of this transformation is that $l(\mathbf{n})$, $c_1(\mathbf{n})$, and $c_2(\mathbf{n})$, taken together, require less storage or transmission capacity than $r(\mathbf{n})$, $g(\mathbf{n})$, and $b(\mathbf{n})$; they are also compatible with the way in which colour video signals are normally transmitted, namely as a luminance and two chrominance signals.

1.4 Image models

It is possible to think of the arrays of numbers in a variety of ways. These *representations* are important, for they constitute the theories that we humans have constructed to help us to devise better image-processing operations. Theories or beliefs about physical systems sometimes help and sometimes constrain progress. The field of image processing is no exception; authors often differ in the image model that they use (sometimes unconsciously), which in turn leads them to employ different algorithms in finding a solution to a problem.

The *stochastic* representation of signals has a number of advantages in classical communication theory (Shannon and Weaver, 1959) and many authors think and talk about their images as arrays of numbers generated by a process in which chance plays a part. Communication networks are performance-designed on the basis of statistical calculations of traffic; it helps considerably if the signal sources can be given probabilistic descriptions. If, however, we are concerned to interpret images in order to understand the three-dimensional object world—as in computer vision or in some recent coding schemes for transmission at very low bit rates—it may be better to think of them as projections or mappings of objects, as discussed above. Images which are synthesized in computer graphics have usually been produced by algorithms that simulate the paths of light rays bouncing off objects on

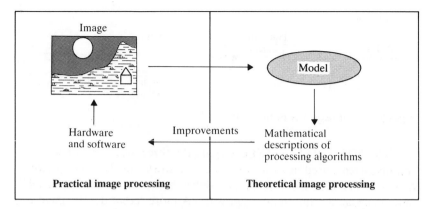

Figure 1.3 The role of theoretical models in image processing.

their way to the eye of the viewer (Magnetat-Thalmann and Thalmann, 1985), though stochastic modelling and the use of fractals are useful in representing some outlines and textures. Analysis and synthesis are two sides of the same coin of image understanding. The subject of pattern recognition is further explored in Chap. 5 and that of image synthesis in Chap. 6. The next chapter contains a more detailed treatment of theories about images.

In image processing we discover two worlds: the practical world of hardware and software, handling operations on arrays of numbers, and the theoretical world of models and mathematics. The two are only in approximate correspondence with one another. What theories *should* do (Fig. 1.3) is to lead to improvements in practical techniques; what they sometimes do is to throw up curious visual artefacts and distortions in the processed images, owing to conflicts between the model and reality. These distortions tend to be more visible to the opponents than to the proponents of the theory that produced them. The way in which technology interfaces with human purpose is pursued in a light-hearted treatment in Chap. 14.

1.5 Image transmission

The stages in the transmission of an image over a channel or network are portrayed in Fig. 1.4. The image-formation process in Fig. 1.1 is the front end of a chain, whose overall purpose is to set up in the brain of the viewer some approximation to the perception that he or she would have had if present at the original scene. The image sequence from the camera is coded into as concise a representation as possible for transmission over the channel.

Most transmission in broadcast television is still in analogue form and analogue coding methods are used to make it as efficient as

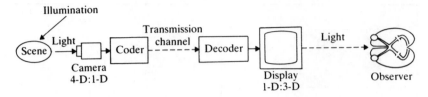

Figure 1.4 Image transmission.

possible. NTSC, PAL, and SECAM are the three major analogue coding systems used in various parts of the world for the transmission of colour signals; each of them modulates the two chrominance signals onto a subcarrier, but in different ways. A more recent development is MAC (multiplexed analogue components), in which the luminance and chrominance signals are time-compressed and sent in sequence; this avoids the interference (cross-colour) between the three signals in the older systems. Further details of broadcast colour image processing are given in Chaps. 3 and 4.

Digital image coding is a high-activity area in image processing (Netravali and Haskell, 1988); it is concerned with the efficient transmission of images over digital communication channels. A variety of ingenious ideas have been developed to compress the large bit rates produced by using pulse code modulation (PCM), i.e straightforward sampling and quantization of the video signal. The subject is treated in some detail in Chaps. 11–13. Coding is influenced by the type of channel used to carry the image signals. Several different physical types of transmission channel are encountered in practice, including cables, terrestrial radio, satellites, and optical fibres. In the future we may see integrated networks which carry voice, video, and data signals on a common physical medium rather than in separate channels, probably in packet form (Schwartz, 1987). The coding of image sequences for transmission over packet networks is treated in *IEEE Journal* (1989) and Chap. 13. There is a good deal of current activity internationally, through organizations such as the CCITT (Comité Consultatif International Télégraphique et Téléphonique), to standardize on coding methods for video signals. References are again made to this later in the book.

After decoding at the receiver, the image sequence is displayed on a screen, which in turn is imaged onto the photosensitive rear interior surface (retina) of the viewer's eye. After that it is subject to further coding by the neural pathways in transmission to the brain—firstly to the back of the viewer's head (the primary visual cortex) and thence to other parts of the cortex.

The human visual system is of considerable interest to image-processing engineers, both as the ultimate receiver of image sequences and as the most compact and powerful image processor known. Concepts from engineering have helped to further an understanding of vision (Campbell, 1968; Marr, 1982) and vision research has in turn stimulated work in engineering. Because the building blocks and transmission paths of the human visual system are different from those used in engineering, it is not necessarily the case that optimal engineering involves duplicating what is known of human vision. Frequently, however, they turn out to be somewhat similar. In fact, many of the fundamental parameters of image scanning and coding systems are directly related to the limitations of human vision (Pearson, 1975).

1.6 Gamma

One complication of note in the image-transmission chain is the non-linear behaviour of many of its elements. If the amplitude of the input signal to a device is x and its output y, the relationship is frequently of the form

$$y = cx^{\gamma}$$

where c is a constant and γ is an exponent (referred to as the *gamma* of the device) varying in practice between about 0.5 and nearly 3. The camera, the display and the eye all have non-unity gammas (Pearson, 1975); to make sure that the perceived grey scale in displayed images is correct, it is usually necessary to insert an additional, compensating non-linear device after the camera called a *gamma corrector*.

It is easily verified that the gammas of devices in cascade multiply together. The figure obtained by multiplying all the device gammas from the camera through to the display (but not including the eye) is known as the *system gamma*. If the conditions of viewing at the scene and at the display are the same (they often are not), the system gamma needs to be unity.

As an approximation, the gamma of a typical cathode ray tube (CRT) (in the range 2–3) and that of the eye (in the range 0.3–0.5, depending on viewing conditions) are inverse to one another (Fig. 1.5). This means that the sensation of brightness we have inside our head is nearly linearly related to the voltage input to the CRT. Equal increments of voltage at the CRT input produce approximately equal increments of subjective brightness (but not of luminance). The implications of this result for image quantization are considered in Chap. 7.

1.7 Sampling and quantization

If, as in Fig. 1.6, an image is sampled using A samples horizontally and B samples vertically, there are AB samples per frame. If the frame rate is C per second and if each sample is quantized into D bits, then each

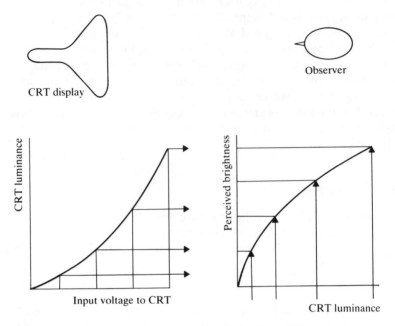

Figure 1.5   The non-linear characteristics of a CRT and of the eye approximately cancel one another.

second's worth of the image sequence generates a bit rate, for transmission or storage, of

$$R = ABCD \text{ bits/s}$$

In reality scanning is usually line-interlaced, with each frame being divided into two interleaved fields of $A/2$ lines. For the higher frame rates, this improves the quality slightly for the same bit rate.

In practice the bit rate may be somewhat higher than R in the formula above because sampling may be continued during blanking intervals in the scanning process, where subsidiary information is sometimes placed. However, the formula $R = ABCD$ provides a rough guide to the throughput requirement of an image-processing system.

Although there are three signals associated with colour images, the bit rate is usually about $2R$ rather than $3R$, since sampling and quantization can be coarser for the two chrominance signals c_1 and c_2.

1.8 Parameter selection in image-processing systems

The parameters A, B, C, and D are fundamental ones which require careful selection in any image-processing system. If large values are

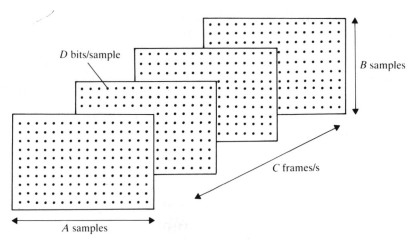

Figure 1.6 Image sampling and quantization.

chosen, a bit rate as high as 0.5–1 Gbit/s can result, as in high-definition television or HDTV (see Chap. 4). High bit rates mean that the hardware and software have to work much faster. This increases the cost and limits the complexity of algorithms that can be implemented in real time.

If small values of A, B, C, and D are chosen, storage and processing become much easier, but the image sequence may have visible defects such as blurring, jerkiness, and contours. This may be quite acceptable in some applications, but not in others. The values of the four parameters should therefore be no higher than is necessary for the particular application in mind. Their proper selection is often bound up with the way human beings use images, and this is not always straightforward. Choosing a set of parameters for a new visual service is therefore not an easy task and may involve some fairly thorough probing into the psychology of potential users.

Table 1.1 lists some parameters for a few systems that have been used in practice and illustrates the wide variety of bit rates encountered—from around 200 kbits/s to nearly 1 Gbits/s for moving images. The reader is referred to more extensive publications (e.g. Netravali and Haskell, 1988) for detailed descriptions of such systems. The parameters for both very low and very high bit-rate systems are still being discussed in international committees and the figures in the table are illustrative only. The table entries refer to the luminance signal only and are 'raw' bit rates. Data compression techniques can be used to reduce bit rates significantly, usually with some slight visible impairment.

Table 1.1 Some examples of approximate scanning and quantization parameters for the luminance signal, with resulting (uncompressed) bit rates

System	A	B	C	D	ABCD (Mbits/s)
Low-quality videophone	64	64	8	6	0.2
Common intermediate format (CIF) videoconference*	352	288	30	8	24
Digital broadcast television	720	576	25	8	83
HDTV	1920	1150	50	8	883
Facsimile/handwriting @ 4 lines/mm, per A4 page	1200	800	0.01	1	0.01

* An image size of one-quarter CIF (176 × 144 pels) is used in lower-resolution systems. Also the chrominance components for a CIF image are typically sampled at quarter-CIF.

1.9 Classification by bit rate

Another way to look at systems is on an ordered scale of bit rate, as in Fig. 1.7. In this figure the rates are those actually achieved, taking into account any data compression used. Near the top of the scale are the systems such as high-definition and current broadcast television. These have very high rates and can be difficult to process because of speed requirements. Image quality needs to be maintained at a high level, with little or no visible impairment. Sampling and filtering (Chap. 7), motion estimation (Chap. 3), the use of data compression techniques (Chaps 11–13), and the interaction with human vision are all topics receiving study at these bit rates.

In the middle of the scale are the commercial systems used for two-way visual communication. In these systems there is visible impairment, partly due to lowered scanning standards and partly due to the severe data compression used. Currently, the limit for the transmission of moving image sequences in colour is around 64 kbits/s, which is achieved by a hybrid of several coding techniques. The rendition of motion is generally poor at this limit.

At and below 64 kbits/s several novel ideas are being explored. One is to extract outlines from the image; a moving line drawing or cartoon can be transmitted at bit rates as low as 9.6 kbits/s (see Chap. 2). Another idea, known as *model-based coding* (Chap. 12), is to represent

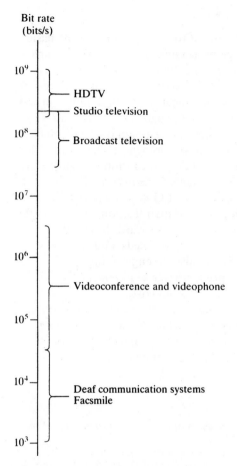

Figure 1.7   Image-sequence scanning systems classified by bit rate.

the three-dimensional object world which the camera sees as a software model (Chap. 6) inside an intelligent processor; when an object moves, the model is updated and the model control signals are coded and sent to the receiver. A third activity is in the area of binary pattern-recognition methods (Chap. 5), which are being investigated, for example, in connection with the next generation of facsimile machines. All these techniques increasingly involve quite complicated image-processing operations.

All along the bit rate scale, the growing complexity of processing algorithms continues to tax the ingenuity of those involved in the software and architectural aspects of image processing. Developments in computing architectures and software for image processing are treated in Chaps 8–10.

1.10 Summary

This introductory chapter has attempted to describe some of the basic concepts and terminology of image processing. Two-dimensional images are related by a mapping process to three-dimensional objects; when images are processed, it can be instructive to give attention to the effect of processing operations on features in object space. Both monochrome and colour images can be represented mathematically as deterministic functions of space-time. However, when transmission over a channel or network is being considered, it is useful to employ a stochastic model.

Widely varying sampling (scanning) and quantization parameters are found in practical image-processing systems. This in turn gives rise to a very large range of bit rates—from around 1 Gbit/s down to a few kbits/s. Selection of the basic sampling and quantization parameters for a particular application is not always straightforward. In fact the characteristics of human beings, their complex needs, and their powers of vision play a significant part. But so also do engineering considerations such as processor speed, storage requirements, algorithmic complexity, channel capacity, and cost.

Many interesting areas in image processing are currently discernible, not least those that interact with contiguous fields such as computer vision, computer graphics, machine architecture, and information networks. These will be explored in subsequent chapters.

References

Campbell F. W. (1968) 'The human eye as an optical filter', *Proceedings of the IEEE*, vol. 56, no. 6, pp. 1009–14.

Dubois E. (1985) 'The sampling and reconstruction of time-varying imagery with application in video systems', *Proceedings of the IEEE*, vol. 73, no. 4, pp. 502–22.

Horn B. K. P. (1986) *Robot Vision*, MIT Press, Cambridge, Mass.

IEEE Journal on Selected Areas in Communications, (1989) issue on packet speech and video, vol. 7, no. 5.

Magnetat-Thalmann N. and Thalmann D. (1985) *Computer Animation*, Springer-Verlag, Berlin.

Marr D. (1982) *Vision*, Freeman, San Francisco.

Netravali A. and Haskell B. (1988) *Digital Pictures: Representation and Compression*, Plenum Press, New York and London.

Pearson D. E. (1975) *Transmission and Display of Pictorial Information*, Pentech Press, London.

Pratt W. K. (1978) *Digital Image Processing*, Wiley, New York.

Schwartz M. (1987) *Telecommunication Networks: Protocols, Modelling and Analysis*, Addison-Wesley, Reading, Mass.

Shannon C. E. and Weaver W. (1959) *The Mathematical Theory of Communication*, University of Illinois Press, Urbana.

PART I

Concepts

In this section the reader is introduced to a number of fundamental concepts that are important in the understanding of modern image communication systems. Such understanding involves a variety of (sometimes conflicting) mathematical theories about images and image-processing operations, which Don Pearson discusses in Chap. 2. These theories encompass space-time and frequency representations as well as stochastic and object-related viewpoints; they serve as an introduction to later chapters.

There is no doubt that the availability of cheaper storage has aroused considerable interest in processing operations along the time axis of image sequences. Some unexpected relationships have been identified between space and time, as in the detection of moving objects. Graham Thomas gives an account of recent ideas in this area in Chap. 3, including methods for the representation, estimation, and detection of motion. Another very important and promising trend is that towards high-definition television (HDTV), in which images of significantly higher resolution will be available to viewers. The planning and implementation of an HDTV service presents fascinating theoretical and systems considerations, which are discussed by Gary Tonge in Chap. 4. Frequency-domain image descriptions have proved to be quite useful in understanding both motion and scanning standards.

Chapters 5 and 6 offer the reader a taste of recent trends in image communication. In the future, operations on images are likely to become more complex and more 'intelligent'. Pattern recognition is likely to play an increasing role in detecting moving objects, segmenting scenes, identifying features, or putting a label on faces and printed characters. The three main techniques are described by Graham Leedham in Chap. 5 and some examples of systems are given. In Chap. 6 Adrian Clark introduces the concepts of computer graphics: how to synthesize an image from a 3-D model stored in a computer. Such models can be made to resemble an actual scene quite closely, so that in the future we may see transmission channels carrying animation rather than pixel data. But there are still many problems to be solved.

2 Image-processing theories

DON PEARSON

2.1 The power and limitation of theories

There is a great deal of fascination in the world of image-processing theories. Theories have an extraordinary power to inspire change and progress and have been responsible in image processing for very significant advances. On the other hand, they have at times tended to establish certain ideas too firmly in the minds of those concerned with the subject. One example is to be found in multidimensional Fourier theory; this is both an elegant and a practically useful way to characterize sampling and filtering in images, but it has tended at times to make people overemphasize the importance of aliasing. Another example is to be found in the ideas of that great communication theorist, Claude Shannon. Shannon's view was that communication signals could be described as a series of symbols generated according to a stochastic process. Thinking about image sequences as arrays of stochastically generated numbers has led to very useful data-reducing codes such as Huffman and transform codes; but it could be said that it has also lent credence to the widespread but dubious usage of mean-square error as a distortion criterion. Recently there has been a shift to object-related theories about images as part of a trend towards understanding and analysing what is transmitted.

In the treatment that follows we shall first of all consider theories about images themselves and thereafter representations of processing operations.

2.2 Image representation: analogue images

Before it is scanned, an image is a rectangular patch of light. A first and very considerable simplification in its representation is possible using the trichromatic property of human vision, namely that the colour appearance of any small patch of light is specifiable in terms of three numbers (Hunt, 1975). These numbers are the equivalent amounts of three chosen primary colours which, when mixed, create the same colour appearance for an average observer as the original. In image processing, the widely used *transmission primaries* L, C_1 and C_2, into which scene colours are analysed, are mathematical concepts; their convenience is that the first contains all the luminance and no colouring or chrominance, while the other two are of zero luminance but contain all the chrominance. While it is not possible to create physical primaries that have these properties, it is possible to generate a luminance signal l and two chrominance signals c_1 and c_2 that represent the amounts of each of these non-physical primaries needed to match any given colour. At the receiver they are transformed into signals that are appropriate for the physical CRT display phosphors (Pearson, 1975).

Coloured filters in the camera with appropriate analysis characteristics are used to generate l, c_1 and c_2. If the dimensions of the image sequence are X cm wide by Y cm high by T s long, each of the luminance and two chrominance components of the image is often represented before scanning as a deterministic function

$$g(\mathbf{x}) = g(x_1, x_2, x_3,) - X/2 \leq x_1 \leq X/2, - Y/2 \leq x_2 \leq Y/2, 0 \leq x_3 \leq T$$
$$= 0, \qquad \text{otherwise}$$

Why do we seek to represent images in this way and what justification is there for it? The attractiveness of the approach is that it accords with that of classical signal theory, which has been found over many years to provide useful insights into processing operations such as filtering and sampling (Carlson, 1986). These operations are certainly of fundamental importance in image processing; they are often most easily described in the frequency domain via the multidimensional Fourier transform. There is in fact an extensive and very interesting series of extensions of signal theory to the multidimensional case which can be used not only for images but also for signals such as electromagnetic waves (Cattermole, 1985).

If we are given a particular image sequence—say on film—it is possible to find out experimentally what the function $g(\mathbf{x})$ is, although it will not in general be possible to express it in closed form. But is not so easy to extrapolate from measurements to a general functional representation for images. The justification for the use of *particular types* of function $g(\mathbf{x})$ is therefore more difficult. In the course of the chapter we shall look at some different assumptions about $g(\mathbf{x})$ associated with various processing operations.

2.2.1   Multidimensional Fourier transforms

The Fourier transform of $g(\mathbf{x})$ is defined as

$$G(\mathbf{u}) = \int_{-\infty}^{\infty} g(\mathbf{x})\, e^{-j2\pi\mathbf{u}\mathbf{x}}\, d\mathbf{x}$$

$$= \int_{-\infty}^{\infty} \int_{-\infty}^{\infty} \int_{-\infty}^{\infty} g(x_1, x_2, x_3)\, e^{-j2\pi(u_1 x_1 + u_2 x_2 + u_3 x_3)}\, dx_1\, dx_2\, dx_3$$

This transform can be thought of as replacing a representation based on the vector space **x** with another based on **u**. The points in **u**-space represent complex multidimensional sine waves, as given by the kernel of the transform; they are easier to picture if taken in complex-conjugate pairs for positive and negative frequencies. In this case they represent real functions, since

$$(e^{-j2\pi \mathbf{ux}} + e^{j2\pi \mathbf{ux}})/2 = \cos(\mathbf{ux}) = \cos(u_1 x_1 + u_2 x_2 + u_3 x_3)$$

These three-dimensional cosine waves can be thought of as moving gratings, whose wavelength, orientation, and speed of movement are determined by the value of **u**. Near the origin of **u**-space the gratings have long wavelengths and move slowly. Further away from the origin they have shorter wavelengths and move more rapidly. The characteristic of quite a large variety of image sequences is that as we go further and further away from the origin of **u**-space, so the amplitude $|G(\mathbf{u})|$ becomes smaller. Travelling out from the origin along any straight line whose angles to each of the axes are specified by the vector $\boldsymbol{\theta}$, we eventually get to a point W where the amplitude is negligible. We call this point the *bandwidth*; since it is a function of the angle made by the straight line, we write it as $W(\boldsymbol{\theta})$. In the idealized world of mathematics, $W(\boldsymbol{\theta})$ defines a region in **u**-space, outside of which $G(\mathbf{u}) = 0$; images whose spectra can be characterized in this way are said to be *bandlimited*.

One of the fascinations of multidimensional signal theory is that the bandwidth is not just a number—it has a shape, as the examples in Fig. 2.1 illustrate. Apart from the constraint that $W(\boldsymbol{\theta}) = W(-\boldsymbol{\theta})$, which

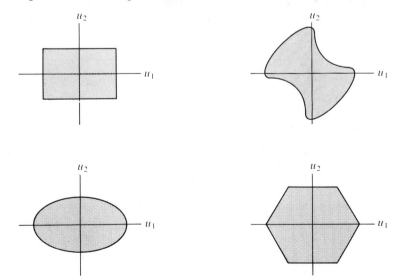

Figure 2.1   Two-dimensional examples of possible image bandwidths.

occurs because $g(\mathbf{x})$ is real (the Fourier transform of any real function is Hermitian, i.e. the negative-frequency components are the complex conjugates of the positive-frequency components), W can have a large variety of forms. Tables of multidimensional Fourier transforms can be used to transform simple images in which $g(\mathbf{x})$ is modelled as a sum or product of common mathematical functions.

2.3 Digital images

2.3.1 Sampling

The conversion of continuous source images into the digital images used in most processing operations is accomplished by sampling the image function $g(\mathbf{x})$ and quantizing the amplitudes of each sample into as many discrete levels as are necessary for the particular application in mind. The practical aspects of image sampling and quantization are further discussed in Chap. 7.

Two sampling patterns are commonly used—rectangular and interlaced—as shown in 2-D form in Fig. 2.2. The interlaced lattice is often called a *quincunx* sampling pattern, because a group of five samples resembles the pattern of dots representing the number 5 on the side of a die. If the horizontal and vertical spacings between samples are equal, a quincunx pattern is just a rectangular lattice rotated through 45°. It is often convenient to analyse quincunx patterns in this way. With another ratio of horizontal to vertical sample spacing, as shown in Fig. 2.2(b), it is also possible to describe a quincunx sampling pattern as hexagonal; it can be seen that around each sample are six other samples

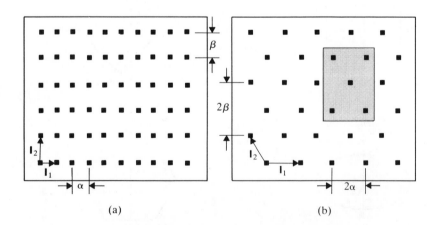

(a)   (b)

Figure 2.2 Common image sampling patterns: (a) is usually described as rectangular or orthogonal, while (b) is termed interlaced, quincunx (the quincunx is highlighted) or hexagonal.

forming a regular hexagon. The descriptor terms *interlaced, quincunx,* and *hexagonal* are therefore synonymous, apart from a scaling factor.

2.3.2   The multidimensional sampling theorem

In general, n-dimensional sampling can take place on any regular lattice of points. A sampling lattice can conveniently be described by an $n \times n$ matrix (termed the *sampling matrix*):

$$\lambda = [\mathbf{l}_1 | \mathbf{l}_2 | \mathbf{l}_3 | \ldots | \mathbf{l}_n]$$

where the $\mathbf{l}_i$ are column vectors of dimension $1 \times n$ specifying the direction of and sample spacing along each of the axes of the lattice (Petersen and Middleton, 1962). In fact the way this is done is to take one image sample as being the origin and draw vectors to the two nearest samples (Fig. 2.2). Thus in Fig. 2.2(a) $\mathbf{l}_1$ is oriented horizontally and of length α, while $\mathbf{l}_2$ is vertical and of length β. So

$$\lambda_a = \begin{bmatrix} \alpha & 0 \\ 0 & \beta \end{bmatrix}$$

Similarly, the sampling matrix that describes the lattice of Fig. 2.2(b) is

$$\lambda_b = \begin{bmatrix} 2\alpha & -\alpha \\ 0 & \beta \end{bmatrix}$$

As we have seen in the previous chapter, it is important to sample images as economically as possible in order to avoid high bit rates and their associated processing problems. How do we solve this problem theoretically? *If* an image can be represented as some deterministic function *and if* it is bandlimited, then a solution is given by the multidimensional sampling theorem. This theorem (Petersen and Middleton, 1962) tells us that if an image $g(\mathbf{x})$ is sampled on a lattice λ, its Fourier transform $G(\mathbf{u})$ is replicated throughout frequency space $\mathbf{u}$ on the *reciprocal* lattice Λ.

What is a reciprocal lattice? Mathematically, Λ is specified by the fact that the product of λ (transposed) and Λ is the unit matrix (Cattermole, 1985; Dudgeon and Mersereau, 1984), i.e.

$$\lambda^T \Lambda = \mathbf{I}$$

We can calculate the reciprocal matrix corresponding to λ_a by transposing its rows and columns and then finding its inverse. Sampling matrices that describe rectangular sampling lattices are diagonal matrices, which are unaffected by transposition. So we merely have to find the inverse of λ_a, which is

$$\Lambda_a = \begin{bmatrix} \dfrac{1}{\alpha} & 0 \\ 0 & \dfrac{1}{\beta} \end{bmatrix}$$

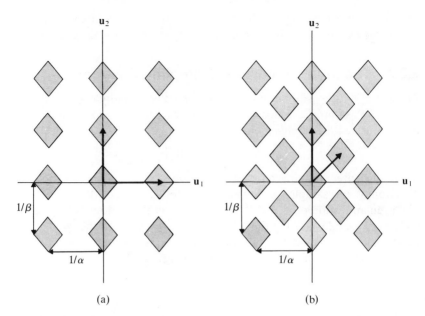

Figure 2.3 Replication patterns in frequency space due to sampling with (a) the rectangular lattice and (b) the quincunx lattice of Fig. 2.2. The vectors shown—which determine the structure of the replication lattice—are those of the reciprocal matrices in each case.

By a similar process we can calculate the reciprocal matrix corresponding to λ_b, namely

$$\Lambda_b = \begin{bmatrix} \dfrac{1}{2\alpha} & 0 \\ \dfrac{1}{2\beta} & \dfrac{1}{\beta} \end{bmatrix}$$

What this means geometrically is illustrated in Fig. 2.3 for the two lattices in Fig. 2.2. In general, the rule is that the first component vector of Λ is orthogonal to *all component vectors of λ except the first* (Cattermole, 1985); this determines its direction. The same rule applies by extension to other components. As with unidimensional sampling, the image can be recovered exactly (this may not be necessary) provided there is no overlap (aliasing) of the replications. In the multidimensional case, however, the most efficient sampling lattices can in general be arrived at only by inspection.

The interesting aspect of the multidimensional sampling theorem, as compared with its unidimensional counterpart, is that it does not not tell us *explicitly* how we should sample images. It tells us how to calculate the replication pattern, but the rest is a sort of jigsaw puzzle that has to be solved for any image with a particular $W(\theta)$. It can be seen from Fig. 2.3 that if the bandwidth shape is that of a diamond, a quincunx sampling lattice with half the sampling density of the rectangular lattice succeeds in fitting in all the replications without overlap. There is also some blank space around each one to allow for an imperfect recovery filter. The reader may like also to verify, however, that a hexagonal bandwidth shape is also appropriate, illustrating that there may be more than one solution to the problem.

2.3.3 Comparison of rectangular and quincunx sampling lattices

It is apparent that the rectangular sampling lattice of Fig. 2.2 has twice the sampling density of the quincunx lattice; images sampled in this way therefore require twice the storage or transmission capacity of those sampled using a quincunx pattern. A fairer comparison between the two types of lattice would be to increase both the horizontal and vertical sample spacings in the rectangular lattice until the total number of samples in each was the same. Under these conditions, quincunx or interlaced sampling is generally found to be superior in terms of subjectively judged image quality. This may be because those measurements that have been made of image spectra indicate a closer correspondence to a diamond than to a rectangular shape (though there are always individual exceptions). The eye's low-pass spatial-filtering recovery action is also more nearly diamond-shaped than rectangular.

The convenience of rectangular sampling, however, is that it makes processing easier. Operations such as prediction or filtering are more simply carried out on a rectangular lattice. It is for this reason that basic source standards for video signals often specify rectangular sampling, though the widespread incorporation of line interlacing into scanning standards means that a quincunx pattern in the plane of time and vertical space is unavoidable.

2.3.4 Model assumptions underlying the use of Fourier descriptions

Some difficulties arise with the model description $g(\mathbf{x})$ used in the treatment above. One is that the content of images varies very widely. A simple image such as that of a ball moving against a plain background is capable of being described by an explicit function, but an image sequence of, say, an orchestra playing music or athletes participating in some sporting event has never been satisfactorily modelled by any particular mathematical function or set of functions. Common unidimensional mathematical functions such as $\sin(x)$ or x^2 can be defined in multidimensional form, but the question is whether they can or should be used, singly or in combination, to describe images. Thus, it could be argued, the theory can really only be applied to synthetic images.

A development of this argument is to say that the image is a projection of an object world that is made up of planes, cylinders, cubes, spheres, and other mathematically describable objects, illuminated by light that varies gradually over space and time. The function $g(\mathbf{x})$ is then the sum total of the separate projections. Marr (1982) has suggested that the human brain may analyse the visual world in this way and has given examples of 3-D models for a number of animals, including horses, giraffes, and humans. Computer-graphic images, which have now reached a startling degree of reality, rely on similar specifications, though in simple form such modelling makes objects look as if they are made of plastic. The basic justification probably lies in the fast-developing field of image synthesis. If we can generate good approximations to the visual world of our experience, then there is reason to have confidence in the model.

Another difficulty arises because much of the classical theory of signals in communications applies to bandlimited signals. A fundamental property of signals is that they cannot be both time-space limited and bandlimited; since therefore images are of finite spatial extent and usually of limited duration, they are not bandlimited. This is a lesser difficulty, since engineers are used to dealing with imperfectly bandlimited signals and have accepted the fact that the theory will only give them approximate results. Nevertheless, with some of the very small (64×64) images that are beginning to be used in low-data-rate systems, some caution is necessary.

2.4   Multidimensional filtering

2.4.1   Description and uses

For an image $g(\mathbf{x})$ with spectrum $G(\mathbf{u})$, the process of linear multidimensional filtering is simply and economically described as

$$K(\mathbf{u}) = G(\mathbf{u})\ H(\mathbf{u})$$

where $H(\mathbf{u})$ is the frequency response of the filter and $K(\mathbf{u})$ is the filtered image. In image processing we may be concerned with 1-D, 2-D, or 3-D filtering, in combinations of space and time.

Filtering is a common and important operation and occurs at several points in the transmission chain (Fig. 2.4). Spatial low-pass filtering by the camera lens, together with both spatial and temporal low-pass filtering by the photosensitive camera target, form an initial 3-D electro-optical filter (Pearson, 1975). Further low-pass pre-filtering may be introduced prior to sampling so as to avoid significant aliasing.

Once the image is in digital form, it may meet a variety of other filters in operations such as sampling-rate conversion, feature extraction, and motion detection. Several examples are to be found in later chapters in

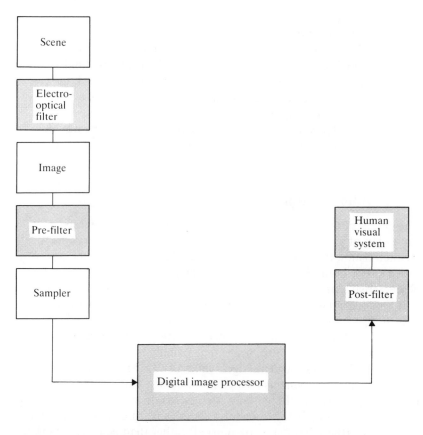

Figure 2.4   Filters (shaded) in the image-processing chain.

the book. Filters that operate in three dimensions are now fairly common.

Recovery of the image from its samples takes place by means of an electro-optical low-pass post-sampling filter in cascade with the human eye, which is itself a low-pass filter (Pearson, 1975). If the whole processing–transmission system is designed correctly, the processed image should appear continuous in space and time, without visible defects. In practice, this only occurs with high values of the parameters A, B and C (see Fig. 1.6), such as are encountered in broadcast television and HDTV. In other systems, particularly those viewed at short distances (when the image in the retina is larger and the spatial filtering action of the eye has less effect), defects caused by inadequate filtering can be quite visible. In practice, electro-optical filters are rather slow cut-off filters and most of the recovery filtering is done electronically or by the eye. The eye's spatial-frequency bandwidth is equal for horizontal and vertical stripes, but slightly attenuated at 45°; as an approximation, engineers often represent this as a square turned through 45°, i.e. as a diamond. This representation is used in Chap. 3 in explaining the effect of sampling on moving objects.

One of the very interesting characteristics of the eye as a filter, which was discovered by Campbell and Robson (1968), is that within its passband there are several spatial-frequency channels. Indeed, the primary visual cortex appears to analyse retinal images into a large number of Fourier components at various spatial and temporal frequencies and at various orientations (Robson, 1983). The way in which this information is used in order to recognize objects is not fully understood.

2.4.2   Filter design

The design of multidimensional filters for images is still regarded as somewhat of a black art. This is because, over and beyond two basic characteristics, there is a good deal of flexibility possible in the design process. For both analogue and digital image filters, the two desirable characteristics are *linear phase* and a *smooth impulse response.*

If the filter phase is a linear function of frequency, this guarantees that the space or time displacement suffered by each of the frequency components $G(\mathbf{u})$ of the image is the same, irrespective of the value of the frequency $\mathbf{u}$. This in turn means that visually important image features of the image, such as edges, valleys and ridges, emerge with their frequency components located at the same point in space-time (though they may be differentially attenuated). In short, what this does is to maintain roughly the same form for each feature; an edge will look like an edge (though it may look blurred) rather than being turned into something else. Since the human visual system is thought to make use of these features in interpreting images (Marr, 1982), this is an important invariant.

Ringing is the decaying oscillation at edges which results from using a filter with a sharp cut-off. For example, a 2-D rectangular spatial filter in the frequency domain has a 2-D sinc function impulse response, with a slow $1/|\mathbf{x}|$ rate of decay. Small defects in the immediate neighbourhood of an edge are not visible due to spatial masking in the human visual system, but the slow decay associated with ringing produces objectionable patterning. Ringing can be avoided by choosing an $H(\mathbf{u})$ for which $h(\mathbf{x})$ is smooth.

There are many mathematical functions that satisfy the two criteria above and therefore many possible ways to design an image filter. A commonly encountered approach is to approximate a Gaussian impulse function $h(\mathbf{x}) = \exp(-\pi\mathbf{x})$, which has a frequency response $H(\mathbf{u}) = \exp(-\pi\mathbf{u})$; this satisfies both the linear-phase and smoothness criteria. Such filters can be designed to have a fairly sharp cutoff.

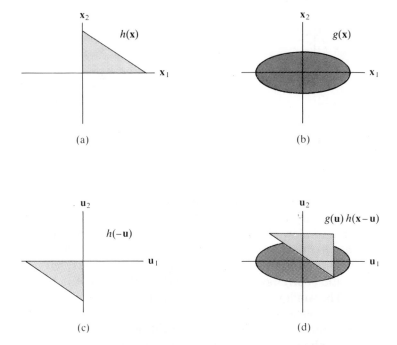

Figure 2.5 Graphical representation of convolution in two dimensions. The two functions to be convolved, $h(\mathbf{x})$ and $g(\mathbf{x})$, are portrayed in (a) and (b). In (c), the first function is rotated by 180° and represented in terms of the dummy variable $\mathbf{u}$ to give $h(-\mathbf{u})$, while (d) shows the product $g(\mathbf{u}).h(\mathbf{x} - \mathbf{u})$. The volume under the product function is the evaluation of the convolution for the particular value of $\mathbf{x}$ chosen.

2.4.3 Multidimensional convolution

The equivalent operation in space-time to that of linear filtering in the frequency domain is multidimensional convolution

$$g(\mathbf{x}) * h(\mathbf{x}) = \int_{-\infty}^{\infty} g(\mathbf{u}) h(\mathbf{x} - \mathbf{u})\,d\mathbf{u}$$

This is illustrated graphically for the 2-D case in Fig. 2.5.

2.4.4 Digital image filters

In the case of digital filters, the convolution integral is replaced by a convolution sum of the sampled image $g(\mathbf{n})$ and the filter impulse response $h(\mathbf{n})$

$$g(\mathbf{n}) * h(\mathbf{n}) = \sum_{\mathbf{k}=-\infty}^{\infty} g(\mathbf{k}) h(\mathbf{n} - \mathbf{k})$$

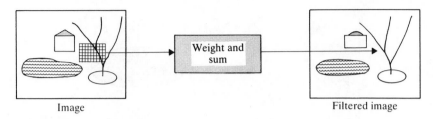

Image   Filtered image

Figure 2.6 Implementation of an FIR digital image filter by convolution.

This constitutes a direct and practical way to implement a finite impulse response (FIR) filtering operation, as is illustrated in Fig. 2.6. A section of the image in a window of $M \times N$ elements is weighted by the impulse response of the filter (if Gaussian, the weighting is an approximation to a Gaussian function) and then summed over the window. The result is placed in a location corresponding to the centre of the window in the output image. The window is then scanned over the input image, generating the complete output image. It is easy to ensure that the filter has linear phase; this is accomplished by choosing an even (symmetrical) impulse response about the centre point of the window. The reader is referred to texts such as Dudgeon and Merserau (1984) for ways in which general multidimensional digital filters can be designed and to Chaps 7 and 9 of this book for more details about implementation. In addition to the FIR filter portrayed in Fig. 2.6, there are a variety of other linear and non-linear filters for images, some of which the reader will encounter in later chapters.

2.4.5 Motion

Multidimensional convolution has other uses, for example in the representation of moving objects. If a stationary object has a description $g(\mathbf{x})$ and its trajectory at constant velocity $\mathbf{v}$ in $\mathbf{x}$-space is along a line $\delta(\mathbf{x} - \mathbf{v}t)$, the moving object itself has a description

$$g(\mathbf{x}) * \delta(\mathbf{x} - \mathbf{v}t)$$

from which its spectrum is easily calculated as

$$G(\mathbf{u}) . \delta(\mathbf{u} + f\mathbf{v}^{-1})$$

This can be interpreted as a *slice* through $G(\mathbf{u})$, the angle of the slice being determined by the velocity $\mathbf{v}$. The concept is further explored in Chap. 3. It enables the multidimensional Fourier transform of a moving object, as a function of velocity, to be found quite readily. This in turn makes possible some interesting analyses of motion-dependent interpolation and coding.

2.5 Discrete transforms

A frequently encountered operation in image processing is that of dividing up the image into (usually square) blocks, each of some selected size $N \times N$ and then performing a discrete transformation on each block. Examples will be encountered in later chapters concerned with motion estimation (Chap. 3) and data compression (Chap. 11).

When the authors of conference papers describe such operations, they sometimes do so without so much as the bat of an eyelid. This indicates either that they have not thought very much about what an image is, or else that they believe that image arrays are just collections of stochastically generated numbers. Whether or not a person feels uneasy when using block-processing of image sequences is an interesting test of that person's own theory about images.

The idea of slicing up an image into squares that bear no relation to the content of the image (and certainly no relation to objects in the field of view of the camera) is an operation that is difficult to justify on any grounds other than practical convenience. There is no doubt, however, that it is convenient, in both hardware and software terms, to do this; scene-dependent segmentation is often plagued by noise and requires more addressing overhead. The use of this technique could therefore be justified as a triumph of pragmatism over belief, with such difficulties and distortions as occur at block edges being accepted as one of life's vicissitudes!

Any particular block of elements can be considered to be an $N \times N$ matrix $\mathbf{X}$. A discrete transformation is such as to convert $\mathbf{X}$ into another $N \times N$ matrix $\mathbf{Y}$. Such a transformation can often be expressed by means of the matrix multiplication

$$\mathbf{Y} = \mathbf{TXT'}$$

where $\mathbf{T}$ is the transformation matrix and $\mathbf{T'}$ is transpose. This operation can be understood as a cascade of unidimensional transformations; the first, $\mathbf{TX}$, is one in which the columns of $\mathbf{X}$ are unidimensionally transformed to produce some intermediate matrix $\mathbf{X_1}$, while the second, $\mathbf{X_1 T'}$, transforms the rows of the intermediate matrix. It is possible to extend the idea of block transformation to three dimensions, though not with the convenient matrix notation that is usable in one and two dimensions.

A variety of multidimensional discrete transformations is encountered in image processing and the reader is referred to Chap. 11 and to books such as that by Pratt (1978) for the numerical details of the basis vectors which distinguish one transform from another. Among the common transforms are the discrete Fourier transform (used, for example, in block motion estimation) and the discrete cosine transform or DCT (pre-eminent in data compression using transform coding).

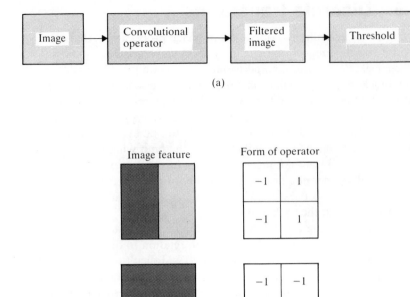

(a)

(b)

Figure 2.7 (a) Feature detection using a convolutional operator and (b) examples of simple 2 × 2 operators for detecting vertical and horizontal edges.

2.6   Operators

An operator is a particular kind of filter which seeks to extract image features such as edges or valleys. Feature-extracted binary images are used in image segmentation, pattern recognition, in the location and recognition of objects and in visual communication at very low data rates. Their attractiveness lies in the economy of representation; with only two levels of luminance and relatively sparse occupation in the image array, they are quick and convenient to use. It is, however, possible to cite a number of papers in the image-processing literature in which the authors employ such operators without having a clear idea of what the operator is doing. When, as a consequence, the system in which the operator is incorporated does not work (or occasionally, does work), they are at a loss to give a coherent explanation. Since the theory of operators is tied up with the theory of images, it is evident that a clear understanding of one is dependent on the clear appreciation of the other.

A simple and common form of operator can be realized as a linear convolution followed by thresholding, though there are many variants on this, some being concerned with the ability of the operator to discriminate against noise. The theory and implementation of a simple edge operator are illustrated in Fig. 2.7(a), with the window coefficients being shown in Fig. 2.7(b). If, as the window is being scanned over the image, it encounters a feature to which it is matched or 'tuned', a peak in response is generated in the filtered image. When this exceeds the threshold, a binary indication of an edge is given.

2.7   Operators and three-dimensional shape

In recent times work has been done on relating the form of operators to the shape of solids in object space. The way in which light reflects from 3-D solids can be studied using the so-called Gaussian sphere (Horn, 1986; Koenderink, 1990). The idea behind this concept is that for objects with a specified illumination from a particular direction and a constant surface-reflectance characteristic, the light reflected towards the eye or camera is a function only of the surface orientation, provided there is no mutual illumination, i.e. light bouncing off one surface onto another. Thus the study of highlights, lowlights, and shading on complicated shapes can be simplified by mapping all surfaces onto a unit sphere so that the surface normal on the sphere and that on the object point in the same direction. A 2-D plot of surface luminance as a function of its orientation, for a particular illumination source, is known as a *reflectance map* (Fig. 2.8). The two reflectance maps in Fig. 2.8 are derived from measurements made in the author's office, which is rectangular with a large north-facing window in the outside wall and overhead fluorescent lighting. The luminance of white, matt paper at various angles (α, β) was measured, where $\alpha = \beta = 0$ represents a direction of the surface normal parallel to the floor and walls, pointing towards the window; α is the horizontal rotation angle and β the vertical rotation angle from this direction. The value at the origin of the reflectance map represents the luminance of the paper, as seen from the window side, relative to the peak recorded value. The difference between Figs 2.8(a) and 2.8(b) is that (a) was measured in daylight and (b) in the evening. In the daytime the peak luminance (1.0) was obtained with the surface normal pointing towards the window but at a slight elevation from horizontal. At night the peak is obtained with the surface normal at about 75° to the horizontal.

Consider now an actual sphere with some uniform, matt surface as seen by a camera against a uniform background, as in Figs 2.9(a) and 2.9(b). In both figures the illumination is from the direction of the camera. The sphere can be taken to be what it physically is: a sphere, but it can also be considered to be a Gaussian sphere, representing all possible surface orientations of a more complex matt solid. Such a solid

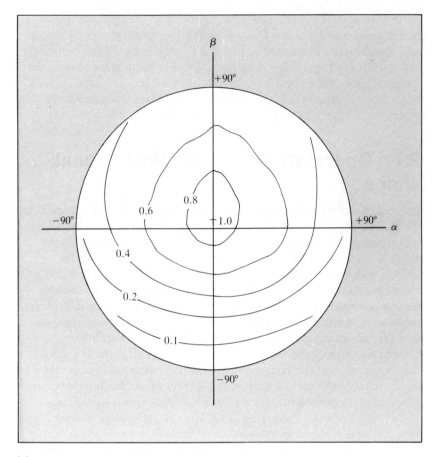

(a)

Figure 2.8(a) Reflectance map measured in the author's office at noon.

would map to some subsection of the total surface area of the sphere. The image of the sphere on the photosensitive target of the camera in Fig. 2.9 would essentially be the same as the reflectance map portrayed in Fig. 2.8. The difference between Figs 2.9(a) and 2.9(b) is that the background is dark in one case and light in the other. The relationship between image operators and 3-D objects can now be explored.

2.7.1 Edge detection

Consider the form of operator required in Fig. 2.9(a) to pick out the circular bounding shape of the sphere from the image (or the occluding contour of some general object). The luminance profile of the image of the sphere shows a peak in the middle where the surface normal points

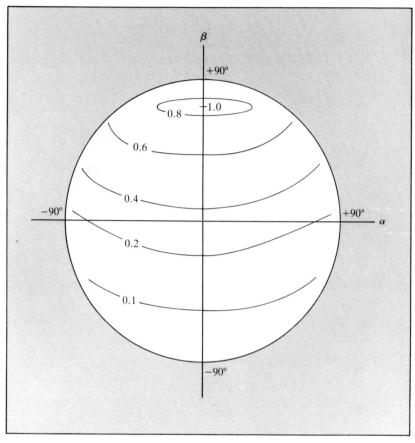

(b)

Figure 2.8(b) Reflectance map measured in the author's office at night.

towards the direction of the illumination; on either side it falls off in accordance with an assumed approximate cosine law as the angle between the surface normal and the illumination direction increases. Finally it drops to the background level. To detect the outline of the sphere it is apparent that an operator in the form of an edge detector is appropriate. Since, however, the orientation of the edge changes around the circular boundary, the edge detector has to check for both vertical and horizontal changes (Fig. 2.7), as well as, perhaps, some intermediate angles.

2.7.2 Thresholding

It is interesting to note, with reference to Fig. 2.7(a), that the thresholding operation alone, without any linear operator preceding it,

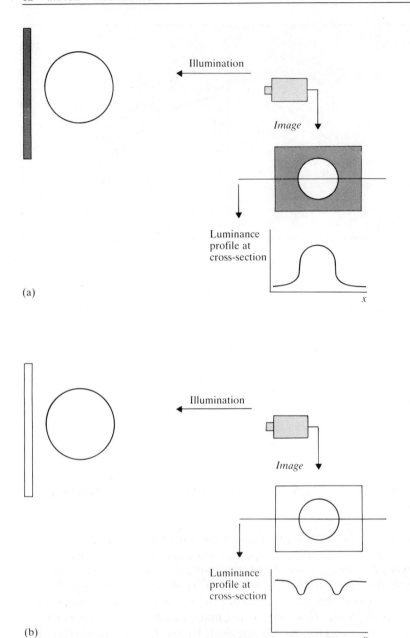

Figure 2.9 The images of a light-coloured sphere illuminated from the direction of the camera seen against (a) a dark background and (b) a light background, with cross-sections of the image luminance profile.

also picks out the boundary shape of the sphere in Fig. 2.9(a).This assumes that the slicing level is set appropriately, but given a sufficiently large difference between the luminance factors of the sphere and the background, it is not difficult to arrange for this to work in practice. Simple thresholding is in fact a remarkably powerful extractor of shape under the right lighting conditions and is used in the input binarization of images for pattern-recognition devices such as WISARD (Aleksander *et al.*, 1984). However, variable surface reflectance and shadows can produce spurious shape indications.

2.7.3 Valley detection

Turning now to Fig. 2.9(b), where the background reflectance is assumed to be the same as that of the sphere, we see that a different operator is required. As the surface of the sphere turns away from the incident illumination, so less light is reflected towards the camera. When the surface is parallel to the line of vision, the image luminance is minimum. Thus scanning across the image of the sphere produces a luminance profile which is in the form of two valleys at the bounding surfaces, as shown in the lower part of the figure. The low-pass filtering action of the camera lens and target makes the valleys somewhat wider that they might otherwise be; in addition, if there is mutual illumination from the background onto the sphere, the depth of the valleys is affected.

To detect the boundaries of the sphere, we use a valley detector, as shown in simplified form in Fig. 2.10(a). A valley detector looks for a thin line of slightly darker image elements against a slightly lighter background. As with edge detection, a search has generally to be made in several orientations in image space, as valleys can occur at any angle. If this is done in the situation portrayed in Fig. 2.9(b) and a black dot placed at the lowest point of each valley, the circular outline of the sphere is obtained as shown.

Also shown in Fig. 2.10 is the inversion of a valley, i.e. a ridge, together with the form of the operator required to detect it. There are no ridge features in Fig. 2.9 because the surfaces are assumed to be matt, but on specular objects, highlights may be formed at surface inflexional points and are a rich source of information about solid shape (Koenderink, 1990).

2.7.4 Operator size and scale

In the illustrations above, simple 2×2 and 3×3 operators have been used. With small windows such as this, however, the operator is not sharply tuned to the feature it is desired to detect. A valley operator, for example, will have some response to edges. As we shall shortly see, this can be a useful feature, but if it is desired to increase the sharpness of response, a larger value of N in an $N \times N$ operator can be chosen.

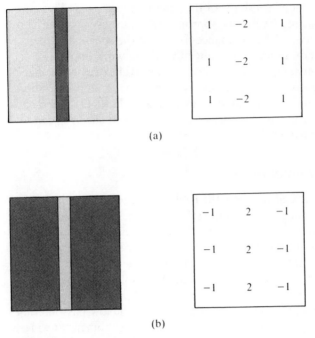

(a)

(b)

Figure 2.10 (a) A vertically running luminance valley and (b) a luminance ridge, together with the convolutional operators required to detect them.

It is important to match the size of the operator to the scale of the feature being detected. If an image is very densely sampled, then a particular edge or valley may spread over quite a large number of image elements. If an operator is mismatched for scale, it tends either to miss features or to insert spurious ones. It may be advantageous in practice to extract features using several operators, each working to a different scale.

2.7.5 Combination of valley detection and thresholding

A composite operator comprising the logical OR of a valley detector and a threshold is good for detecting facial features (Pearson and Robinson, 1985). This is demonstrated in Fig. 2.11 using a 5 × 5 operator which incorporates non-linear operations to suppress noise. The thresholding brings out dark hair on the head or in the eyebrows, together with shadowed areas such as the nostrils or the interior of the mouth when open. The 'valledge' detector (i.e. a valley detector with some residual response to large edges by virtue of the finite size of the operator window), following the explanations given above, is good at picking out the outline of the nose and chin and also the hands. The

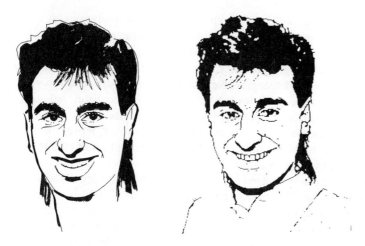

Figure 2.11 Line drawings or cartoons produced from the same grey-level photograph of the subject by a human artist (left) and electronically (right) using a composite valledge-threshold operator (from Pearson et. al., 1990).

clues to 3-D shape given by the right choice of detector are thought to be a reason for the success of the composite operator. In respect of the remarkable similarity of the artist-drawn and machine-generated cartoons, it has been noted (Pearson *et al.*, 1990) that the early stages of human vision involve a form of operator rather like the valley operator.

2.8 Coding

The subject of image coding is a large one which is treated in Chaps 11–13 and in Netravali and Haskell, (1988). Since this chapter is about image-processing theories, however, it is appropriate that we should briefly examine the theories that underlie coding.

The aim of image coding is to represent an image sequence efficiently and robustly by a stream of binary digits, so that it may be reliably transmitted over a given (usually noisy) communication channel or network, or stored compactly in digital memory. Two strands are discernible in the history of image coding, associated with two different theories.

In the first, attributable to the work of Claude Shannon, images are thought of as stochastically generated arrays of numbers. This approach has given rise to variable word-length coding techniques and to others (such as transform coding) in which the aim is to decorrelate blocks of input data and thus effect compression. More recently, vector quantization has been used with the same theoretical model in mind. There is no doubt that very useful advances have been made by stochastic modelling, but there is a question as to its limitations. A number of erudite papers have been published characterizing video sources as Markov models, but their authors have frequently not thought it necessary to program the model onto a computer in order to see whether it produced recognizable images. Such experimental work as has been done in this area leads to the tentative conclusion that simple Markov models are satisfactory only for selected areas of image texture such as grass or clouds. In recent times, however, more complex multicomponent stochastic models and the approximation of selected areas of images by fractals (Mandlebrot, 1983) have been developed.

The second strand in image coding—which appeared very early on—is one in which 2-D image features are recognized. This is evident in the invention of DPCM (Cutler, 1952, 1955), where edges are coded differently from slowly changing regions, and in two-component coding (Schreiber, 1967), in which edges and low-frequency information are separated. Subsequently conditional replenishment coding (Mounts, 1969) identified moving and non-moving areas for different treatment. All three techniques have been very successful at a practical level.

A recent trend in image coding is one in which the *three-dimensional* structure of the scene is used in the coding process. One example has been given in terms of object-related operator-generation of cartoons, which can be transmitted in moving form at bit rates as low as 9.6 kbits/s (Whybray and Hanna, 1989). Another is in the use of a software model of the 3-D world within the coder (Aizawa *et al.*, 1989; Musmann *et al.*, 1989). This field of model-based coding is treated in more detail in Chap. 12; it seems likely that coding methods using sophisticated 3-D modelling and analysis will continue to develop (Liedtke *et al.*, 1990).

In the end it seems, all models, however sophisticated, have a variable correspondence with reality. Fortunately developments in packet networks may allow image information to be transmitted at a variable bit rate. This is another recent field which is known as *packet video* and is described in Chap. 13. Systems such as this are in principle highly efficient; they are reminiscent of the human nerve-impulse transmission system in so far as its impulse rate tends to be related to change in the exterior world, which in turn appears to be modelled within the brain. A possible future synthesis of model-based coding and packet video is illustrated in Fig. 2.12.

2.9 Summary

In this chapter we have looked at the variety of theories or models that have been used to characterize images and image processing. Such theories have been very influential in shaping the direction of research into new image-processing techniques, as for example in sampling, filtering, discrete tranformation, feature extraction, and coding.

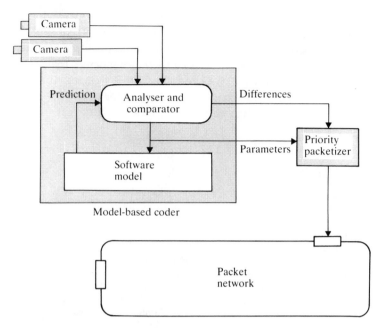

Figure 2.12 A speculative future image-coding system in which a 3-D model of the external world as seen by the camera is compared with reality. Differences between the model and the analysed input are transmitted in packet form at a highly variable bit rate and update an identical software model at the receiver.

The understanding of sampling and filtering has been facilitated through the representation of images as multidimensional deterministic functions $g(\mathbf{x})$ having a Fourier transform $G(\mathbf{u})$. An outline of this approach has been given, together with some indications as to how it can be applied in practice to the design of sampling lattices and image-sequence filters. These matters are pursued in later chapters.

The widespread practice of dividing up images into rectangular blocks for processing purposes has been looked at in the light of image models. It was noted that block-oriented processing is used in multidimensional discrete transforms such as the Fourier and cosine transforms.

More recent work in the use of operators to extract object-related features from images has been reviewed. This is an interesting interface area between traditional image processing and computer vision. The way in which edge, valley, and threshold detectors extract shape has been described using a simple application of the concepts of the Gaussian sphere and reflectance map.

Finally, some of the history of image coding has been reviewed in the light of different image models. The motivational force for the development of source models came initially from a theoretical characterization of communication channels that was largely stochastic. Stochastic models continue to be important; however, in recent times, very high-compression coding methods that use object-centred models have been developed or suggested. Among these are schemes that extract a primitive in the form of a cartoon and those that set up a moving software model of the exterior world inside the coder, transmitting only the differences between the model and the camera input.

References

Aizawa K., Harashima H. and Saito T. (1989) 'Model-based analysis synthesis coding system for a person's face', *Image Communication*, vol. 1, no. 2, pp. 139–52.

Aleksander I., Thomas W.V. and Bowden P.A. (1984) 'WISARD, a radical step forward in image recognition', *Sensor Review*, pp. 120–4, July.

Campbell F.W. and Robson J.G. (1968) 'Application of Fourier analysis to the visibility of gratings', *Journal of Physiology*, vol. 197, pp. 551–66.

Carlson A.B. (1986) *Communication Systems*, McGraw-Hill, New York.

Cattermole K.W. (1985) *Mathematical Foundations for Communication Engineering*, vol. 1: Determinate Theory of Signals and Waves, Pentech Press, London.

Cutler, C.C. (1952, 1955) 'Differential quantization of communication signals', US Patents 2 605 361 (1952) and 2 724 740 (1955).

Dudgeon D.E. and Merserau R.M. (1984) *Multidimensional Digital Signal Processing*, Prentice Hall, Englewood Cliffs, NJ.

Horn B.K.P. (1986) *Robot Vision*, MIT Press, Cambridge, Mass.

Hunt R.W.G. (1975) *The Reproduction of Colour*, Fountain Press, London.

Koenderink J.J. (1990) *Solid Shape*, MIT Press, Cambridge, Mass.

Liedtke C.-E., Busch H. and Koch R. (1990) 'Automatic modelling of 3D moving objects from a TV image sequence', *SPIE/SPSE Symposium on Sensing and Reconstruction of 3D Objects and Scenes*, Santa Clara, Calif.

Mandlebrot B.B. (1983) *The Fractal Geometry of Nature*, Freeman, New York.

Marr D. (1982) *Vision*, Freeman, San Francisco.

Mounts F.W. (1969) 'A video encoding scheme with conditional picture-element replenishment', *Bell System Technical Journal*, vol. 48, no. 7, pp. 2545–54.

Musmann H.G., Hötter M. and Ostermann, J. (1989) 'Object-oriented analysis–synthesis coding of moving images', *Image Communication*, vol. 1, no. 2, pp. 117–38.

Netravali A.N. and Haskell B.G. (1988) *Digital Pictures: Representation and Compression*, Plenum Press, New York.

Pearson D.E. (1975) *Transmission and Display of Pictorial Information*, Pentech Press, London.

Pearson D.E. and Robinson J.A. (1985) 'Visual communication at very low data rates', *Proceedings of the IEEE*, vol. 73, no. 4, pp. 795–812.

Pearson D.E., Hanna E. and Martinez K. (1990) 'Computer-generated cartoons', in *Images and Understanding*, ed. Barlow H.B., Blakemore C. and Weston-Smith M., Cambridge University Press, Cambridge, pp. 46–60.

Petersen D.P. and Middleton D. (1962) 'Sampling and reconstruction of wave-number-limited functions in *N*-dimensional Euclidean spaces', *Information and Control*, vol. 5, pp. 279–323.

Pratt W.K. (1978) *Digital Image Processing*, Wiley, New York.

Robson J.G. (1983) 'Frequency domain visual processing', in *Physical and Biological Processing of Images*, ed. Braddick O.J. and Sleigh A.C., Springer-Verlag, Berlin.

Schreiber W.F. (1967) 'Picture Coding', *Proceedings of the IEEE*, vol. 55, no. 3, pp. 320–30.

Whybray M.W. and Hanna E. (1989) 'A DSP based videophone for the hearing-impaired using valledge processed pictures', *Proceedings of the IEEE International Conference on Acoustics, Speech and Signal Processing*, Glasgow, Scotland.

3 Motion and motion estimation

GRAHAM THOMAS

3.1 Introduction

The temporal axis of an image signal has a number of different properties compared with the spatial axis. For example, there can be a lot of temporal aliasing in the signal; the overall subjective effect of this may be beneficial, whereas spatial aliasing rarely is. There can also be a lot of redundancy in the temporal components of a moving image.

In order to perform image-processing operations successfully in the temporal domain, it can be very useful to know which areas of the picture are moving and to know their motion vectors.

Many kinds of image coding or bit-rate reduction systems can benefit from motion compensation. For example, DPCM systems can use motion compensation to form a prediction of the signal by extrapolation from the preceding frame. The use of motion compensation can reduce drastically the prediction error compared with that generated using a non-motion-compensated predictor; this reduces the bit rate required for the error signal and can improve the picture quality. Another way of using motion compensation in a bandwidth reduction system is to omit alternate frames from the transmitted signal, and reconstruct the dropped frames at the receiver using motion compensation.

Motion compensation can be used in other applications where images need to be interpolated along the temporal axis. For example, the conversion of a television signal from a 60 Hz to a 50 Hz scanning standard requires the interpolation of new fields. This is usually done with a fixed spatio-temporal filter, which causes rapidly moving objects to judder or become blurred. Some converters use a motion detector to switch between filters with different characteristics, which can give a better compromise between sharpness in stationary areas and smooth motion in moving areas. Motion compensation can be used to eliminate almost all motion artefacts. In these kinds of applications it is important that the estimated motion refers to the *true* motion in the scene; in applications such as predictive coding it is only necessary to determine

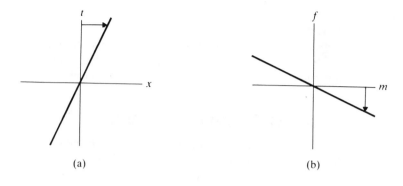

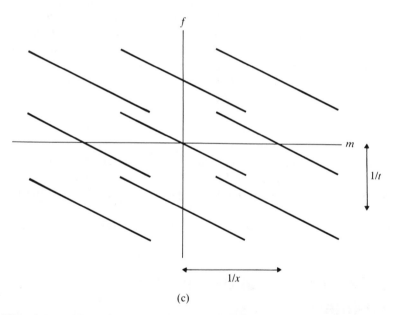

Figure 3.1 The spectrum of a moving object. (a) Space-time description of a moving point. (b) Spatio-temporal frequency spectrum (before sampling). (c) Spatio-temporal frequency spectrum (after sampling)

vectors that indicate which portion of one picture is a good match for a portion of another.

Other processes such as image segmentation and scene analysis can also benefit from motion information. For example, such information can play an important role in distinguishing an object from the background, and in estimating the 3-D structure of an object. Motion estimation techniques can be used to process stereo pairs of images in order to determine depth information.

This chapter opens with a brief discussion of the spatio-temporal spectrum of moving objects and the effect of sampling and aliasing. Motion detection and estimation techniques are then considered.

3.2 Spectrum of a moving object

Consider an image of a point moving horizontally at a fixed speed. A plot showing the position of the point in 1-D space is shown in Fig. 3.1(a). The line would be vertical if the velocity was zero; the angle of skew would increase for higher velocities.

The spatio-temporal frequency content of this scene is shown in Fig. 3.1(b). The spatial and temporal frequency axes are labelled m and f, respectively. If the point were stationary, its spectrum would lie along the $f = 0$ axis. The motion of the point causes the spectrum to become skewed as shown. The reason for the skew can be readily understood by considering the temporal frequency at a fixed point in the image: the contribution to the temporal frequency from a given spatial frequency is the product of the spatial frequency and the speed of movement, so higher spatial frequencies therefore give rise to higher temporal frequencies. It should be stressed that the spectrum is skewed and not rotated.

When the image is sampled in space and time, the spectrum is replicated at intervals of the reciprocal sampling frequencies. Figure 3.1(c) shows such a replicated spectrum in the case of orthogonal sampling. In this example, insufficient pre-filtering has been performed prior to sampling to prevent the repeat spectra from overlapping both spatially and temporally at particular motion speeds.

The following section considers the effect of spectral overlaps on an observer.

3.3 The effects of temporal pre- and post-filters

3.3.1 Post-filters

The most significant temporal post-filtering in a system consisting of human observer and a normal CRT display occurs in the human eye itself (the same is true of almost all other display systems except those using long-persistence phosphors). Therefore let us consider the effect of the post-filter in the eye; first for a fixed gazing point, then for an eye tracking an object. (Data on the spatio-temporal response of the eye can be found in Budrikis, 1973.)

Figure 3.2(a) shows the approximate spatio-temporal response of a

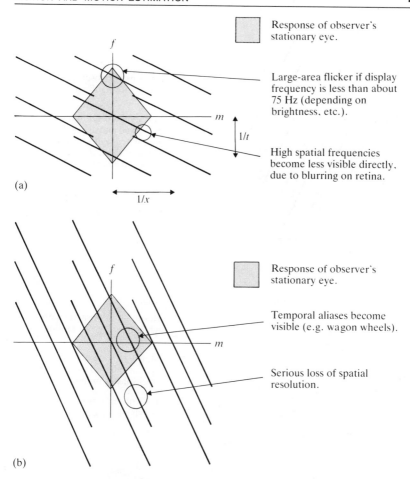

Response of observer's stationary eye.

Large-area flicker if display frequency is less than about 75 Hz (depending on brightness. etc.).

High spatial frequencies become less visible directly. due to blurring on retina.

(a)

Response of observer's stationary eye.

Temporal aliases become visible (e.g. wagon wheels).

Serious loss of spatial resolution.

(b)

Figure 3.2 The stationary eye as a spatio-temporal post-filter. (a) Low motion speed. (b) High motion speed.

fixed human eye superimposed on the spectra produced from feeding the sampled signal described in the previous section into a display (assuming negligible post-filtering occurs in the display). The sampling frequencies chosen are such as to render the first temporal repeat spectrum just visible; an example of such an effect is 'large-area' flicker on a 50 Hz television picture (so termed as it is most visible in large bright areas). High spatial frequencies are no longer visible due to blurring (or the production of multiple images) on the retina.

Figure 3.2(b) shows an exaggerated example of very fast motion, still with a fixed gazing point. At this speed of motion, components from the first temporal repeat spectrum lie near the axis of zero temporal frequency. They thus appear as almost stationary objects; a well-known example is the appearance of wagon wheels slowly rotating backwards

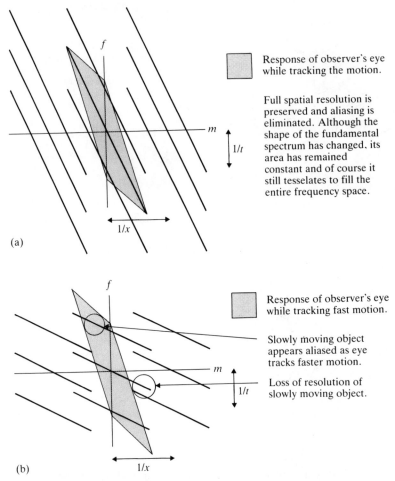

Response of observer's eye while tracking the motion.

Full spatial resolution is preserved and aliasing is eliminated. Although the shape of the fundamental spectrum has changed, its area has remained constant and of course it still tesselates to fill the entire frequency space.

(a)

Response of observer's eye while tracking fast motion.

Slowly moving object appears aliased as eye tracks faster motion.

Loss of resolution of slowly moving object.

(b)

Figure 3.3 The moving eye as a spatio-temporal post-filter. (a) Eye tracking fast motion. (b) Eye tracking fast motion, but slower motion also present.

in Western films. The loss of spatial resolution at this motion speed is now very severe.

When the eye tracks an object, the response of the eye's post-filter is skewed in the same way as the spectrum of the object being tracked. This amounts to changing the reference frame of the eye to render the object stationary. It is sometimes useful to consider such motion as motion of the image-processing system relative to a fixed object and eye rather than motion of the object and eye; thus the sampling structure moves and the responses of the temporal filters in the system are skewed.

Figure 3.3(a) shows the spectra from the same moving image as Fig. 3.2(b), but now the observer's eye is assumed to be tracking the motion perfectly. The loss of spatial resolution has been eliminated; the only remaining temporal artefact is the large-area flicker.

A typical moving scene contains several different types of motion, although the eye can only track one sort of motion at a time. Thus effects such as blurring, flicker, and the formation of multiple images will be visible when the eye tracks one object and other types of motion are also present. Figure 3.3(b) illustrates some of these problems. An example in the context of television would be an observer whose eye was tracking the background as the camera is panned to follow an ice-skater; the observer would see multiple images of the skater on the periphery of his or her vision.

Most of the problems encountered when a moving image is reconstructed by the combination of display device, eye and brain can be overcome by the use of a sufficiently high frame rate in the display. This is simply because the degree of aliasing is reduced as the field rate is increased, and the temporal repeat spectra are at a higher (and hence less visible) frequency.

3.3.2 Pre-filters

The degree of temporal pre-filtering required depends on the camera and display frame rate; the only pre-filtering that usually occurs is due to the integrating action of the camera and is determined by the shutter time. In a typical television camera, light is integrated for one field period, so the temporal response is a sinc function with its first null at 50 Hz. The highest temporal frequency that can be supported by this sampling rate is 25 Hz, so there is quite a lot of aliasing in the sampled signal. However, this aliasing is beneficial when the observer's eye tracks motion, as indicated in Fig. 3.3(a). Use of a shorter shutter time increases the degree of aliasing, allowing more spatial resolution on moving objects. However this aliasing will give rise to multiple images of objects that are not tracked by the eye, as shown in Fig. 3.2(b). A further discussion of the fundamental requirements of cameras, transmission links, and displays for accurate motion portrayal is given in Tonge (1986).

It should be clear from this section that the ability to detect and track motion is the key to making best use of the information in a temporally sampled image. This is one important reason for developing motion detection and estimation techniques. The following sections discuss possible techniques.

3.4 Motion detection

For many applications, it is sufficient simply to detect which areas of a picture are moving; different types of processing algorithm can then be applied to stationary and moving areas.

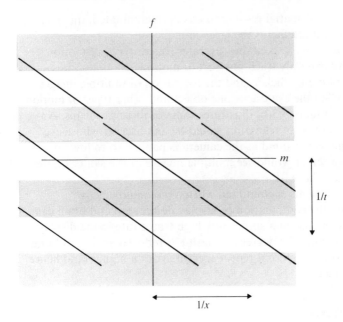

Figure 3.4 Areas of the spatio-temporal spectrum that can be used to detect motion.

A temporal high-pass filter can be used to detect the presence of motion by passing signals shown in the shaded regions of Fig. 3.4. At its simplest, such a filter would consist of taking the difference between successive pictures. It should be said that complications arise in the case of an interlaced signal, where high vertical detail can give rise to energy in the same part of the sampled spectrum as motion. With such a signal, it is generally better to compare information over a picture period rather than a field period, so that samples are co-sited. The signal from a temporal high-pass filter cannot be used directly as an indication of the amount of motion because of noise. One way of reducing the problem of noise is to filter spatially the r.m.s. value of the filtered signal. The filtered signal can be thresholded to indicate motion; the threshold can be adjusted dynamically according to the noise level in the picture. A block diagram of such a system is shown in Fig. 3.5. An

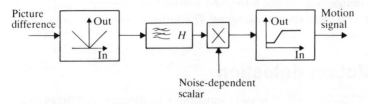

Figure 3.5 A block diagram of a motion detector based on the use of picture difference signals.

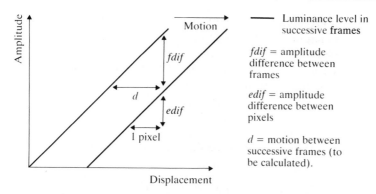

Figure 3.6 The estimation of displacement using the method of differentials.

account of the development of a video noise reduction system that incorporates a motion detector using these principles is given in Drewery *et al.* (1984).

3.5 Motion estimation

A number of techniques have been developed to estimate motion in video sequences. Each has its own strengths and weaknesses, in terms of the type and complexity of motion that can be dealt with and the hardware complexity. This section outlines four general methods; details of variations and enhancements to these methods will be found in the literature.

3.5.1 Method of differentials

This technique involves measuring the spatial and temporal luminance gradients at each point in the picture, and from them deriving an estimate of the motion. It is generally necessary to make the following assumptions:

1 Luminance is a linear function of position over the distance an object might move in a frame period (i.e. the displacement is small compared to the wavelength of the highest image frequency component present).

2 The luminance of objects remains constant as they move.

The principle is most easily explained by reference to Fig. 3.6, which illustrates the process in one dimension. The luminance difference between corresponding pixels in successive frames (*fdif*) and adjacent pixels in one frame (*edif*) is calculated. The ratio *fdif* : *edif* gives the displacement in pixels over one frame period, as can be seen by simple geometry from the diagram. The quantities *fdif* and *edif* are best obtained by summation over a block of pixels.

This technique was first proposed as a method for obtaining an approximate measure of the magnitude of the motion in an image, as described by Limb and Murphy (1975). This measure was used to control the switch between two different processing modes; one optimal for stationary or slowly moving areas, the other optimal for areas containing rapid movement.

More generally, the assumptions behind this method can be explained by modelling the image by the equation

$$I(x, y, t + \Delta t) = I(x - v_x\Delta t, y - v_y\Delta t, t)$$

where

$I(x, y, t)$ is the intensity (brightness) of the image at a point (x, y) and time t

v_x, v_y are the average components of the velocity of the object at the point (x, y) between times t and $t + \Delta t$

for all regions of the image, except those through which an object boundary has passed between the times t and $t + \Delta t$. A Taylor expansion of the above equation gives

$$v_x \frac{\partial I}{\partial x} + v_y \frac{\partial I}{\partial y} + \frac{\partial I}{\partial t} + E(x,y,t) = 0$$

where $E(x,y,t)$ represents higher-order terms of I.

If the spatial and temporal derivatives of the image brightness can be estimated at two locations at which the velocity is assumed to be related, then in principle the two unknown velocity components v_x and v_y may be found, assuming that the higher-order terms E can be ignored. This latter condition is equivalent to assuming that the brightness of each image is a linear function of position.

One way of enhancing the performance of this technique is to introduce recursion, as described by Netravali and Robbins (1979). The displacement estimate from the previous frame can be used as an initial estimate of the current displacement (so that the algorithm is looking for *changes* in velocity). The displacement estimate can be updated on a pixel-by-pixel basis, which helps to allow for objects changing shape as they move.

Although such techniques work well for sub-pixel shifts, they can fail for larger movements when assumption (1) becomes invalid. The use of recursion can improve the performance, but sometimes convergence can be slow or may not occur at all. One possible way around this problem is spatially to pre-filter the source picture to remove high-frequency components, thus enabling an initial motion estimate to be obtained. A second estimation process is then applied to the original picture, using the first estimate as a starting point. Such an algorithm is described by Bierling and Thoma (1986).

This algorithm (in common with many others) tends to give inaccurate estimates at object boundaries. To some extent this problem is fundamental, as the appearance or disappearance of picture material does not fit into the simple image model inherent in most motion estimation algorithms. Recursive algorithms tend to be more sensitive to boundary problems than non-recursive ones, as the initial motion estimate for the region beyond the boundary is almost certain to be wrong.

One advantage of this type of algorithm is that the hardware implementation can be fairly simple, although the incorporation of refinements can increase the complexity significantly.

This algorithm tends to minimize the difference between luminance levels in the current frame and the previous frame displaced by the motion vector. The minimization is usually carried out over a small area of the picture. This often results in vectors that do not correspond to the actual motion in the scene, but merely work as a frame-to-frame predictor. Techniques based on block matching (described below) often behave in the same way. Such 'motion' information can be used to good effect in a predictive coding scheme, in which both the coder and decoder use a predictor to estimate the value of each picture sample based on previously transmitted information, and only the difference between the predicted and actual value is transmitted. However, in applications where the motion information is to be used to perform temporal interpolation, it is important that the vectors correspond to the actual motion in the scene, rather than simply indicating which area of one frame is a good match for an area in the following frame.

3.5.2 Block matching

This class of technique works by dividing the picture into small blocks and summing the mean square difference (or similar function) between each pixel of corresponding blocks in adjacent frames. This calculation is performed with a range of different spatial offsets between the blocks and the offset that gives the minimum error is taken as the motion vector for that block. Figure 3.7 illustrates this process.

The function that is to be minimized can be written

$$\sum_{\text{block}} \{I_2(x, y) - I_1(x - x', y - y')\}^2$$

where

I_1, I_2 are the luminance levels in the successive frames
x, y are the coordinates within the block in the current frame
x', y' are the displacement components with respect to which the function is minimized.

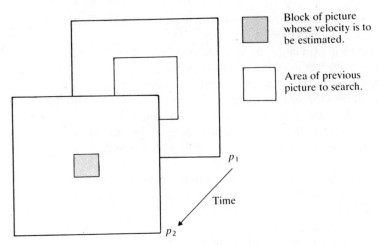

Block of picture whose velocity is to be estimated.

Area of previous picture to search.

p_1

Time

p_2

Figure 3.7 Motion estimation using block matching.

This is equivalent to maximizing the cross-correlation function

$$\sum_{block} \{I_2\,(x, y)\,I_1\,(x - x', y - y')\}$$

assuming that the blocks are large compared to the displacement.

One of the main problems with this method is that it is computationally very intensive; some implementations of the method employ various techniques to reduce the number of comparisons required.

In one implementation of this technique described by Ninomiya and Ohtsuka (1982), the match error is computed at 25 different offsets, and the one giving the least match error is chosen. The offset measured for the corresponding block in the previous picture is used as a starting point. The trial offsets are chosen to give reasonable resolution (1 pixel) for small displacements, while still covering relative shifts up to 5 pixels in any direction.

Recently, however, the advent of cheap VLSI has made it possible to consider performing exhaustive searches over a wide range of displacement values. Some researchers are now concentrating on methods of post-processing vector fields in order to reduce false assignments. As discussed above, motion estimation methods that only work on local areas of the picture do not always generate vectors that refer to the true motion in the scene. Operations such as median filtering can be used to reduce false assignments by detecting blocks whose vector differs significantly from those around it. A median filter returns the value of the median sample in its aperture; in other words, the value of the central sample if all the samples were sorted into ascending order. Such filters are good at removing occasional noisy samples and have the useful property of preserving edges.

Generally speaking, block matching methods have the potential to deal with larger movements and greater accelerations than gradient methods. However, they are confined to assigning vectors on a block-by-block basis unless the computations are repeated for blocks centred on each pixel, which implies a vast increase in hardware. They are also limited to integer-pixel accuracy unless image interpolation is applied during the matching process.

3.5.3 Fourier methods

In this class of technique, the 2-D Fourier transform of each field is calculated and the phase information from the transforms is used to determine the relative displacement between successive fields.

Consider two successive fields I_1 and I_2 of a scene undergoing translatory movement with a motion vector (v_x, v_y) pixels per field period. If we ignore edge effects and any effects due to interlace,

$$I_2 (x, y) = I_1 (x - v_x, y - v_y)$$

Taking the Fourier transform of each side of this and invoking the shifting theorem gives

$$F_2(m, n) = F_1(m, n)\, e^{- \pi j(mv_x + nv_y)}$$

where F_1 is the Fourier transform of I_1 and m, n represent spatial frequencies.

The Fourier transform of the (circular) cross-correlation of the images is

$$\mathcal{F}(C) = F_1 \cdot F_2^*$$
$$= F_1 \cdot F_1^* \cdot e^{2\pi j(mv_x + nv_y)}$$

where $\mathcal{F}(.)$ represents the Fourier transform.

If we divide this expression by $F_1 \cdot F_1^*$ before taking the reverse transform, we obtain the useful result

$$C(x, y) = \delta(x - v_x, y - v_y)$$

i.e. the correlation function has become a delta function situated at the required displacement. More generally, if I_2 was not a pure translation of I_1 but differed in overall luminance, we would calculate

$$C (x, y) = \mathcal{F}^{-1} \left\{ \frac{F_1 F_2^*}{|F_1 F_2^*|} \right\}$$

where $\mathcal{F}^{-1}$ represents the inverse Fourier transform.

What we have done is to normalize the spectrum of I_1 and I_2 before performing a cross-correlation; we can consider the normalizing process to have extracted the phase information from the transforms.

There are several advantages of this type of correlation (which is called *phase correlation*) over cross-correlation:

1 The sharpness of the peak makes it possible to distinguish several peaks from different types of motion.

2 The shape of the maxima is largely scene-independent, and it is therefore easier to choose an interpolation method to enable the sub-pixel portion of a shift to be estimated.

3 Brightness changes in the scene do not affect the measurement if they have a narrow spectral bandwidth (i.e. if the illumination in the whole scene drops or large diffuse shadows move across the scene).

4 Use of fast Fourier transforms to perform the calculation results in less multiplications than would be required to perform a cross-correlation 'long-hand', particularly for larger shift values. Other computationally efficient implementations of the Fourier transform can result in even greater savings.

Figure 3.8 shows a typical correlation surface for a scene showing a

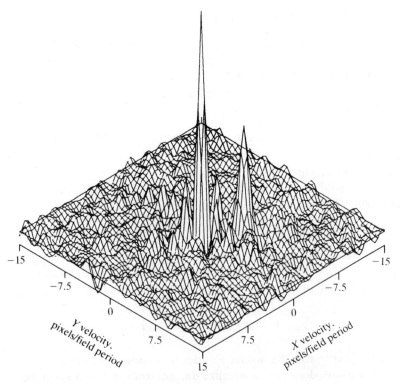

Figure 3.8 Phase correlation surface for an object moving over a stationary background.

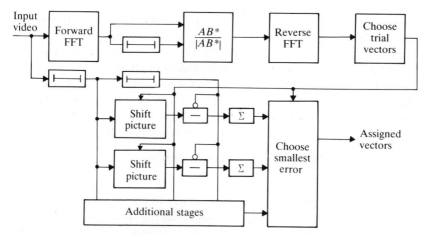

Figure 3.9 Block diagram of a vector measurement system that uses phase correlation to measure the dominant motion in the image.

small object moving over a stationary background. The large central peak corresponds to the stationary background; the next largest peak is due to the moving object and is situated at a point corresponding to its displacement between the two images that were correlated. In this example, the object moved 3 pixels horizontally and 3 pixels vertically. The heights of the peaks are determined by the area and spectral content of the object and the background. The noise is due to the fact that the two images were not related by pure translation; the revealed and obscured background around the moving object also contribute. The images that were correlated had dimensions 64×64 pixels; the resulting correlation surface thus corresponded to shifts in the range ± 32 pixels; only the central portion of this surface is shown. Points corresponding to half-integer pixel shifts have been interpolated; some of the ringing visible around the peaks is due to the impulse response of the interpolator.

This technique was originally used in image registration problems (Pearson *et al.*, 1977) where the requirement was to measure global picture shifts to high accuracy.

However, the technique can be applied to scenes containing many types of motion by using it to generate lists of trial vectors which can then be assigned on a block-by-block or pixel-by-pixel basis using a technique similar to block matching. The development of such a technique is described in Thomas (1987), an outline of which is given below.

Figure 3.9 shows a block diagram of how phase correlation can be used to estimate motion vectors for pixels in a scene containing many moving objects. The incoming fields are divided into blocks of 64×64 pixels for the purpose of performing phase correlations. The phase correlation functions (or 'surfaces') are examined to locate the dominant peaks, and interpolation is performed to evaluate the sub-pixel part of the displacement. A number of trial displacements are selected for each region of the image; these are presented to a number of modules which shift the current field by the given displacement relative to the previous field. The modulus of the difference signal between the shifted and the previous field is calculated and integrated over a small aperture; the vector giving the smallest error is then assigned.

Some of the advantages of this technique are the following:

1 Vectors can be assigned to individual pixels rather than to blocks of pixels.

2 Vectors tend to correspond more closely to the actual motion in the picture than with gradient or block matching techniques because the trial vectors are measured over a relatively large area of the picture.

One of the disadvantages is that rotations and fast zooms can generate too many vectors for the correlation technique to find; it is rarely possible to distinguish more than three individual peaks in each correlation surface.

3.5.4 Techniques based on feature extraction

The basis of feature extraction methods is to identify particular features in the scene (often edges or corners of objects), and to follow the movement of these features from one picture to the next. This provides motion information at various points in the picture, and an interpolation process is used to assign motion vectors to the remaining picture areas. This class of technique is often applied to problems such as the determination of the 3-D structure of a scene from a number of photographs taken from different locations; an example of such work is given in Buxton *et al.* (1985).

One way of measuring the movement of the edge or corner features is by first applying a high-pass filter to the image to isolate the edge, and then using techniques based on the method of differentials to measure the amount of movement. The edge information can be smoothed with a low-pass filter to reduce the effects of noise and enable large movements to be measured.

A more sophisticated approach to detecting features in an image prior to motion estimation is to convolve the image with the Laplacian of a Gaussian and to use the resulting zero-crossing contours. It has been suggested that such zero-crossings are tied more closely to physical features of the image than are other intensity changes. Also, as such points correspond to points in the image at which the gradient of the intensity is a local maximum, the accuracy of the following motion component estimation process is improved. The perpendicular motion component at each point on the contour can be calculated using the method of differentials as described above. These estimates can then be combined to form a 2-D motion estimate. An example of this approach is given in Hildreth (1984).

This class of technique is useful for specialized scene analysis tasks, but is not often used to measure motion in more general scenes. As these techniques rely on the extraction of particular features of the scene (such as edges), they can fail to measure the correct velocity in picture areas that do not contain such features.

3.5.5 Motion estimation in 3-D space

The motion estimation techniques described in the preceding sections are applicable to 2-D images; however, there are a number of applications in which the motion of objects in 3-D space needs to be derived from two or more successive 2-D images. An example of such an application is passive navigation, in which a vehicle is guided using information from an on-board camera. Another application is model-based image coding, in which a 3-D model of the scene is formed from 2-D images and parameters describing this model are transmitted. The decoder then generates a 2-D picture from the 3-D model.

Consider a point on an object whose position vector changes from $\mathbf{X}$ to $\mathbf{X}'$ between two images. The motion can be described as a rotation followed by a translation:

$$\mathbf{X}' = \mathbf{R}\mathbf{X} + \mathbf{T}$$

where

$\mathbf{R}$ is a 3×3 rotation matrix
$\mathbf{T}$ is the translation vector.

In order to describe the motion fully, a total of $9 + 3 = 12$ parameters must be estimated. However, for small rotations, $\mathbf{R}$ becomes

$$\mathbf{R} = \begin{bmatrix} 1 & \phi & -\psi \\ -\phi & 1 & \theta \\ \psi & -\theta & 1 \end{bmatrix}$$

where ϕ, ψ, and θ are the angular rotations about each of the axes. This reduces the number of parameters to six. The assumption that the angles of rotation are small may be made by assuming that the time between the two images is short.

These parameters can be calculated from estimates of the observed motion of a number of different points in the 2-D image; such estimates may be obtained using some of the techniques discussed in the preceding subsection. Various methods have been used to perform the calculation. A large number of points may be needed to give reliable estimates, using regression analysis.

At the time of writing there is much activity in this field, particularly for applications such as low bit-rate image coding applied to videoconferencing. An example of such work is given in Musmann *et al.*, (1989).

3.6 Summary

When considering image-processing operations in the time domain, it is important to understand the way in which the spatio-temporal spectrum of the signal behaves in the presence of motion. Global motion causes the spectrum to be skewed, with each spatial frequency giving rise to a temporal frequency proportional to the product of its magnitude and the motion speed.

Almost all of the temporal variation in typical scenes is due to motion. Motion can give rise to temporal frequencies far beyond the Nyquist limit for typical temporal sampling rates; the aliases so produced can cause serious problems for many types of processes. The 'out of band' signals produced by these aliases do not usually present a problem for human observers, as the tracking eye itself has a skewed spatio-temporal frequency response that can make full and correct use of these signals.

The ability to compensate for motion effectively reduces the temporal components to very low levels. This allows processing such as interpolation and bit rate reduction to be used very effectively in the time domain.

A number of techniques to detect and estimate motion have been described. Motion detection can be based around the use of temporal high-pass filters, although the effects of noise must be taken into account. Motion estimation can be performed in a number of ways; techniques based on spatio-temporal gradients, block matching, Fourier methods, and feature extraction have been described. A brief outline of the principles of 3-D motion estimation has also been given.

At the time of writing, research is continuing into many aspects of motion estimation and compensation. Some work is concentrating on post-processing of motion vector fields in order to eliminate false assignments and ensure that vectors correspond to the actual motion in the scene. Other workers are looking at ways of identifying picture areas for which a valid vector cannot be found, such as areas of uncovered background. Most image-processing operations that use motion compensation need to incorporate a fallback mode to use when reliable motion information is not available; the use of an incorrect motion vector can produce serious impairments on processed images. Ideally, algorithms should be used that are tolerant to incorrect vectors, so that an explicit determination of validity is not required.

Acknowledgement

The author would like to thank the Director of Engineering of the BBC for permission to publish this chapter.

References

Bierling M. and Thoma R. (1986) 'Motion compensating field interpolation using a hierarchically structured displacement estimator', *Signal Processing*, vol. 11, no. 4, pp. 387–404.

Budrikis Z. L. (1973) 'Model approximations to visual spatio-temporal sine-wave threshold data', *Bell System Technical Journal*, vol. 52, no. 9, pp. 1643–67.

Buxton B. F., Buxton H., Murray D. W. and Williams N. S. (1985) 'Machine perception of visual motion' *GEC Journal of Research*, vol. 3, no. 3, pp. 145–61.

Drewery J. O., Storey R. and Tanton N. E. (1984) 'Video Noise Reduction', BBC Research Department Report, no. 1984/7.

Hildreth E. C. (1984) 'Computations underlying the measurement of visual motion', *Artificial Intelligence*, vol. 23, no. 3, pp. 309—54.

Limb J. O. and Murphy H. A. (1975) 'Measuring the speed of moving objects from television signals', *IEEE Transactions on Communications*, vol. COM–23, no. 4, pp. 474–8.

Musmann H. G., Hötter M and Ostermann J. (1989) 'Object-oriented analysis–synthesis coding of moving images', *Image Communication*, vol. 1, no. 2, pp. 117–38.

Netravali A. N. and Robbins J. D. (1979) 'Motion compensated television coding: part 1', *Bell System Technical Journal* , vol. 58, no. 3, pp. 631–70.

Ninomiya Y. and Ohtsuka Y. (1982) 'A Motion-compensated Interframe Coding Scheme for Television Pictures' *IEEE Transactions on Communications*, vol. COM-30, no. 1, pp 201–11.

Pearson J. J., Hines D. C., Golosman S. and Kuglin C. D. (1977) 'Video-rate image correlation processor', Application of Digital Image Processing, International Optical Computing Conference, San Diego, published in *SPIE Proceedings*, vol. 119, pp. 197–205.

Thomas G. A. (1987) 'Television motion measurement for DATV and other applications', BBC Research Department Report, no. 1987/11.

Tonge G. (1986) 'Time-sampled motion portrayal', *Second IEE International Conference on Image Processing*, IEE Conference Publication no. 265, pp. 215–19.

4 Higher-definition television

GARY TONGE

4.1 Introduction

Of the many developments in digital image processing, one that will
have an impact on most of the population is in the area of consumer
television. Digital storage and processing are already finding their way
into consumer television equipment (teletext memories,
picture-in-picture facilities, etc.) and the future promises much more.
This chapter addresses the increasing amount of research and
development with the goal of higher definition television ('hi-fi TV').
Some of the image processing being considered is of a complexity that is
currently hard to imagine in the consumer environment. Nevertheless
the prospect of VLSI volume production makes it possible to consider
some of the relatively complex approaches, provided that the
improvement is worthwhile.

4.2 Picture quality targets

In a general sense the target is to produce a picture presentation in the
home that is a sufficient improvement over the current norm to justify
the extra expense. Typically the improved quality will not be exploited
to give a better picture definition as seen by the eye, but rather to enable
a larger screen presentation.

Subjective tests in Japan and in Europe have shown that a larger
viewing angle can increase the sense of involvement in a televised scene.
Given that domestic television viewing distances are typically set more
by practical constraints (room size, furniture, etc.) than by technical,
this implies an increased screen size. The Japanese work also
highlighted the importance of having a wider aspect ratio for
large-screen television.

More specifically, targets for 'high-definition television' (HDTV) have
been set as an improvement in comparison with conventional television
systems in both vertical and horizontal resolution of about 2 : 1 in
conjunction with a wider aspect ratio of around 5 : 3. This implies that
for the same picture definition as seen by the eye at a fixed viewing

distance, an increase in screen height by a factor of about 2 and screen width by a factor of around 2½.

The image-processing techniques described here can be used to achieve a broad range in the degree of improvement over conventional systems. The specific targets discussed above represent a tangible benchmark of quality which has been called 'HDTV'. It is not clear, however, what reduction in picture quality is necessary before an image ceases to be HDTV. With conventional television standards, for example, a domestic videocassette recorder provides a degraded picture. Nevertheless from a user's point of view this does not imply a destruction of the service. In practice, any improvements that can be provided by image-processing techniques in a cost-effective way are likely to find definite application, and an increasing future trend toward higher-quality consumer television can be predicted.

4.3 Compatibility

Image-processing techniques for picture quality improvement can be applied in a number of different ways. At one extreme they can be applied retrospectively to current television services by processing in the receiver alone. At the other extreme they can be particular to a proposed new and completely different television service. In the technical description that follows, the techniques are subdivided into four categories of 'compatibility' with current systems.

Compatible level 1

These are techniques that can be applied to current NTSC/PAL/SECAM broadcasts by receiver processing alone. Such techniques are often referred to as IDTV (improved definition television).

Compatible level 2

These are techniques that can be applied to the current NTSC/PAL/SECAM broadcast formats but require processing both at the receiver and at the source.

Compatible level 3

These are techniques that can be applied to 625 or 525 line systems only in channels using MAC colour coding. Multiplexed Analogue Components (MAC) is a time division multiplex format for colour TV coding using time compression which is standardized in Europe for direct broadcast satellite transmissions (IBA, 1988). In North America such formats are under discussion in the ATSC (Advanced Television Systems Committee) and in Australia they are used for services on the AUSSAT satellite.

Non-compatible systems

These are techniques that assume a different scanning format from those used in conventional television transmission. The only constraints considered here are those of transmission or storage bandwidth.

These subdivisions are important since they concern broadcasting system concepts that affect significantly the receiver cost and also have political implications for standardization. From a technical point of view they represent constraints on the extent to which the wide range of possible image-processing techniques can be applied. Of particular importance in Europe are techniques in the third category—i.e. compatible with MAC. The goal is the introduction of very high quality television pictures via direct broadcast satellite by a method that is operationally very similar to the introduction of colour television.

4.4 Aspect ratio

In this section we consider methods of achieving a transition from the current aspect ratio of 4 : 3 to a wider aspect ratio picture format. Although a wider aspect ratio is normally considered in conjunction with improved definition, it is in its own right a valid target. Indeed as far as the general public is concerned, a wider picture format is likely to be a major distinctive feature of any new 'hi-fi' service. It remains a property of the system, however poor the signal strength or however poor the viewing conditions! The precise picture aspect ratio considered in most cases is 16 : 9 (5.33 : 3). This format (33 per cent wider than the current 4 : 3) is the one now generally agreed for HDTV production in preference to the earlier assumed figure of 5 : 3.

Despite their importance, the image-processing content of methods for achieving a wide aspect ratio is not great and so techniques are described here only very briefly.

For existing broadcast formats (NTSC/PAL/SECAM) there are broadly four ways of introducing a wider aspect ratio:

1 Simply change the geometry of the source pictures leaving the transmitted signal unchanged. This would result in the display of geometrically distorted pictures on normal 4 : 3 shaped receivers. This technique was used in the United Kingdom in 1950 when the aspect ratio was changed from 5 : 4 to 4 : 3. In this case the 7 per cent distortion was tolerable. However, it is unlikely that the 33 per cent distortion resulting from a change from 4 : 3 to 16 : 9 would be acceptable.

2 Increase the active line length (i.e. the picture width) in transmission.

3 Reduce the number of active picture lines per frame (i.e. the picture height) in transmission.

4 Separate off the widescreen picture 'side panels' (i.e. those parts of the picture outside the current 4 : 3 window) and encode them into some other part of the transmission signal such as an additional subcarrier or on lines in the field blanking interval.

These four approaches are all used to varying degrees in current proposals for compatible widescreen television NTSC. In PAL and SECAM countries these approaches are also being considered, although in Europe there is a greater emphasis on the new service possibilities available with MAC transmission by satellite. The MAC system has built in from the start a dual aspect ratio specification (4 : 3 or 16 : 9) and so a transition from one to the other can readily be achieved: decoders recognize the aspect ratio of the transmitted signal via a digital data flag and respond accordingly.

4.5 Vertical resolution improvement

We turn now to our core topic—methods for improving television picture definition by digital image-processing techniques. We start by considering improvements in the vertical direction. The descriptions are categorized according to the compatibility headings introduced in Sec. 4.3.

4.5.1 Compatible level 1—increasing vertical resolution by receiver processing

Current resolution limits

Clearly the current limits to vertical resolution are set by the number of lines in the system. If we assume a perfect sampling process, then the 575 active lines (vertical samples) in the 625 line system should be able to carry vertical frequencies up to the Nyquist limit of 288 cycles per picture height. This corresponds to an 'equivalent' horizontal frequency of 383 cycles per picture width, or 7.4 MHz. The comparable calculation for 525 line systems yields a figure of 6.1 MHz. It has been evident from the early days of television that these ideal figures are not provided in practice and that a reduction factor (the 'kell factor') applies. The scanning imperfections that give rise to the kell factor are discussed in Tonge (1984). It emerges that a significant contribution to the perceived loss of resolution with current television standards is due to the use of interlace—especially in the display. This is because any high vertical frequencies in the source tend to be dominated on display by 'interline flicker' effects. In the extreme case of a 'Nyquist' frequency of 288 cycles per picture height, the display shows alternate lines as 'black' and 'white', which due to interlace appear as alternate plain black and white fields. In this way a purely vertical frequency of 288 cycles per picture height (c/ph), 0 Hz is aliased to appear as a purely temporal frequency of 0 c/ph, 25 Hz. In a similar way a frequency of 200 c/ph, 0 Hz for example, is aliased to appear as a lower vertical frequency flickering at 25 Hz, i.e. 88 c/ph, 25 Hz. These aliasing defects tend to mask the high vertical frequencies and hence limit vertical resolution in interlaced systems. If an electronic vertical frequency sweep (gamma-corrected to provide an optical sine wave sweep on display) is used as a test, then the 'kell factor' for the 525 or 625 line systems can be put at something just below 0.5, i.e. they are achieving less than 50 per cent of their theoretical potential.

Receiver processing for display scan conversion

Receiver processing can be applied to increase the scanning standard for display so as to overcome some of these limitations. The potential for picture improvement in this way has been recognized widely and this area is one of active research worldwide (Long and Tonge, 1984; Nishizawa and Tanaka, 1982; Uhlenkamp and Guttner, 1982). In particular, scan conversion for non-interlaced (progressive or sequential) display has received attention. If interpolation is used to provide additional display lines for 625/50 or 525/60 non-interlaced display as illustrated in Fig. 4.1, then the quality of static pictures improves significantly. The improvement applies for static pictures since in this case all of the information in the two interlaced fields can be combined into each single non-interlaced field ('temporal interpolation'). With pictures containing significant movement this would produce multiple-image or blurring defects and so an alternative strategy is applied for moving images.

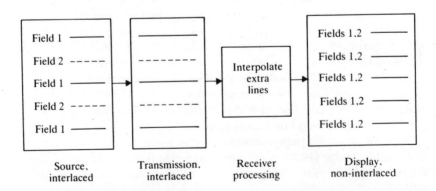

Figure 4.1 Increasing vertical resolution by interlaced to non-interlaced display scan conversion.

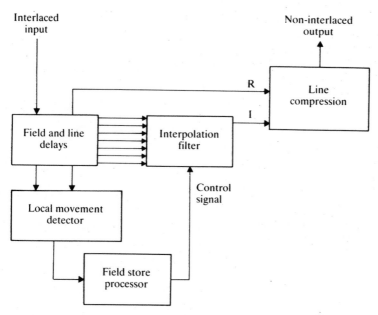

Figure 4.2 The interlaced to non-interlaced scan conversion technique developed at the IBA. Processing for the digital luminance signal.

Many people have commented on the high-definition appearance resulting from such scan conversion using component-coded television signals. Not only is interline flicker removed for static pictures, but also a noticeable absence of 'busyness' occurs in the line structure of the non-interlaced display. If the electronic vertical frequency sweep referred to above is used as a test, then the improvement in vertical resolution offered by this technique is almost the full factor of 2 : 1. With real picture material the improvement is not so great and a factor more in the region of 1.5 : 1 results. This is primarily because the modulation depth of the high vertical frequency detail in conventional scenes is much less than the extreme case (100 per cent) of the electronic sweep.

Improvement in perceived resolution is not achieved, however, in parts of scenes that have significant motion. If the algorithm that is used to interpolate the extra lines for display is fixed, then any improvement in static picture quality is offset by a motion degradation. For this reason, most of the research has pursued the option of a motion-adaptive interpolation procedure to achieve the improvement for static pictures described above, while maintaining the conventional motion portrayal capabilities of interlace. Other work has been aimed at arriving at a compromise algorithm using a linear spatio-temporal filter to interpolate the extra lines. Unfortunately, such a technique is not

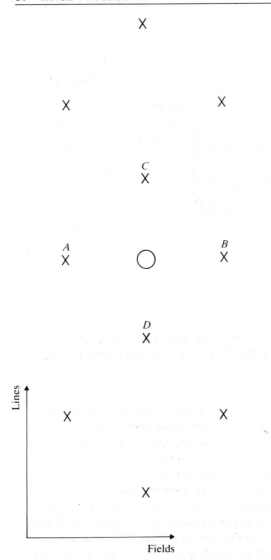

Figure 4.3 Line positions (marked by **X**) available for the interpolation of the 'missing' line marked by O.

able to remove all interline flicker from static scenes without corresponding motion degradation.

We shall now describe briefly the specific approach for non-interlaced scan conversion developed at the Independent Broadcasting Authority (IBA) by Long and Tonge (1984). The processing operates on digitized decoded luminance and colour difference signals. For the colour difference components the techniques used are simple and non-adaptive.

A block diagram of the adaptive processing for the digital luminance component is shown in Fig. 4.2. The block labelled 'field and line delays' contains two field delays and several line delays to make available to the interpolation filter the line positions indicated in Fig. 4.3. Appropriate weighted sums of the signal values from these positions are used in the interpolation filter to provide the signal value for the interpolated line whose position is marked by a circle. The field and line delay block also provides the 'real' (unfiltered) lines (R), suitably delayed to be combined with the interpolated lines (I), and outputs to the movement control loop (consisting of a local movement detector and a field store processor).

The interpolation filter

For the interpolation filter, it was found that it was sufficient to use only points A, B, C, and D in Fig. 4.3. When the control signal indicates no motion then temporal interpolation is used (averaging A and B), and when the control signal indicates full motion, vertical interpolation is used (averaging C and D). Intermediate states involving a weighted sum of A, B, C, and D are used for intermediate levels of the control signal, but in practice these are in operation for only a small proportion of the time.

The local movement detector (LMD)

The local movement detector is the first part of the control loop and indicates to the interpolation filter the most suitable interpolation to apply for a given picture point.

The basis of the local movement detector is an absolute frame difference signal $|A - B|$ (Fig. 4.3). This is followed by a 'coring threshold' which minimizes the effect of low value difference signals occurring due to noise in the picture. This threshold can be adapted according to measures of scene brightness and accumulated noise statistics.

The non-local field store processor

Certain types of motion would bypass the local detection technique if this were used alone to provide the control signal. A simple example, which occurs in practice within electronically generated moving captions, is a moving narrow bar. Consider a horizontally moving vertical bar as illustrated in Fig. 4.4. The task is to interpolate the 'missing lines' within this bar in field 0. By comparing the frame difference signal that results (Fig. 4.5(a)) with the signal amplitude of the bar itself (Fig. 4.5(b)), it can be seen that during the bar the frame difference value is zero (indicating no change) even though the bar is moving. Thus if the frame difference signal were used to control directly the interpolation to be used, then a wrong result would emerge. It has

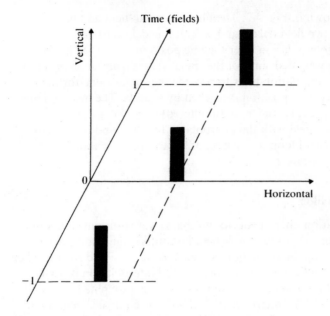

Figure 4.4 A horizontally moving bar over three television fields.

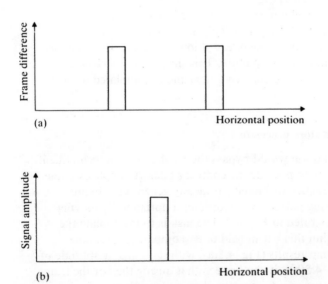

Figure 4.5 The frame difference signal (a) compared with the picture signal itself (b) for the moving bar of Fig. 4.4 in field 0.

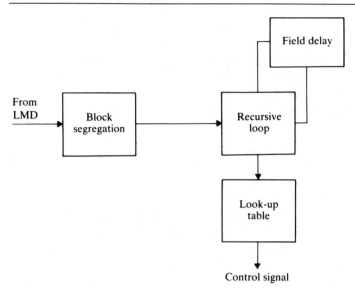

Figure 4.6   The field-store processor in the IBA display scan converter of Fig. 4.2.

been shown (Tonge, 1983) that this effect is a fundamental feature of the processing being attempted and cannot be suitably overcome on a purely local basis. The purpose of the field-store processor is suitably to 'spread' the local detection signal so that the 'gaps' left by such types of movement are filled, and hence the correct (vertical) interpolation method is used within the bar.

A block diagram of the processor is shown in Fig. 4.6. The local movement detection signal is separated into blocks since very fine spatial resolution is not required for this part of the processing. The signal values within a block are accumulated and coded with few quantization levels. The block signals are then modified according to previous field values by use of a recursive loop containing a field delay element. This results in a 'spreading' of the signal in areas of motion. Finally, the output of the recursive loop is fed into a look-up table which performs a second 'coring threshold' function. By suitable choice of block size (e.g. 6 samples × 4 lines), and the use of horizontally and vertically overlapping blocks, it is found that the same control signal value can be applied to the interpolation process for all positions within a block without detrimental effects on the picture quality.

This technique has been found to be effective with all electronically generated moving captions tested so far and also with less critical motion. Furthermore, the immunity of the motion detection process to noise is good and effective down to luminance signal-to-noise ratios of around 30 dB. For higher noise levels than this the system is configured to be able to adapt its coring thresholds according to an accumulated measure of noise statistics.

Line compression

The final stage in the conversion process (Fig. 4.2) is to combine the 'real' and 'interpolated' lines to give the non-interlaced output. This implies time compression by a factor of 2 and a doubling of bandwidths. In our implementation the luminance input bandwidth is 10 MHz (sampling frequency is 22.5 MHz) while the output bandwidth is 20 MHz ($f_s = 45$ MHz).

Discussion

Despite the complexity of the motion detection in the above description, techniques such as these could be able to be implemented in domestic television receivers since the techniques lend themselves to large scale integration. Indeed consumer television sets incorporating motion-adaptive display scan conversion techniques were first introduced in Japan in 1988.

4.5.2 Compatible level 2—vertical resolution improvement by pre- and post-processing

Further improvements should prove possible if a higher scanning standard is introduced also at the source, as shown in Fig. 4.7. Following on from the previous example, the source and display formats could be 625/50 or 525/60 non-interlaced. Alternatively, the source and display formats could be 1250/50 or 1050/60 interlaced. This latter case has received more attention recently, combined with motion-adaptive pre- and post-filtering. Despite the promise of further improvements beyond the use of display scan conversion alone, subjective tests on simulations by Wendland and Schroeder (1985) showed very little difference between the results of this approach and that of the previous section.

4.5.3 Compatible level 3—opportunities with a MAC signal

For the luminance component, the MAC system offers no difference with respect to composite systems in terms of vertical resolution. One

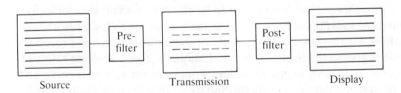

Figure 4.7 Pre-processing and post-processing for vertical resolution improvement.

feature of the system that could be used in this context, however, is the presence of a digital channel to carry audio and data services. This digital channel could be used to convey motion detection control information from the source to the receiver (Storey, 1986; Tonge, 1983). This would be of particular use for the case of pre- and post-processing since it is desirable to have source and receive motion detectors locked together.

For the colour difference components, the MAC system has inferior vertical resolution since each component is carried only on alternate lines. In fact the particular arrangement of alternate-line colour used in MAC (a frame-reset sequence) limits the vertical resolution not to one-half of the luminance potential but to one-quarter. Compatible pre- and post-processing techniques can be used, however, to change the effective transmitted colour line structure to a better format which can provide half the potential of the luminance vertical resolution (Tonge, 1983). In this way a balanced solution is provided with colour components having half the resolution of the luminance in both horizontal and vertical directions.

4.6 Horizontal resolution improvement

4.6.1 Compatible level 1—receiver processing for composite systems

Composite systems are impeded in picture quality by cross-colour (the misinterpretation by the receiver of high-frequency luminance detail as colour) and cross-luminance (the misinterpretation by the receiver of colour information as high-frequency luminance detail). These impose effective limitations to luminance and colour difference horizontal resolution that can be reduced by improved decoding techniques. Improved decoding incorporating line-delay 'comb-filters' has been known for some time, while more recently processing (fixed or motion adaptive) incorporating field stores has been studied (Achiha et al., 1984). The improvements potentially offered by these more complex NTSC and PAL decoding techniques are measurable, but not of very high significance in terms of the targets set in Sec. 4.2.

4.6.2 Compatible level 2—pre- and post-processing with composite systems

It is fundamentally impossible completely to remove the cross-effects described above by receiver processing alone. It is possible, however, to eliminate cross-effects altogether by a combination of improved NTSC or PAL coding and decoding. The nature of the precise subcarrier frequencies in NTSC and PAL implies a frequency offset in horizontal, vertical, and temporal frequency for the colour information with reference to the luminance (Drewery, 1976; Dubois et al., 1982). This means that by using digital 2-D or 3-D pre- and post-filtering for the luminance and colour difference signals it is possible to convey 'clean' NTSC or PAL signals while maintaining the full horizontal resolution specification. This can be illustrated by considering the spectrum of the television image in three-dimensional terms. *Horizontal* frequencies (f_h) are spatial variations that may be normalized to the television picture width and expressed in cycles per picture width (c/pw). *Vertical* frequencies (f_v) can be expressed in cycles per picture height (c/ph) and *temporal* frequencies (f_t) are dynamic variations measured in cycles per second or Hz. The relationship between 'one-dimensional' signal frequency f and the image frequencies f_h, f_v, and f_t is given by the equation

$$f = (f_h - f_v/N)\, f_L + f_t$$

where N is the number of lines per field and f_L is the line frequency. Blanking is ignored in this equation. A single signal frequency f (e.g. 5 MHz) does not correspond to a unique image frequency (f_h, f_v, f_t), but there are various solutions. This reflects the spectral-repeating effect of television scanning as a sampling process.

Taking the example of a 5 MHz signal in the 625 line system (f_L = 15 625 Hz, N = 312.5) gives one solution for the image frequency as being (320, 0, 0), or a purely 'horizontal' frequency of 320 c/pw. Taking blanking into account would give a frequency of 260 cycles per *active* picture width. Increasing the frequency very slightly from 5 MHz could correspond to such a frequency grating moving; as the frequency increases further, vertical elements come in to make the grating pattern diagonal. Eventually another static horizontal frequency grating is reached at 5.015 625 MHz (321 c/pw).

One solution for the PAL subcarrier frequency of 4.43 3618 75 MHz is (284, 78, 18.75), i.e. f_h = 284 c/pw, f_v = 78 c/ph and f_t = 18.75 Hz. This is illustrated in Fig. 4.8, which shows the spectrum of a PAL signal on 3-D frequency axes. The vertical–temporal frequency offset of the subcarrier frequency can be seen by the position of the carrier for the 'U' signal. The alternate-line switching of the phase of the 'V' component in PAL results in a separate vertical–temporal frequency offset as shown. The shaded block shown bounded by separate lines in Fig. 4.8 represents the limits to the 3-D frequency spectrum of the luminance signal with 'ideal' pre- and post-filtering for complete separation between the luminance and colour components. The smaller blocks shown bounded by dotted lines represent the corresponding limits for the chrominance signals.

Further improvements in horizontal resolution beyond those of the normal specifications for NTSC (4.2 MHz) and PAL (5–6 MHz) have been suggested by introducing extra-high-frequency luminance information in a further subcarrier within the band. In one example, the

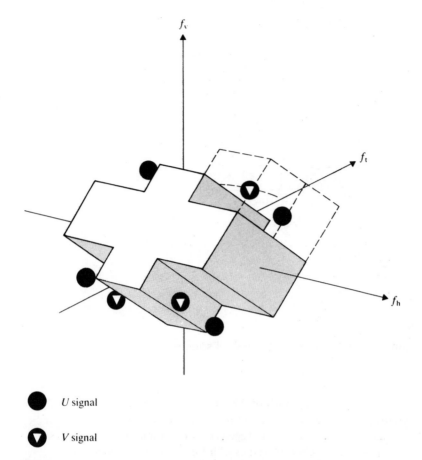

U signal

V signal

Figure 4.8 The spectrum of a PAL signal in terms of horizontal (f_h), vertical (f_v), and temporal frequency (f_t).

subcarrier frequency is chosen to be essentially the same as the colour subcarrier frequency, but with a shifted phase.

4.6.3 Compatible level 3—approaches based on MAC transmission

While efforts towards compatible high-definition television in North America are tending to concentrate on NTSC-based approaches (Hopkins, 1988), in Europe the emphasis is clearly on MAC, which offers a significantly greater flexibility in signal-processing terms.

Firstly, the absence of subcarriers for colour or sound with MAC make it easier to widen the bandwidth of the video signal. The 'basic' specification for the European MAC/packet family of systems gives a transmission video bandwidth of 8.4 MHz. This gives a decoded luminance bandwidth of 5.6 MHz (time compression factor 1.5) and

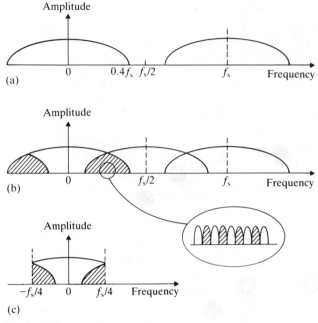

Figure 4.9   A 1-D frequency view of spectrum folding. See text for explanation.

colour difference bandwidth of 2.8 MHz (time compression factor 3). These figures in themselves represent a significant improvement over composite systems as typically received in the home. By suitable attention to the r.f. characteristics of a direct broadcast satellite channel, it is possible to widen the transmission video bandwidth as far as 14 MHz, which corresponds to around 9 MHz for the luminance. The non-linear techniques that can achieve this rely on the fact that signal amplitude at these high frequencies will not be 100 per cent.

Secondly, the absence of a colour subcarrier with MAC enables a much greater flexibility in the use of 'spectrum folding' techniques in which high-frequency luminance detail is carried on a suppressed 'subcarrier' at the top of the band.

4.6.4 Spectrum-folding techniques

The horizontal sampling along each television line in digital processing introduces the opportunity to convey a reduced-rate non-orthogonal sampling structure on a transmission channel, in order to enable transmission bandwidth efficiency in a MAC transmission channel. The same basic technique has been referred to as sub-Nyquist sampling, offset sampling, 3-D filtering, frequency-interleaved coding, or colloquially as 'spectrum folding'. The basic concept is illustrated in 1-D frequency terms in Fig. 4.9. A television signal with bandwidth B is sampled with frequency f_s where $B = 0.4f_s$, say. As shown in Fig. 4.9(a), this represents 'super-Nyquist' sampling with no spectral overlap between the baseband spectrum and those generated by the sampling process.

Assume that half the samples are omitted to give a sampling rate of $f_s/2$. There then appears to be spectral overlap which leads to confusion (aliasing) in the signal (Fig. 4.9(b)). However, it is possible to apply filtering to the signal prior to subsampling which has a fine 'comb' structure based on the harmonics of line and/or field or frame frequency. If the subsampling is then based on a non-orthogonal (offset) structure it is possible to arrange that the 'teeth of the comb' in the filtered spectra of the baseband and the adjacent repeats do not overlap but instead interleave, as illustrated in the expanded illustration of Fig. 4.9(b). In reconstruction it is then possible to use another comb filter spectrum. In this way signal frequencies of up to $0.4f_s$ are conveyed by a sampling frequency of $0.5f_s$, appearing to violate the Nyquist limit of $0.25f_s$. All of the signal information can now be carried in a bandwidth of $0.25f_s$ (Fig. 4.9(c)), which represents a bandwidth saving of nearly 40 per cent compared with the original $0.4f_s$. An infinitely sharp transmission filter with cut-off at $0.25f_s$ cannot be realized, but any filter that has an amplitude response of 0.5 at $0.25f_s$ with skew-symmetry around this point enables accurate transmission of the samples.

With MAC transmission, this approximately achieves the target for HDTV set in Sec. 4.2. This improvement is merely an example. The extent to which the horizontal resolution is improved depends solely on the extent to which the spectrum is 'folded back'. Indeed, it is possible to fold the spectrum a second time by performing a further subsampling process. This would reduce the bandwidth requirements even further to $f_s/8$. However, the additional comb filtering would remove more information from the signal (typically relating to vertical to temporal resolution) and would furthermore increase the likelihood of the 'folded information' (e.g. the hatched part of the spectrum in Fig. 4.9(c)) being visible on a simple receiver that has no reconstruction comb filters.

Another way of viewing the process illustrated in Fig. 4.9 is to look at the television signal spectrum in 3-D terms (horizontal, vertical, and temporal frequency) (Tonge, 1981).

The original sampled signal of Fig. 4.9(a) is shown in Fig. 4.10. The block shape represents the extent of the baseband spectrum in three dimensions. The horizontal limits are set by the filtering applied with cut-off at $0.4f_s$, while the vertical/temporal boundaries are purely notional ones representing the capabilities of interlace. We consider now the effect of a 3-D 'comb' filter. An example digital filter using 35 taps spread over a grid of 11 samples horizontally, 5 lines vertically, and 3 fields temporally can be implemented with a frequency response as indicated in Fig. 4.11 (Tonge, 1982).

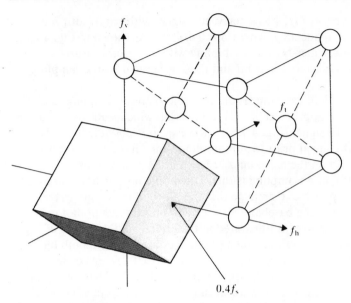

Figure 4.10 The sampled television signal spectrum of Fig. 9(a) shown in 3-D frequency terms. The axes are horizontal frequency (f_h), vertical frequency (f_v), and temporal frequency (f_t).

Figure 4.11(a) shows the horizontal–vertical frequency amplitude response, while Fig. 4.11(b) shows the horizontal–temporal frequency amplitude response. There is no filtering applied in the vertical–temporal frequency sense. The response of Fig. 4.11(a) indicates a loss in diagonal resolution while maintaining full horizontal resolution. The response of Fig. 4.11(b) indicates a loss of 'temporal resolution' with high horizontal frequencies. This is difficult to interpret and so in Fig. 4.11(c) the horizontal frequency response of the filter is illustrated as a function of motion velocity, measured in picture widths per second (pw/s). (The response is shown here within the constraints of a temporal frequency of less than 25 Hz. Beyond this frequency the response repeats. This is not shown in the diagram for clarity.) It is seen that the horizontal bandlimiting effect of the filter is more severe as the motion velocity increases. In practice the most significant loss noticeable (especially with television camera pictures, which are significantly temporally filtered in any case due to the light integration effect) is with fairly slow motion of a finely detailed image.

The effect of this filtering on the 3-D view of the baseband spectrum is indicated in Fig. 4.12: the 'corners' are removed. If the signal is now

Figure 4.11 Amplitude versus frequency response for a 3-D comb filter applied in the spectrum-folding example. (a) Horizontal and vertical frequency. (b) Horizontal and temporal frequency. (c) Horizontal frequency and motion velocity.

(a)

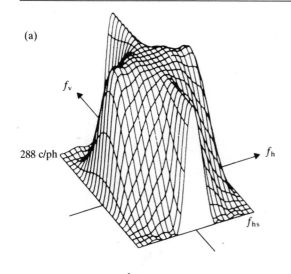

(b)

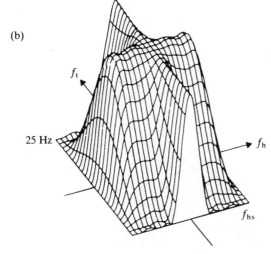

(c)

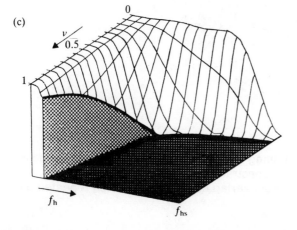

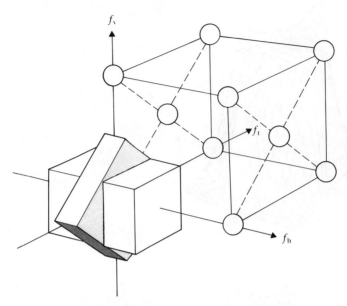

Figure 4.12 The effect of the 3-D filter of Fig. 4.11 on the sampled television signal spectrum of Fig. 4.10.

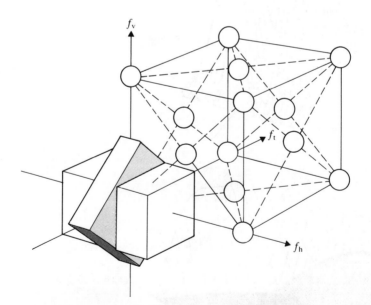

Figure 4.13 Downsampling the signal of Fig. 4.12 in a field-quincunx pattern introduces extra spectral repeats. The filtered spectrum shape illustrated does not overlap its neighbours when repeated on this pattern.

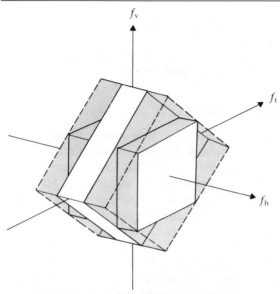

Figure 4.14 The transmitted signal spectrum, analogous to Fig. 4.9(c).

downsampled by a factor of two in a field-quincunx pattern (Tonge, 1981), then the filtered baseband spectrum is repeated on a different pattern of repeat spectra as illustrated in Fig. 4.13, (this is now analogous to Fig. 4.9(b)). The filtering is such that the shape tesselates on the pattern of repeat spectra.

The sampling frequency is now $0.5 f_s$ and it is possible to transmit the signal in an analogue channel of bandwidth $0.25 f_s$ (-6 dB). The 3-D transmitted signal spectrum is as illustrated in Fig. 4.14 (analogous to Fig. 4.10(c)). The shaded corners are now the extra horizontal resolution 'folded' within the band.

At the receiver a simple decoder merely displays the information as transmitted; the shaded corners are spurious information. However, an improved decoder samples the signal in a field-quincunx pattern and uses a 3-D filter similar to the one at source to reconstruct the spectrum of Fig. 4.12—with the improved horizontal resolution.

Discussion

Despite the elegance of this example, which uses non-adaptive 3-D filters, efforts have more recently tended to concentrate on the use of motion-adaptive filtering. These promise slightly improved performance but at the expense of the need for motion detection. Where adaptive techniques promise to show a significant improvement is in the area of motion compensation (see Chap. 3). By determining local motion velocity information, it is possible, in principle, to adapt the pre- and post-filtering and the downsampling pattern according to *velocity* and thus maintain more horizontal resolution with motion.

The opportunity offered by the digital channel in the MAC system is perhaps particularly important here. Motion velocity information can be derived at source (perhaps at great expense) and conveyed to the receiver using part of the MAC data signal (Storey, 1986).

4.6.5 Non-compatible systems

Spectrum folding techniques have also been proposed as a means of bandwidth compression for non-compatible HDTV systems. For example, the MUSE system (Ninomiya *et al.*, 1984) compresses an 1125/60 interlaced signal with 5 : 3 aspect ratio into around 8 MHz by these methods. In this system a 'double downsampling' is used to reduce the sample rate of the initially sampled digital signal by 4 : 1.

Motion-adaptive filtering is used with motion compensation for the special case of translatory motion for the whole scene (simple camera pans and tilts). Although there are no limits on the extent of 'folding' due to compatibility constraints, it is found that it is necessary to keep the bottom 2 MHz of the transmitted spectrum 'clean' to enable the receiver motion detector to function satisfactorily.

An alternative to spectrum folding that has also been considered for 'non-compatible' systems is sub-band coding (Schreiber and Lippman, 1989). In this approach the 3-D frequency spectrum of the image is subdivided into a number of 'blocks' or sub-bands. Bandwidth reduction is achieved by transmitting only a portion of these sub-bands, or by transmitting the higher-frequency sub-bands with less signal-to-noise capability. In one adaptive approach only the sub-bands with greatest energy content are transmitted at any one time. Other alternatives being considered for non-compatible transmission involve digital coding using the DCT (discrete cosine transform), for example.

4.7 Combined horizontal–vertical resolution improvement

Although the foregoing discussions on compatible systems have assumed separable improvements to vertical and to horizontal resolution, it is possible to consider an approach where both methods are combined into one. For example, the double-downsampling approach of MUSE described above could be applied in a very similar way for a 1250-line, 50 Hz system as opposed to the 1125/60 system. By 'shuffling' alternate samples into a 625-line grid it is then possible to transmit a 1250-line signal in a manner that is compatible with MAC (Vreeswijk *et al.*, 1988). Combining these techniques with sophisticated motion compensation maintains the full 1250-line resolution even on moving scenes.

4.8 Non-linear correction and constant luminance

The picture quality of current composite (PAL/SECAM/NTSC) and MAC colour television systems is restricted not only by simple limitations in luminance and colour horizontal and vertical resolution but also by effects resulting from the 'failure of constant luminance', i.e. the transmitted luminance signal is not, when displayed, a true representation of luminance perceived by the eye. Some of the 'true' luminance information is in fact conveyed in the colour difference signals—which are more severely bandlimited. This implies that some defects due to colour bandlimitation (especially with highly saturated colours) affect the perceived luminance, and are hence more visible. A second drawback relates to the visibility of transmission noise introduced in the colour signals. Since the transmitted colour signals contain some true luminance content, the transmission colour noise becomes visible as perceived luminance errors. This significantly affects the noise visibility.

The reason for the failure of constant luminance is twofold. The first relates to gamma-correction. The light output versus signal input characteristic of a CRT display follows an approximately exponential ('gamma') law. The approximately linear red–green–blue signals generated by a television camera are 'gamma-corrected' at source rather than at the display for practical reasons. The colour matrix that calculates the transmitted luminance and colour difference signals operates on these non-linearly corrected signals rather than on linear versions, and hence the outputs do not represent true luminance and colour difference in the linear domain.

The second reason relates to the use of the wrong colour matrix at source, at least in Europe. The matrix values used are based on NTSC display phosphors, while the more typical PAL displays give rise to a completely different matrix. Despite this, errors due to this mismatch tend to be less significant than those due to gamma-correction.

During the early days of the definition of colour television standards much fundamental work was done on these aspects (Livingston, 1954). More recently, work towards future improved television systems is addressing this topic again in an attempt to restore—at least partially—the constant luminance principle. Non-compatible systems clearly have the advantage here, although there is still an opportunity for improvements by signal processing in a compatible manner. Most work in this area is still at an early stage, although progress so far is promising (Schafer et al., 1988).

4.9 Summary

This chapter has surveyed some of the digital image-processing techniques being studied for television picture quality enhancement. The end goal is a television picture capable of large-screen display with wide aspect ratio to give a completely different viewing experience. In the transition from today's television towards this improved quality, it is unclear how many stages will be passed through. One school of thought says that a 'clean' 525 or 625 line signal in its own right is an impressive improvement over what is currently achieved and is a sufficient target for the next few years. Another says that the next step should be a big one—immediately to large screen, wide aspect ratio with full 'high definition' quality. Digital image processing is central to either philosophy and will inevitably play an ever increasing role in the consumer television field.

References

Achiha M., Ishikura K. and Fukinuki T. (1984) 'A motion adaptive high definition converter for NTSC colour TV signals', *SMPTE Journal*, vol. 93, no. 5, pp. 470–6.

Drewery J. O. (1976) 'The filtering of luminance and chrominance signals to avoid cross-colour in a PAL colour system', *BBC Engineering*, pp. 8–39.

Dubois E., Sabri M. S. and Ouellet J. Y. (1982) 'Three-dimensional spectrum and processing of digital NTSC color signals', *SMPTE Journal*, vol. 91, no. 4, pp.372–8.

Hopkins R. (1988) 'Advanced television systems', *IEEE Transactions on Consumer Electronics*, vol. CE-34, pp. 1–15.

IBA Technical Review (1988) Issue on the D-MAC/packet system for satellite and cable, no. 24.

Livingston D. C. (1954) 'Colorimetric analysis of the NTSC color television system', *Proceedings of the IRE*, vol. 42, pp. 138–50.

Long T. J. and Tonge G. J. (1984) 'Scan conversion for higher definition television', *Proceedings of the 10th International Broadcasting Convention*, Brighton, pp. 116–19.

Ninomiya Y., Ohtusuka Y. and Izumi Y. (1984) 'A single channel HDTV broadcast system—The MUSE', NHK Lab. Note no. 304.

Nishizawa T. and Tanaka Y. (1982) 'New approach to research and development of high definition television', *NHK Technical Monograph*, vol. 32, pp. 98–101.

Schafer R., Chen S. C., le Goff F. and Melwig R. (1988) 'Colorimetry and constant luminance coding in a compatible HD-MAC systems', *Proceedings of the 12th International Broadcasting Convention*, Brighton, pp. 45–8.

Schreiber W. F. and Lippman A. B. (1989) 'Reliable EDTV/HDTV transmission in low-quality analog channels', *SMPTE Journal*, vol. 98, no. 7, pp. 496–503.

Storey R. (1986) 'HDTV motion adaptive bandwidth reduction using DATV', *Proceedings of the 11th International Broadcasting Convention*, Brighton, pp. 167–72.

Tonge G. J. (1981) 'The sampling of television images', IBA Experimental and Development Report no. 112/81.

Tonge G. J. (1982) 'Three-dimensional filters for television sampling', IBA Experimental and Development Report no. 117/82.

Tonge G. J. (1983) 'Signal processing for higher definition television', *IBA Technical Review*, vol. 21, pp. 13–26.

Tonge G. J. (1984) 'The television scanning process', *SMPTE Journal*, vol. 93, no. 7, pp. 657–66.

Uhlenkamp D. and Guttner E. (1982) 'Improved reproduction by standard television systems', *NTZ Archiv.*, vol. 4, pp. 313–21.

Vreeswijk F. W. P., Fonsalas F., Trew T. I. P., Carey-Smith C. and Haghiri M. (1988) 'HD-MAC coding of high definition television signals', *Proceedings of the 12th International Broadcasting Convention*, Brighton, pp. 62–5.

Wendland B. and Schroeder H. (1985) 'Signal processing for new HQTV systems', *SMPTE Journal*, vol 94, no. 2, pp. 182–89.

5 Pattern recognition

GRAHAM LEEDHAM

5.1 Introduction

Pattern-recognition techniques are increasingly being used or proposed in image processing for telecommunication and information systems. Two specific examples are discussed elsewhere in this book. One has already been encountered in Chap. 3: to estimate the interframe motion of an object, a search is made in successive frames for a pattern of light that corresponds to the object. The other example is discussed in Chap. 12 and concerns the analysis of an image sequence in model-based coding: image patterns corresponding to the eyes, mouth, etc., of a human subject are automatically located in order to create a wire-mesh software model of the camera image.

In the storage or transmission of documents by facsimile (fax), advanced techniques for recognizing patterns are being developed; instead of having to transmit a whole array of image pixels to specify a pattern, a single coded symbol representing the pattern may be used, with considerable saving in the amount of data required to represent the document image. In addition, pattern-recognition techniques are used to recognize the individual characters and symbols in document images to enable both machine-printed and handwritten documents to be efficiently converted to a machine-compatible form. Approaches to both of these problems are discussed later in this chapter.

It is computationally simpler to look for patterns in binary (black and white) images, so that where source images have a fully grey or colour scale, operators are often used to extract binary features, as described in Chap. 2. Some neural-net architectures for recognizing faces and scenes—discussed later in the book—extract binary representations of the scene as a primary operation.

This chapter introduces the topic of automatic pattern recognition and discusses three general techniques used in its implementation: template matching, statistical classification, and structural classification. This introductory discussion is followed, in Sec. 5.6, by a consideration of two practical examples of pattern-recognition implementations for binary images: coding of document images for fax transmission and character recognition. The treatment does not cover automatic pattern

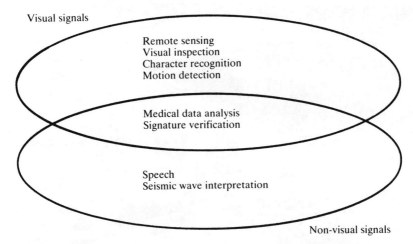

Figure 5.1 Example areas of study in pattern recognition.

recognition in depth but there are a number of published textbooks dedicated to this subject; pointers to further information are provided for the reader seeking more detailed information.

5.2 Definition and scope of pattern recognition

Due to the wide range of patterns encountered, pattern recognition is by no means a narrow subject; rather, it is a multidisciplinary research topic and is studied by psychologists, computer scientists, engineers, and others. It encompasses in its entirety both visual and non-visual signals. Some examples of the application areas studied in pattern recognition are shown in Fig. 5.1. A detailed treatment of these applications can be found in Fu (1982), Young and Fu (1986), and Plamondon *et al.* (1989).

Before considering approaches to automatic pattern recognition it is instructive to attempt a definition. After a survey of the definitions of pattern recognition, Verhagen (1975) reviewed many definitions and concluded that all the definitions in published work tended to be specific to the particular patterns under consideration. The statement by Guiliano (1967) summarizes the problem of definition 'For a human it is probably not possible to give a better definition than: a pattern is something which one recognizes as a pattern'!

Apart from the difficulty in defining the term and scope of pattern recognition, a limiting factor on the design of automatic pattern-recognition systems is the fact that psychologists do not understand how people perform the task. For example, Sayre (1965) observed that, 'We simply do not understand what recognition is. And

Figure 5.2 Spotty dog. (Original photograph by R. C. James.)

if we do not understand the behaviour we cannot reasonably hold high hopes of being successful in our attempts to simulate it.' It is possible, however, to say that to recognize a pattern it must have previously been perceived and remembered, and the past and present experiences related. For example, at first glance, or even after careful study, many people find it difficult to put any meaning to the image in Fig. 5.2. If, however, the reader has seen this picture before, he or she recognizes it immediately and is therefore relating that past experience to his or her present experience in order to describe it. To those who have never seen this picture before it appears totally unintelligible. Calling on these readers' past experience by associating the image with the word 'dog' or more specifically 'Dalmation dog' may help. Having located the dog, further study of the picture uncovers even more detail. Once such basic perceptual cues have been provided, people apply a great deal of information gained from past experience and knowledge of the world in general to classify even the most distorted or poorly defined image. This view is supported by many psychologists: Biederman (see Rosenfeld, 1986) notes people's ability to attempt to classify an unknown object by reference to previously perceived objects and knowledge whilst Schwab and Nusbaum (1986) term this phenomenon 'perceptual glue'.

Current computer technology and advances in pattern recognition and artificial intelligence are a long way from achieving the pattern-recognition and image-classification ability of humans. This

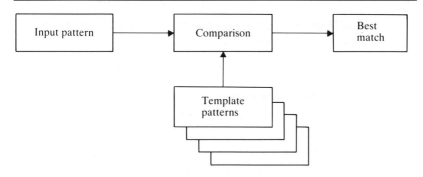

Figure 5.3 Template matching.

does not deter researchers from trying to achieve automatic pattern recognition, as there are many simpler pattern-classification problems that can be tackled effectively by automatic techniques (see Fig. 5.1).

5.3 General pattern-recognition techniques

There are a number of basic techniques that can be applied to almost any pattern-recognition problem whether it is a visual image of a scene or object or a 1-D time-varying signal such as speech. These basic techniques are discussed below.

5.3.1 Template matching

Template matching is perhaps the simplest pattern-recognition technique. Patterns are identified by comparing the input pattern to a list of stored pattern representations. The stored pattern representations are the templates. This principle is illustrated in Fig. 5.3 where an isolated input pattern is passed to a comparator which performs a similarity measure between it and each of a set of pre-stored template patterns; the comparison that produces the best match is deemed to be the recognized pattern if the match exceeds a predefined threshold of similarity. If none of the matches exceeds this threshold, the pattern is rejected as not being the same as any of the stored templates.

If we assume that we have an input pattern $P = \{p(x_1, y_1), p(x_2, y_2), \ldots, p(x_n, y_n)\}$ and an identically dimensioned template pattern $R = \{r(s_1, t_1), r(s_2, t_2), \ldots, r(s_n, t_n)\}$ where $p(x, y)$ and $r(s, t)$ are individual pixels, the Euclidean distance is defined as

$$D_E(P, R) = \sum_n \sqrt{(x_n - s_n)^2 + (y_n - t_n)^2} \qquad (5.1)$$

Frequently the square and square root are removed and just the magnitudes of the distances between individual pixels used for the template match, producing what is known as the 'city-block' or D4 distance, which can be expressed as

$$D_C(P, R) = \sum_n (|x_n - s_n| + |y_n - t_n|) \tag{5.2}$$

The Hamming distance is defined as

$$D_H(P, R) = \sum_n e_n \tag{5.3}$$

where e_n is defined as

$$e_n = \begin{cases} 1 & \text{if } p(x_n, y_n) \neq r(s_n, t_n) \\ 0 & \text{if } p(x_n, y_n) = r(s_n, t_n) \end{cases} \tag{5.4}$$

Each of these distance measures is a minimum for the template pattern that most closely resembles the input pattern. If patterns P and R were identical, then $D_E(P, R) = D_C(P, R) = D_H(P, R) = 0$.

The Euclidean, city-block and Hamming distance measures can easily be applied to 2-D patterns composed of binary, grey-scale, or colour pixels providing a suitable relationship between the value of pixels is defined in grey-scale and colour images to make the distance measure meaningful.

However, in order for any of these distance or similarity measures to operate successfully it is assumed that both the input pattern and the template pattern are the same size in both x and y dimensions. In reality this is rarely the case and normalization is required to ensure that the size of one pattern (usually the input pattern) is made the same as the template pattern. In addition it is usual to carry out preprocessing to filter out the effect of quantization and threshold noise in the pictures before template matching is performed.

In order to operate effectively the recognizer must be trained with a representative set of template patterns. If this is done and a suitable distance measure is selected, simple template matching produces satisfactory performance when the following conditions hold:

1 The number of different patterns is small, i.e. there are not many different template patterns.

2 There is little variation in the same pattern classes over all occurrences of the patterns, i.e. each time a particular pattern occurs it is always similar to its template.

3 There is not a close degree of similarity between any two or more of the template patterns.

Elastic matching (or dynamic programming template matching) provides a means of relaxing the second constraint to some extent and also removes the need to incorporate exact size normalization prior to performing the template match (Widrow, 1974). Indeed, the need to normalize input patterns frequently degrades the template match because the normalization process is linear and causes expansion or contraction of all parts of the image by the same amount. In many images variation in size from one occurrence to another is non-linear and linear size normalization can distort the significant features of the pattern. Elastic matching operates by stretching the template pattern onto the input pattern and measuring the amount of stretching required. This stretching has the effect of a non-linear normalization process. The less stretching needed, the more similar are the patterns.

In general, however, template matching is only appropriate in simple pattern-matching problems where there is only a small number of distinct dissimilar patterns that vary little from the stored template. Note that pattern variation includes such factors as rotation as well as size and position variation, as simple template matching cannot easily cope with orientation differences between the input and template patterns even if their shapes are identical. For more complex patterns, exhibiting wider variation, statistical or structural techniques must be applied.

5.3.2 Statistical methods

Statistical pattern-recognition techniques (also known as decision-theoretic techniques) determine which class a given input sample belongs to, based on selected measures or features extracted from the pattern. Figure 5.4 shows the main components of a statistical pattern recognizer. It consists essentially of two parts: a feature extractor and a pattern classifier. Each isolated pattern is input to the feature extractor which extracts significant features from the pattern and passes this feature vector to the classifier, which makes a decision as to which class the pattern belongs to. In many ways this is similar to the template-matching technique described above but the statistical method can be less prone to noise and pattern variation as it does not match the whole pattern with a reference pattern but uses a set of features that are resilient to pattern variation. The simple template matching described above is a special case of statistical pattern matching.

The selection of features to form the feature vector is a difficult problem but, in general, they should be chosen such that they are less

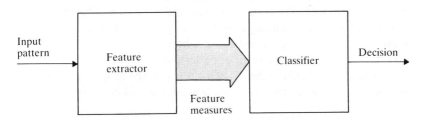

Figure 5.4 Statistical pattern recognizer.

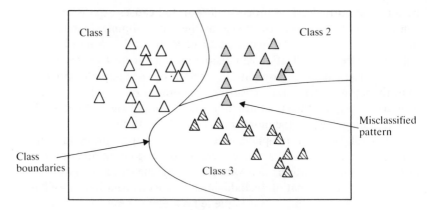

Figure 5.5 Subdividing the feature space.

sensitive to variation in the pattern. The features may not necessarily have any physical meaning but are nevertheless good measures for the pattern classification. There are at present no real, tangible rules for the selection of features (see Chap. 3 of Young and Fu, 1986, and Chap. 5 of Devijver and Kittler, 1982). Selection is based upon experimentation with a training set of known patterns.

In statistical pattern recognition a feature vector containing N feature maps each pattern as a point in an N-dimensional feature space, as shown in Fig. 5.5. Statistical information obtained from observations on a known set of representative patterns (the training set) is used to determine suitable features and the boundaries between one class and another, in order to maximize the recognition performance for each pattern class. If a given pattern is identical to a reference pattern, then they will both be mapped to the same point in the feature space. If this was the case, then the definition of the boundaries between patterns would be trivial. However, this is not the case with real patterns. The requirement is to choose features such that patterns of the same class are tightly clustered in the N-dimensional space and patterns of different classes are in other tightly clustered regions that are well separated from other clusters. If this is achieved the task of the pattern classifier is simplified and the classification performance is improved.

There are two methods of determining whether a pattern belongs to a certain class, namely the non-parametric and the parametric decision methods. In the non-parametric method a discriminant function $\partial_j(X)$ is defined, based on extracted features X where $X = \{x_1, x_2, x_3, \ldots x_F\}$. If $\partial_j(X)$ is a maximum, then the input pattern with feature vector X belongs to the particular class W_j. This is expressed in Eq. (5.5) where the boundary between classes is determined when $\partial_i(x) - \partial_j(x) = 0$.

$$\partial_i(x) > \partial_j(x) \qquad i, j = 1, \ldots, C \quad i \neq 0 \qquad (5.5)$$

where C is the number of distinct classes.

The commonly used discriminant functions are the linear discriminant function, the minimum distance classifier, and the nearest neighbour classifier (these are all described in detail in Chap. 4 of Devijver and Kittler, 1982).

As an example, the linear discrimination function is a weighted linear combination of the F feature measurements as shown in Eq. (5.6)

$$\partial_j(x) = \sum_{k=1}^{F} w_{jk} x_k + w_{j\ N+1} \qquad i = 1, \ldots, C \qquad (5.6)$$

In the parametric classifier the decision rule involves the class conditional densities $[p(X \mid W_j)]$ and the *a priori* probabilities of occurrence of the classes $[P(W_j)]$. The objective is to design a statistical decision classifier to minimize the risk of misclassification. The decision rule to determine the class boundaries is given by

$$P(W_i)p(X \mid W_i) \geq P(W_j)p(X \mid W_j) \qquad \text{for all } j = 1, \ldots, C \qquad (5.7)$$

This is generally referred to as the Bayes classifier. Further discussion of the parametric decision rule can be found in Chap. 2 of Devijver and Kittler (1982) and Chap. 1 of Young and Fu (1986).

Statistical classifiers need to be trained on a large database of known patterns if they are to be effective. This large database is needed to define accurately the feature set and the classifier decision boundaries. Alternatively, if a large data base is available but the number of distinct classes is unknown, the pattern identification can be on the basis of looking for clustering or grouping together of certain samples and thus enabling some automatic pattern grouping to be achieved.

5.4   Structural or syntactic techniques

The principle behind structural pattern recognition is the observation that many patterns contain structure and can be expressed as an ordered composition of simple subpatterns or pattern primitives. That is, patterns can be formed from a sentence or grammar of simple pattern primitives (such as straight and curved lines) in a pattern description language. This is illustrated in Fig. 5.6, where two simple patterns, a square and a brick, are expressed as a combination of three basic straight-line pattern primitives, A, B, and C. Pattern representation is made on the basis of the identification and connectivity or syntax of the subpatterns. That is, the square can be represented as a string of four pattern primitives and a brick can be represented as a string of nine pattern primitives. The connection of the pattern primitives to create the pattern is expressed in a pattern grammar.

The structural pattern recognizer is shown in block diagram form in Fig. 5.7. Each incoming pattern enters a segmenter which splits the pattern into its component pattern primitives. This list of pattern

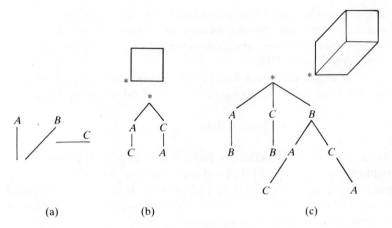

Figure 5.6 Example of a structural classification. (a) Pattern primitives. (b) Square. (c) Brick.

primitives is then passed to the recognizer which classifies the pattern primitives and the relationship between them. This list of pattern primitives and their connectivity is then passed to a syntax analyser which makes the final classification of the pattern based on the observed syntax of the incoming pattern and on its own set of pattern syntax rules, which describe patterns known to the recognizer.

While the overall process of recognition appears as a simple logical progression, there are several difficulties that must be overcome. Primarily, the selection of pattern primitives is a difficult task. There are no general rules available for this task and, in essence, it depends on heuristics and the experience or preference of the user. On the subject of selecting primitives, Fu (1982) has only given the following guidelines:

1 The primitives should serve as basic pattern elements to provide a compact but adequate description of the data in terms of specific structural relations.

2 The primitives should be easily extracted.

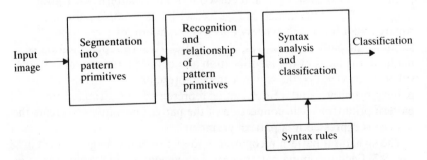

Figure 5.7 Structural recognition.

It is important that the pattern primitives are easily extracted as it is difficult, if not impossible, to correct gross errors at this stage.

As a general rule, selecting simple pattern primitives results in complex syntax grammars, while selecting complex pattern primitives results in simpler syntax grammars. It is the designer who must decide upon the trade-off between these two criteria after a careful study of the patterns that are to be recognized.

5.5 Choosing a pattern-recognition technique

When faced with a particular pattern-recognition problem, deciding which of the three general techniques to apply is not always obvious. In general, if there are a small number of invariant patterns, then template matching is probably most appropriate. But if there is little apparent structure to the patterns or if they are in the presence of high noise, then the statistical pattern recognizer may be most effective. If, however, the patterns have an obvious structure and a certain amount of variability, as for example in handwritten characters, then the structural pattern-recognition technique is usually most appropriate.

It is not always possible to apply such simple rules to the choice of recognizer and a combination of techniques may be needed for many patterns. In fact, in order to obtain high performance many pattern-recognition algorithms use a combination of statistical and structural techniques. For example, the known *a priori* probabilities of occurrence of certain pattern classes can be used to reinforce structural recognition. Knowledge representation and interaction with the pattern recognizer is the key to successful pattern recognition and this knowledge may take the form of both structural knowledge and statistical knowledge.

To attempt to appreciate the factors involved in pattern recognition it is useful to consider how humans recognize patterns. For example, look at the two sets of patterns shown in Fig. 5.8 and locate the two pairs of patterns that are identical. When you have done ask yourself the following questions:

- How did I find the two identical patterns?
- What features did I use to perform this operation?
- How certain am I that I have found the match?

5.6 Examples of pattern recognition in image processing

In this section two particular examples of pattern-recognition problems associated with document images are discussed. The first is concerned

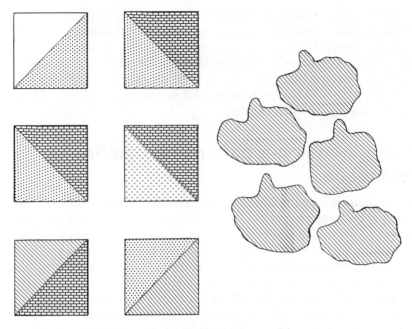

Figure 5.8   Examples of pattern-matching problems.

with the scanning and reading of printed and handwritten characters, and the second is concerned with using simple pattern matching to encode document images for fax transmission.

5.6.1   Pattern recognition for document reading

In this, the first of our two examples of practical pattern-recognition systems, we consider character recognition. In offices throughout the world there are many thousands of millions of pages of printed documents either in the form of magazines, or books, or typed sheets of paper. These piles of stored information are growing larger as time goes by and are becoming increasingly difficult to catalogue and reference. If a general search for specific information is needed, the task is often unjustifiable in terms of both time and cost. With the ever growing use of electronic databases, computer-based search techniques, and transmission methods such as electronic mail, there is a need optically to scan and store these existing printed documents in computer form, in order either to search them by computer or to transmit them to a remote destination in an efficient object-oriented format. Transmission of printed documents is possible by fax machines but current implementations involve no understanding or analysis of the document that is sent.

In a typical scanned A4 size document there may be up to 8 000 000 pixels of information and each pixel may have up to 256 grey scales associated with it. Thus the storage capacity for a single sheet of paper

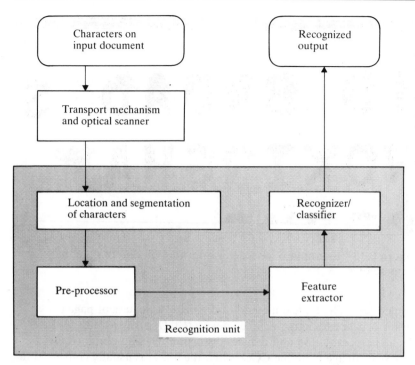

Figure 5.9 The principal components of a document reader.

is vast (even if it is reduced to a binary image). It would be far more compact and also enable computer searching operations to be performed if textual information were automatically recognized and stored as characters using standard ASCII coding and its layout information.

The general structure of an optical character recognition (OCR) system is shown in Fig. 5.9. Documents are delivered beneath a scanner on a transport mechanism and digitized. The scanner converts the reflected image into a binary image to save computational effort and individual characters are located and separated within the recognition unit. A pre-processor is applied to remove noise from the character image and possibly 'thin' each character image to a skeletonized form. A feature extractor then extracts the significant features from the character image and passes them to a recognizer or classifier, which decides which class, if any, each character belongs to.

Digitization of the text

The quality of any recognition algorithm is closely related to the quality of the initial digitization of the text. For OCR applications of many standard fonts it is widely accepted that approximately 10 pixels/mm resolution is needed in both axes to produce good performance. This gives approximately 30 × 30 pixel resolution for 12 point typed or

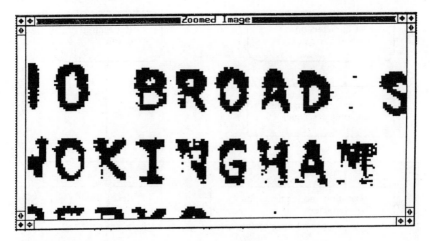

Figure 5.10 Example of character degradation due to poor thresholding.

printed text. The typical method of digitizing a document page is by means of a linear charge-coupled device (CCD) array as this produces the highest resolution and reduces distortion. Having obtained the grey-scale image from the CCD array, the image is usually converted to a binary image using an appropriate thresholding algorithm. For OCR applications it is usually adequate to apply a simple fixed-level thresholding technique when the printing or typing is black lettering on white paper, but with coloured paper or coloured inks or poor quality inking it may be necessary to apply a more sophisticated type of thresholding algorithm. Figure 5.10 illustrates the degradation in character quality caused by applying a simple thresholding algorithm to poor quality inking.

Character location and separation

Most commercially available OCR systems assume that lines of text can be separated by detecting horizontal lines of white space and characters can be isolated within each line by detecting vertical lines of white space. The locations of these horizontal and vertical lines are usually obtained by first taking horizontal histograms to separate the lines of text and then separating each line into words and characters by taking vertical histograms. This is satisfactory for simple documents if they are composed of good quality print (using a simple font) and have horizontal text, but as few documents fall into this category, a number of problems remain in the majority of documents which cannot be resolved by simple horizontal and vertical histogram analysis. For example, in certain fonts, the 'f' and 'i' in words like 'five' became joined together into a composite character—fi.

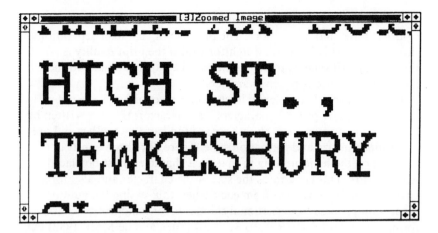

Figure 5.11   Example of joined characters.

Furthermore, with proportionally spaced character fonts there is the danger that if characters such as n and m appear next to each other, and there is merging of adjacent characters, then it can be difficult to locate the boundary between characters. Different locations of the boundaries can produce rnr or rm or nrn, etc. Close printed or typed characters can become joined after they have been digitized and binarized. This problem is illustrated in Fig. 5.11 where the T, E, W, K, and E of TEWKESBURY are joined. Separation of these characters, while readily apparent to the human reader, is not a trivial problem for automatic readers.

Levels of recognition complexity

Some constrained machine fonts have been specifically designed for OCR applications. These include the MICR (magnetic ink character recognition) standard (*Character Recognition Handbook*, 1967) which was originally magnetic material deposited on the paper and is still widely used as a standardized form of characters on such documents as bank cheques. MICR was established around 1966 and was designed such that simple template matching could be performed using relatively low resolution scanning of 9 × 7 pixels per character and therefore high recognition speeds achieved.

More recently two types of OCR printed character font have been designed. There are the American ANSI OCR-A standard (*American National Standard Character Set*, 1981) and the European ECMA OCR-B standard (*Standard ECMA-11*, 1976). Both of these fonts are designed for automatic character recognition and make clear distinctions between such letters as I and 1, 5 and S and O and 0. While these fonts work well for OCR, the vast majority of existing documents are not printed in this form. Most commonly found documents consist of many different machine-printed fonts such as Times, Helvetica, Courier, Elite, and many more. The problem of character separation in these fonts is usually fairly straightforward if the print quality is good, the contrast between character print and the paper is high, and there is a clear white space between characters.

The next level of complexity in character recognition is the use of constrained hand-printed characters, i.e. characters that are written by hand but are written so as to ease separation from each other and are constrained in size and formation style. There have been constraints imposed on the handprinting in that each character must be placed within a box. This constrains the size of the character and also forces characters to be separated from each other, thus easing the automatic separation problem. International standards for handprinted character formation styles for OCR purposes exist (Suen and de Mori, 1982) but these are not widely used as many people find the imposition of these constraints to be unacceptable and do not conform to them, thereby making them ineffective. By far the most common form of writing, however, is cursive script. There are no maintainable standards for this type of script although a number of different styles are taught in schools. There is enormous variation in people's handwriting due to it being an acquired and developing skill, and many features bear personal traits of the writer.

The recognition of unconstrained cursive handwriting remains an unsolved problem that is being investigated in a number of research laboratories, but the realization of high-performance systems remains a dream for the future. Most current research on cursive script recognition is based on looking for significant features in a word, such as ascenders and descenders, which can restrict the list of likely interpretations by searching a dictionary for the words that exhibit those features. This approach attempts to simulate how humans attempt the recognition of handwritten script (Plamondon and Leedham, 1990).

Pre-processing

Once a binary image of the handwriting or printed characters has been obtained, it is necessary to pre-process it to remove unnecessary features and variation in size so that pattern recognition can be performed more precisely. Pre-processing generally falls into two areas: smoothing and normalization (Suen, 1980). The smoothing process involves filling to remove small breaks and gaps or holes, due to perhaps poor quality copy or inadequate binarization techniques, and the removal of noise around the characters. Thinning can be either light or heavy. Light thinning removes noise bumps and isolated bits around the edge of the character, while heavy thinning reduces the character to a single pixel wide skeleton or line drawing image.

The second pre-processing technique is normalization. This involves four operations: size normalization, position normalization, skew normalization and line width normalization. Size normalization involves scaling the input character to fit within a predefined matrix size. This enables template matching to be more easily performed. Position normalization involves placing the input character at a particular position within the input matrix. While the character separation process decides where a particular character is, it is not necessarily correctly positioned within the matrix. Skew normalization involves attempting to place a character in its correct orientation by straightening slanted lines. After only a brief look at handwriting styles it is apparent that many people write with a slope, making it more difficult to recognize individual characters. Skew normalization attempts to determine the baseline of a set of characters and rotates each character such that it is perpendicular to this baseline. Line width normalization involves normalizing the width of the character to a constant value through its whole length. Heavy thinning in the smoothing pre-processing is a form of line width normalization where normalization is a single pixel width.

Feature extraction and recognition

For OCR fonts, and many standard printed fonts, it is possible to use simple template matching for the recognition. For multi-font text, handprinting, and handwriting it is necessary to use either a statistical or syntactic approach for the recognition. Because of the high structural content of printing and handwriting, structural recognition is the most successful technique, although statistical recognition techniques have also been applied successfully.

The types of features that have been extracted for character recognition can be grouped as global features or structural features. The global features are based upon the distribution of points in terms of their position, density, relative distance apart, and the number of crossings; or they can be based upon transformations of either the Fourier, Haar, Hadamard, or Walsh type (see Chap. 11). Global features in the form of physical measurements of the width and height of the character or parts of the character have also been used as features. Structural features take the form of edges and line segments where measures are made on straight and inclined lines, line length, and line endpoints. Alternatively, structural features can be determined on the outline of the character and measurements made of the line directions at any particular point. Other structural features are based on the centreline of the character where line discontinuity points, curves, loops, and the center of gravity of the character are measured. Many character recognition algorithms have been reported in the literature (see journals mentioned in the references). Performance comparison between algorithms is often difficult because of the lack of a common database for handwritten characters and the fact that some algorithms for printed characters are trained on the databases of printed characters, making the quoted results rather optimistic.

In summary, the current state of the art in OCR is that commercial systems do exist that are capable of achieving good recognition performance with many machine-printed character fonts subject to constraints on the printing quality, character size, character orientation, and paper quality. There are also systems that can recognize constrained and even mostly unconstrained hand-printed characters although their performance is less than that for the machine-printed character sets. There are no systems available that can accurately recognize unconstrained cursive script, although such systems do exist in research establishments and operate with some success for constrained cursive script from a cooperative writer.

5.6.2   Pattern recognition for data reduction

Facsimile transmission is becoming more widely used for document transmission because of its high speed in comparison to conventional letter post and carrier methods. In the widely used Group 3 facsimile transmission, a document is optically scanned and converted to a binary image of resolution 200 pixels/inch. This binary image is then transmitted over conventional telephone lines to another facsimile machine which reconstructs the binary image and prints it as a hard copy. To enhance transmission speeds and reduce the cost of the telephone charges, the binarized image is coded by some technique to reduce the amount of data required to represent the image fully. Run-length or predictive coding has conventionally been used to achieve the data reduction. This form of coding does not attempt to recognize any patterns in the image but makes use of the fact that there is a great deal of redundant and repetitive information in a binary image that can be represented more compactly.

One particular coding scheme that has been investigated (Johnsen *et al.*, 1983) attempts to compress further a binary image by locating patterns within the image. The facsimile can be coded by attempting to locate and recognize certain type of patterns such as individual characters. A character is not recognized (as, say, an A or a B), but its pattern can be matched to a previously transmitted pattern; if it is the same, or very similar, a reference to the previous pattern is transmitted along with its position. A block diagram of a pattern-matching encoder is shown in Fig. 5.12. The pattern locator scans the binary image line by line in a raster fashion, and when a black pixel is located the pattern isolator isolates the pattern using a simple contour-tracing algorithm. The pattern can be a complete pattern (i.e. completely surrounded by white pixels) or part of a larger black region. The contour tracing is restricted to a window of 32 × 32 pixels, which is usually sufficient for single characters to be represented as complete patterns. When the

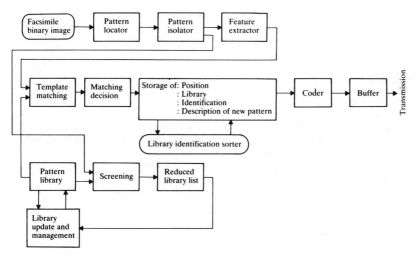

Figure 5.12 Facsimile image coding using pattern matching. (Adapted from Johnsen *et al.*, 1983.).

pattern has been isolated it is erased from the original image and matched against the library of patterns that have already been transmitted. If a similar match is found, information about the position and identification of the pattern are sent to the coder, if no match is found the pattern is added to the library. The pattern matching is accomplished using a template match between the two patterns with specific reference to the pixels that differ between the two representations. Template matching is not performed on all patterns in the pattern library. Instead, a screening operation is performed using features extracted from the pattern to determine the patterns that are likely to form a match and exclude those that are unlikely to form a match.

Simulations of this coding scheme have shown that it produces a compression of up to a factor of 80 and usually more than twice the compression of standard facsimile coding schemes. The drawback of this form of coding is that the transmitted image is not an exact copy of the original binary image due to the tolerances in the pattern matching or slight inaccuracies in the pattern position.

5.7 Summary

In this chapter we have introduced and given outline descriptions of the three main techniques for automatic pattern recognition: template matching, statistical pattern matching, and structural pattern matching. Subsequently, two particular examples of their use are described: one is a document reader that can recognize machine and hand-written or printed characters and the other an advanced system for data compression in facsimile. Other examples can be found elsewhere in this book.

References

American National Standard Character Set for Optical Character Recognition (OCR-A), X3.17-1981.

Character Recognition Handbook 1967, British Computer Society, London.

Devijver P.A. and Kittler J. (1982) *Pattern Recognition: A Statistical Approach*, Prentice Hall, Englewood Cliffs, NJ.

Fu K.S. (1982) *Applications of Pattern Recognition*, CRC Press, Boca Raton, FL.

Guiliano V.E. (1967) 'How can we find patterns', *International Science the Technology*, p. 42, February.

Johnsen O., Segen J. and Cash G.L. (1983) 'Coding of two-level pictures by pattern matching and substitution', *Bell System Technical Journal*, vol. 62, no. 8.

Plamondon R. and Leedham C.G. (eds) (1990) *Computer Processing of Handwriting*, World Scientific, Singapore.

Plamondon R., Suen C.Y. and Simner M. (eds.) (1989) *Computer Recognition and Human Production of Handwriting*, World Scientific, Singapore.

Rosenfeld A. (ed.) (1986) *Human and Machine Vision II*, Academic Press, Orlando, FL.

Sayre K.M. (1965) *Recognition, A Study in the Philosophy of Artificial Intelligence*, University of Notre Dame Press.

Schwab E.C. and Nusbaum H.C. (eds) (1986) *Pattern Recognition by Humans and Machines*, Vol. 2, Academic Press, Orlando, FL.

Standard ECMA-11 for the Alphanumeric Character Set OCR-B for Optical Recognition, 3rd edn, March 1976.

Suen C.Y. (1980) 'Feature extraction in automatic recognition of handprinted characters', in *Signal Processing: Theories and Applications*, Kunt M. and de Coulon F. (eds), North Holland, Amsterdam.

Suen C.Y. and de Mori R. (1982) *Computer Analysis and Perception. Vol. 1: Visual Signals*, CRC Press, Boca Raton, FL.

Verhagen C.J.D.M. (1975) 'Some general remarks about pattern recognition; its definition; its relation with other disciplines; a literature survey', *Pattern Recognition*, vol. 7, no. 3, pp. 1109–16.

Widrow B. (1974) 'The "rubber mask" technique, I and II', in *Learning Systems and Intelligent Robots*, Fu K.S. and Tou J.T. (eds), Plenum Press, New York.

Young T.Y. and Fu K.S. (1986) *Handbook of Pattern Recognition and Image Processing*, Academic Press, Orlando, FL.

Further reading

Books

Pavlidis T. (1977) *Structural Pattern Recognition*, Springer-Verlag, Berlin.

Ballard D.H. and Brown C.M. (1982) *Computer Vision*, Prentice Hall, Englewood Cliffs, NJ.

Gonzalez R.C. and Wintz P. (1987) *Digital Image Processing*, 2nd edn, Addison-Wesley, Reading, Mass.

Zuech N. and Miller R.K. (1987) *Matching Vision*, Fairmount Press, Atlanta, GA.

Journals

IEEE Transactions on Pattern Analysis and Machine Intelligence.
Pattern Recognition.
Pattern Recognition Letters.
Computer Vision, Graphics and Image Processing.

6 Image synthesis from 3-D models

ADRIAN CLARK

6.1 Introduction

Anyone who watches television will be familiar with the animated logos used in advertisements and title sequences. These form the most public face of *image synthesis*, in which a scene is modelled in three dimensions and the observer (and frequently objects within the scene) move. Each frame in the sequence is calculated by a computer, often using special-purpose hardware, and the result recorded on film or videotape. A surprisingly wide variety of effects can be simulated, including rough surfaces, reflections (highlights), and natural objects such as trees and mist, as well as the cartoon-like metamorphosis of one object into another.

However, image synthesis is relevant to many applications of image processing. In seismic work, for example, it can be used to provide a display of the properties of rock strata (Plate 1), determined by setting off a series of controlled explosions and sensing the resulting oscillation of the ground. Similar display techniques are used in medical image processing, where body scanner imagery is processed to provide a 3-D 'picture' of a patient. Pharmaceutical companies use 3-D graphics for visualizing molecules when developing new drugs. This approach can also be used to model macromolecular structures of biological importance in three dimensions, allowing the resulting pictures (Fig. 6.1) to be compared with micrographs. Other applications include the use of 'ray-tracing' (Sec. 6.5) to simulate radar images from a 3-D model of the ground, and the visualization of these 'digital terrain models', which can be determined from images recorded from satellites in the earth's orbit (Plate 2). Chapter 12 discusses the use of image synthesis techniques in model-based coding schemes.

In this chapter, a brief introduction to the fundamentals of image synthesis is presented. The essential geometric aspects are described, followed by a discussion of the way in which objects are usually modelled. The process of *rendering* (displaying the 3-D scene on a 2-D display) is then described, along with details of techniques for simulating surface properties. The chapter concludes with a brief discussion of stochastic techniques, which use a variety of methods

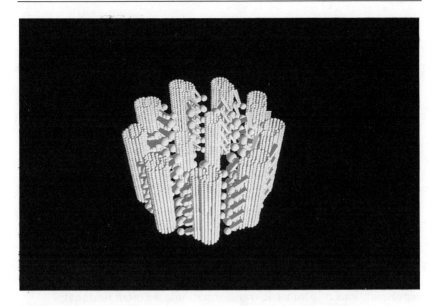

Figure 6.1 Simulation of the macromolecular structure of a flagellum, an organelle (major functional subunit) of a simple microscopic organism.

based on random numbers to simulate the chance complexities of nature.

Image synthesis is usually regarded as an advanced topic in computer graphics and is treated as such in a variety of books (e.g. Foley *et al.*, 1990; Newman and Sproull, 1979; Rogers, 1985). The subject is now sufficiently mature that specialist books are starting to appear (e.g. Hall, 1988; Magnenet-Thalmann and Thalmann, 1987). The reader is referred to these texts for further details and references to original work.

6.2 Geometrical transformations

Although it is quite feasible to model all the objects of a scene in the same coordinate system, this introduces problems when we allow the objects to move. The approach conventionally adopted is to represent objects in their own coordinate systems, then to apply transformations that map one set of coordinates onto another (see Sec. 6.3). It is also fundamental to the positioning of the 'observer' when we wish to display the scene. Hence, the process of geometric transformation is an essential one.

There are three basic types of transformation: translation, scaling, and rotation. (Other types of scaling may be obtained by appropriate combinations of these operations. For example, reflection is simply

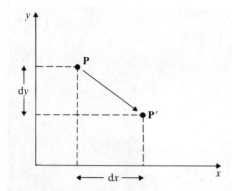

Figure 6.2 Illustration of translation.

scaling by a negative factor.) We shall initially consider these in two dimensions, then generalize the results to three dimensions. It is worth noting that most graphics texts use different notations for the representations of geometric transformations: we often find that coordinates are expressed as row vectors, resulting in transformation matrices that are the transposes of the ones derived here. All these formulations do, of course, lead to equivalent results.

6.2.1 Translation

Consider the movement of the point $\mathbf{P} = (x, y)$ to $\mathbf{P}' = (x', y')$ as indicated in Fig. 6.2. If the distance moved in the x direction is $\mathrm{d}x$ and in the y direction $\mathrm{d}y$, then we have $x' = x + \mathrm{d}x$ and $y' = y + \mathrm{d}y$. We can write this in a matrix notation as

$$\begin{pmatrix} x' \\ y' \end{pmatrix} = \begin{pmatrix} x \\ y \end{pmatrix} + \begin{pmatrix} \mathrm{d}x \\ \mathrm{d}y \end{pmatrix}$$

i.e. as $\mathbf{P}' = \mathbf{P} + \mathbf{T}$, where $\mathbf{T}$ represents the translation.

6.2.2 Scaling

If we have $x' = S_x x$ and $y' = S_y y$, we have *scaled* the point $\mathbf{P}$ to $\mathbf{P}'$ (Fig. 6.3). As with translation, we can write this as a matrix

$$\begin{pmatrix} x' \\ y' \end{pmatrix} = \begin{pmatrix} S_x & 0 \\ 0 & S_y \end{pmatrix} \begin{pmatrix} x \\ y \end{pmatrix}$$

or $\mathbf{P}' = \mathbf{SP}$, where $\mathbf{S}$ is the matrix representing the scaling.

6.2.3 Rotation

Rotating the point $\mathbf{P}$ onto $\mathbf{P}'$ requires a little more effort. From Fig. 6.4, we observe that $x = r \cos \phi$ and $y = r \sin \phi$ and that

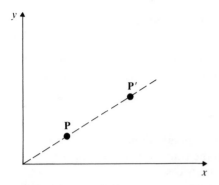

Figure 6.3   Illustration of scaling.

$$x' = r\cos(\theta + \phi) = r\cos\phi\cos\theta - r\sin\phi\sin\theta$$
$$y' = r\sin(\theta + \phi) = r\cos\phi\sin\theta + r\sin\phi\cos\theta$$

Substituting in x and y, we get

$$x' = x\cos\theta - y\sin\theta$$
$$y' = x\sin\theta + y\cos\theta$$

which we can write in matrix form as

$$\begin{pmatrix} x' \\ y' \end{pmatrix} = \begin{pmatrix} \cos\theta & -\sin\theta \\ \sin\theta & \cos\theta \end{pmatrix} \begin{pmatrix} x \\ y \end{pmatrix}$$

or $\mathbf{P}' = \mathbf{RP}$, where $\mathbf{R}$ represents the rotation.

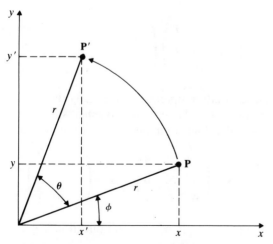

Figure 6.4   Illustration of rotation.

6.2.4 Compound transformations—homogeneous coordinates

Conversion between coordinate systems, in general, involves more than one transformation—e.g. a rotation followed by a scaling. In this case, we would have

$$\mathbf{P'} = \mathbf{SRP}$$

i.e. we *pre-multiply* by a matrix to effect an additional transformation. Hence, we can combine or *compound* the transformations simply by multiplying together their individual matrices.

One noteworthy point is that the order of applying transformations is important. For example, a rotation of 90° followed by a shift of 3 units produces very different results from a shift of 3 units followed by a 90° rotation. Mathematically, we can think of this as being a consequence of the non-commutative nature of matrix multiplication ($\mathbf{M_1 M_2} \neq \mathbf{M_2 M_1}$).

There is, however, a problem with this paradigm. While scaling and rotation are multiplicative operations, translation is additive. To be able to compound transformations in a consistent way, we must make translation into a multiplicative operation. This is done by introducing a *homogeneous coordinate system.*

For any combination of rotation, scaling, and translation required to transform $\mathbf{P}$ onto $\mathbf{P'}$, we can always write the overall transformation in the general form

$$x' = r_{11}x + r_{12}y + t_x$$

$$y' = r_{21}x + r_{22}y + t_y$$

This may be written as a simple matrix multiplication by expressing the point $\mathbf{P}$ as a *three-element* vector whose final value is always unity; i.e. as

$$\begin{pmatrix} x' \\ y' \\ 1 \end{pmatrix} = \begin{pmatrix} r_{11} & r_{12} & t_x \\ r_{21} & r_{22} & t_y \\ 0 & 0 & 1 \end{pmatrix} \begin{pmatrix} x \\ y \\ 1 \end{pmatrix}$$

This allows us to manipulate translation operations in exactly the same way as rotation and scaling (and hence the term 'homogeneous' coordinate). We can write the individual component transformations as

$$\mathbf{R} = \begin{pmatrix} \cos\theta & -\sin\theta & 0 \\ \sin\theta & \cos\theta & 0 \\ 0 & 0 & 1 \end{pmatrix}; \quad \mathbf{S} = \begin{pmatrix} S_x & 0 & 0 \\ 0 & S_y & 0 \\ 0 & 0 & 1 \end{pmatrix}; \quad \mathbf{T} = \begin{pmatrix} 1 & 0 & t_x \\ 0 & 1 & t_y \\ 0 & 0 & 1 \end{pmatrix}$$

Any transformation is then applied simply by pre-multiplication, e.g.

$$\mathbf{P'} = \mathbf{STSRP}$$

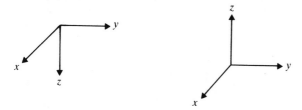

Figure 6.5 Left-handed and right-handed coordinate systems.

If we now turn our attention to the homogeneous representation of 3-D coordinates, we are obviously concerned with 4 × 4 matrices. For scaling and translation, the forms of these matrices are direct extensions of their 2-D counterparts:

$$\mathbf{S} = \begin{pmatrix} S_x & 0 & 0 & 0 \\ 0 & S_y & 0 & 0 \\ 0 & 0 & S_z & 0 \\ 0 & 0 & 0 & 1 \end{pmatrix}; \quad \mathbf{T} = \begin{pmatrix} 1 & 0 & 0 & t_x \\ 0 & 1 & 0 & t_y \\ 0 & 0 & 1 & t_z \\ 0 & 0 & 0 & 1 \end{pmatrix}$$

For rotations, we now have the possibility of rotations about any of the three axes. Moreover, we have to define our coordinate system as being left- or right-handed (Fig. 6.5). Mathematical analysis conventionally uses the latter, but the former is in widespread use in computer graphics, where the x and y axes lie along the edges of the display screen and z represents 'depth' into the screen (Fig. 6.6). The convention adopted here is a right-handed one where positive angles are anticlockwise when looking towards the origin, so that a rotation of $+90°$ around the z axis maps the $+x$ axis onto the $+y$ axis. The rotations about the three axes may then be written as

$$\mathbf{R}_x = \begin{pmatrix} 1 & 0 & 0 & 0 \\ 0 & \cos\theta & -\sin\theta & 0 \\ 0 & \sin\theta & \cos\theta & 0 \\ 0 & 0 & 0 & 1 \end{pmatrix}$$

$$\mathbf{R}_y = \begin{pmatrix} \cos\theta & 0 & \sin\theta & 0 \\ 0 & 1 & 0 & 0 \\ -\sin\theta & 0 & \cos\theta & 0 \\ 0 & 0 & 0 & 1 \end{pmatrix}$$

$$\mathbf{R}_z = \begin{pmatrix} \cos\theta & -\sin\theta & 0 & 0 \\ \sin\theta & \cos\theta & 0 & 0 \\ 0 & 0 & 1 & 0 \\ 0 & 0 & 0 & 1 \end{pmatrix}$$

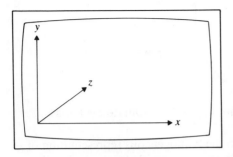

Figure 6.6   A left-handed coordinate system on a computer display.

6.3   Hierarchical modelling

Although synthesized imagery can take a wide variety of forms, the number of basic building blocks is few—typically points, straight lines, and planar polygons, frequently triangular. It is possible to render certain types of curved surfaces directly but they are more often approximated by a combination of the arrangement of polygons in a mesh and suitable shading.

Models of objects can easily contain 20 000 polygons, so it is important that they be stored efficiently. A significant saving can be made by using the fact that adjacent facets share common vertices. This is usually achieved in a data structure known as a polygon mesh or *polymesh*. (An illustration of such a data structure is shown in Fig. 6.7.) It contains three separate lists: the first, the *coordinate list*, contains the x, y and z coordinates of all the vertices of all the polygons. The second list, the *vertex list*, describes which vertices belong to which polygons, while the third, the *polygon list*, indicates where the vertices of a particular polygon are to be found in the vertex list. For example, in Fig. 6.7 the polygon P_7 has vertices V_{31} to V_{35}, which consists of coordinates C_{16}, C_{15}, C_7, and C_8. The vertex list in the figure contains an explicit null entry to terminate each polygon; a more efficient alternative is to negate the final entry, so that V_{34} would contain $-C_8$. The polymesh representation has additional advantages when performing smooth shading (Sec. 6.5), since it contains information regarding the relationships between facets.

Bearing in mind the complexity of even simple objects, and hence the effort involved in constructing a geometrical description, a versatile way of arranging objects in the scene is essential, particularly when generating animated sequences. For example, consider an image of teapots standing side-by-side (Fig. 6.8). It would obviously be very wasteful to store the absolute coordinates of all the vertices of all the facets. Instead, we model the teapot in its own coordinate system (termed an *object coordinate system*), then make it appear in the *world*

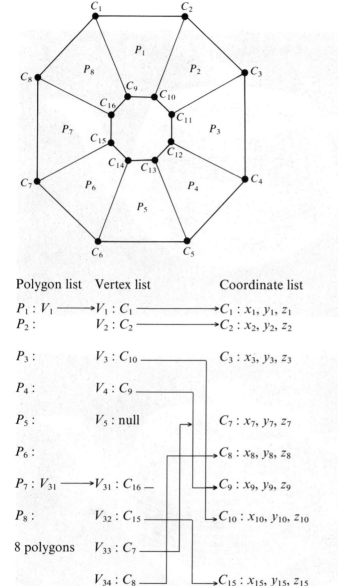

Polygon list   Vertex list   Coordinate list

$P_1 : V_1 \longrightarrow V_1 : C_1 \longrightarrow C_1 : x_1, y_1, z_1$

$P_2 : \qquad\qquad V_2 : C_2 \longrightarrow C_2 : x_2, y_2, z_2$

$P_3 : \qquad\qquad V_3 : C_{10} \qquad\qquad C_3 : x_3, y_3, z_3$

$P_4 : \qquad\qquad V_4 : C_9$

$P_5 : \qquad\qquad V_5 : \text{null} \qquad\qquad C_7 : x_7, y_7, z_7$

$P_6 : \qquad\qquad\qquad\qquad\qquad\qquad\qquad C_8 : x_8, y_8, z_8$

$P_7 : V_{31} \longrightarrow V_{31} : C_{16} \qquad\qquad C_9 : x_9, y_9, z_9$

$P_8 : \qquad\qquad V_{32} : C_{15} \qquad\qquad C_{10} : x_{10}, y_{10}, z_{10}$

8 polygons $V_{33} : C_7$

$\qquad\qquad\qquad V_{34} : C_8$

$\qquad\qquad\qquad V_{35} : \text{null} \qquad\qquad C_{15} : x_{15}, y_{15}, z_{15}$

$\qquad\qquad\qquad\qquad\qquad\qquad\qquad C_{16} : x_{16}, y_{16}, z_{16}$

40 vertices   16 coordinates

Figure 6.7   Illustration of the construction of a polymesh.

coordinate system of the scene by means of a geometric transformation. This process is known as *instancing*, and the mapping of coordinate

(a)

(b)

Figure 6.8   Teapots rendered by: (a) wire-mesh, no hidden lines;
(b) wire-mesh with hidden lines.

(c)

(d)

Figure 6.8 Teapots rendered by: (c) flat shading; (d) Gouraud shading.

(e)

(f)

Figure 6.8 Teapots rendered by: (e) Phong shading;
(f) Torrance–Cook shading.

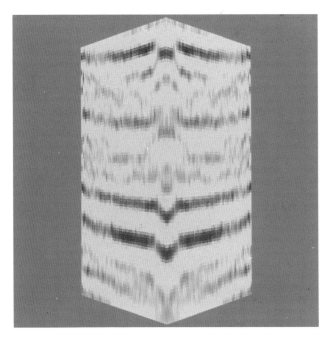

Plate 1 Seismic section, consisting of vertical sections 'texture mapped' onto polygonal facets.

Plate 2 Digital terrain model determined from stereo satellite images. (Reproduced by kind permission of Prof. C. Elachi, Jet Propulsion Laboratory and California Institute of Technology.)

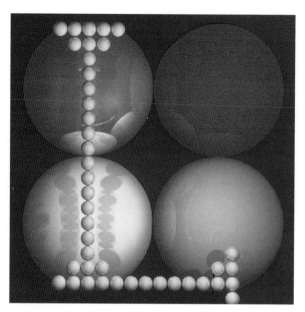

Plate 3 Ray-traced scene consisting of a number of spheres illuminated by several coloured light sources. Note particularly the shadows and multiple reflections. (Courtesy of Array Productions Limited.)

Plate 4 Image of a steel mill calculated using the radiosity technique. (Photograph courtesy of Prof. D. Greenberg of Cornell University, USA.)

Plate 5 Image of a fractal mountain rendered by recursive subdivision. (Courtesy of Array Productions Limited.)

Plate 6 Image of a garden sprinkler rendered using a particle system. (Courtesy of Array Productions Limited.)

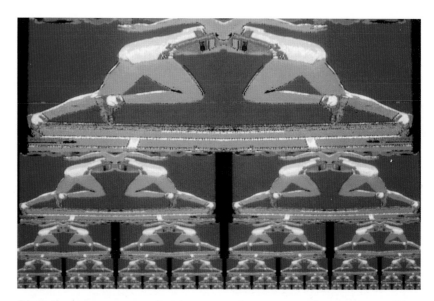

Plate 7 Image processing by computers can produce some striking effects with the simplest algorithms — as we see in this fractal version of Fig. 14.1. Image processors sometimes wonder if more money could not be made out of their specialism by submitting some of the by-products of their work to avant-garde art galleries. Meaningless rubbish could be passed off as unfathomable profundity by the writing of some pretentious covering note generated by a random walk through a few trendy art journals.

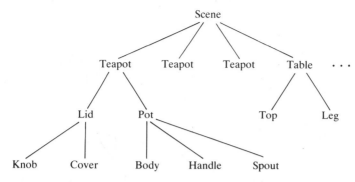

Figure 6.9   Illustration of the hierarchical modelling process.

systems as an *instance transformation*. Hence, the various teapots in Fig. 6.8 are instances of the same model.

The concept of instancing forms the basis of hierarchical modelling. For example, we could use the set of teapots in an image of a pottery factory's warehouse, with the teapot itself being constructed from a number of separate components (Fig. 6.9). Each line in that figure represents a different instance transformation. The only nodes that contain 3-D coordinates are the 'leaves' of the tree, such as 'knob', 'spout', and 'body'.

6.4   Rendering

Having built a 3-D model, we must display it on a 2-D raster device such as a framestore (see Chap. 8), a process known as *rendering*. We shall first discuss the most commonly used approach, based on *scan conversion*. Conceptually, three steps are involved:

1   Projecting the 3-D facets onto a 2-D view plane.

2   Determining which facets are wholly or partially visible.

3   Calculating the intensity (or colour) value of each pixel in the image (*scan conversion*).

In practice, these steps are not separated, and the calculations required for shading (Sec. 6.5) are also involved. The process of rendering can be quite slow: 45 min/frame would be a reasonable figure for a scene of reasonable complexity using a purely software implementation on a one-MIP computer. Most of this time is spent on the shading calculations, which are performed using floating-point arithmetic. There are, however, several commercially available products that perform all these steps in hardware. These can (with some limitations) display an entire scene several times per second.

Two types of projection are commonly used when rendering:

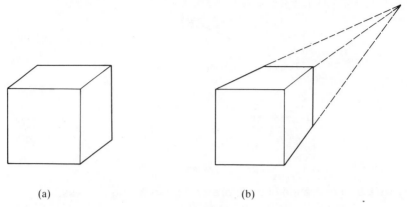

(a)   (b)

Figure 6.10   (a) Orthographic and (b) perspective projections.

orthographic projection, in which parallel lines in 3-D remain so in 2-D (Fig. 6.10(a)) and *perspective projections*, in which parallel lines in depth meet at a 'vanishing point' (Fig. 6.10(b)). Perspective projections are more realistic, but orthographic projections are sometimes used in engineering applications, since measurements may be taken from them.

There are many ways of solving the hidden surface problem; only two approaches will be outlined here. The projection step converts all facets into the appropriate 2-D projection with associated depth values at the vertices. For software implementations, these depth values are usually represented as floating-point numbers, while firmware generally uses integers—this can give rise to errors where facets meet.

The simplest algorithm, and the one most suitable for hardware implementation, is the *depth buffer* or *z-buffer*. This uses a region of memory, of the same dimensions as the final image, to associate a depth value with every pixel. This buffer is initially set to 'infinity'. For every pixel of every polygon, the algorithm compares the depth value already in the buffer with that calculated for the pixel; if it is greater than the pixel's depth, that pixel will be visible, so it is written into the frame buffer and the new depth stored in the z-buffer. At every comparison, pixels that have a smaller depth value (i.e. are closer) are visible and overwrite the buffer's contents. The main advantage of this approach is that it allows the facets to be rendered in any order; its main disadvantage is that transparent objects are difficult to handle.

An alternative approach is the use of a *scan-line algorithm*. This has the advantage that only one line of the image has to be buffered in memory. It achieves this at the expense of storing some representation of the geometry of the entire scene in memory (or, at least, on some mass storage device where it may be quickly accessed).

Let us consider the display screen to be a rectangular element lying in front of the scene. We can then imagine a scan line drawn across the display surface to be the line at which a *scan-line plane* intersects the display surface (Fig. 6.11). This plane is normal to the display surface

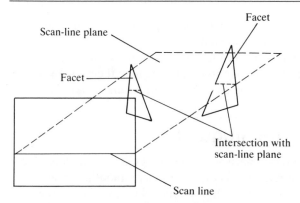

Figure 6.11   Illustration of the scan-line algorithm.

and passes through the scene, intersecting the facets from which the scene is composed. The line of intersection between the scan-line plane and each facet is an *intersection span*. We can now determine the visibility of facets by considering the relationships of their intersection spans in the 2-D coordinate system associated with the scan-line plane. Visibility may be determined at each pixel by means of a one-line depth buffer; alternatively, the intersection spans may be tested for intersection with one another and split into *visibility spans* (Fig. 6.12), each of which has a definite depth relationship to every other visibility span. The run of pixels corresponding to each visibility span can then be filled with appropriate values. This latter approach (with refinements) is known as *Watkins' algorithm*.

Normally, a scan-line algorithm represents the entire scene in terms of the *edges* of facets. Each edge is described in terms of the first scan line at which it becomes *active*, the number of scan lines it crosses, the x and z values when it becomes active, and increments in x and z that need to be added to the current x and z when moving to the next scan line. The

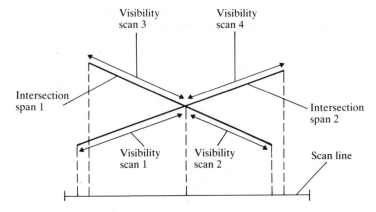

Figure 6.12   Visibility scans across a scan-line plane.

use of simple increments when scan converting a scene is known as *edge coherence*. This, together with efficient management of the edge descriptions, means that scan-line algorithms can be very efficient, especially for high resolutions. Another advantage in their favour is that all the information to account correctly for transparency is available.

6.5 Shading techniques

We have already seen that objects are generally built up from a mesh of planar polygons. Most real objects, however, have smooth, curved surfaces, so we have to render our faceted model to give the impression of smoothness. The most obvious way is to model the curved surface with smaller and smaller facets, approximating the true surface more and more closely. But this necessarily makes the model much larger, greatly increasing storage requirements and execution times, and so this approach is not often used. Instead, we build some sort of smooth shading model into the renderer. In this section, we consider some of these shading models.

6.5.1 Basic shading model

The simplest shading model (Fig. 6.13) assumes that the incoming illumination is absorbed by the surface and re-emitted isotropically in all directions: we call the surface a *diffuse reflector*. The intensity of light emitted in any particular direction is then described by Lambert's law:

$$I_\theta = I_L K_D \cos \theta$$

where I_θ is the intensity observed at an angle θ from the surface normal, I_L is the incident intensity and K_D is the *diffuse reflection coefficient* or *diffusivity*. Typically, K_D depends on the material and on the light's wavelength.

However, there is a fundamental problem with this model: any object that does not receive direct illumination will be invisible! This does not

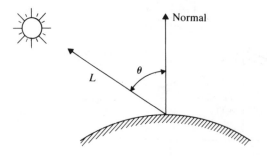

Figure 6.13 Basic shading model.

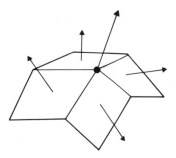

Figure 6.14   Adjacent facets and their normal vectors.

happen in nature because the atmosphere scatters light, producing
ambient illumination. So the total illumination may be modelled as the
sum of the ambient term, which is the same everywhere, and the
Lambertian term. Using this simple shading model, we can shade each
facet according to the positions of any light sources (Fig. 6.8); we obtain
a result that is much more realistic than a wire-frame, but contains
distinct edges.

6.5.2   Gouraud shading

Gouraud shading simulates smooth shading by interpolating the
shading intensity value across a facet. If we consider four facets placed
next to each other (Fig. 6.14), we see that each facet has its own normal
vector. At the vertex where the facets meet or along any of the common
edges, we can *average* the normals, then calculate the corresponding
intensity values at the vertex, based on the simple shading model
(including the ambient term) outlined above. We then *interpolate* the
intensity linearly between these four values as we render the facet. This
smooths the intensity variation as we go from one facet to its neighbour.
This comparatively simple algorithm makes it reasonably
straightforward to implement Gouraud shading in hardware (or, at
least, in firmware).

Unfortunately, there are a few problems with Gouraud shading. If
one looks closely near significant edges, one may see a band which
tracks the edge. This is known as a *Mach band*; it may not be very
apparent on still images, but on moving images a rippling effect is often
visible. Mach banding is a visual effect caused by the fact that the
derivative of the intensity is not continuous between facets. To alleviate
this problem, a different interpolation technique is commonly used,
known as *Phong shading*.

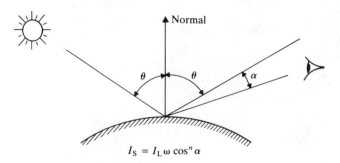

Figure 6.15   The Phong shading model.

6.5.3   Phong shading

There are two aspects to Phong shading: interpolation of the normal vector across facets, reducing (but not eliminating) Mach banding; and use of an improved illumination model which permits highlights (Fig. 6.15). This is described by the equation

$$I_S = I_L \omega \cos^n \alpha$$

where I_S is the observed intensity and I_L the incident intensity; ω is the *reflectance*. An ambient term is also included in practice, as for Gouraud shading. The power, n, to which the cosine term is raised determines the width of the highlight: a small value of n gives a broad highlight and vice versa. Value of $n \approx 10$ are typical. Objects rendered using Phong shading appear somewhat more realistic than with Gouraud shading, and the obtrusive Mach banding is greatly reduced.

6.5.4   Torrance–Cook shading

This shading model incorporates the work of Sparrow (Torrance and Sparrow, 1967) and Blinn (1977). It assumes that a surface is composed of randomly oriented 'micro-facets', a model that is physically quite valid. These micro-facets are mirror-like, so specular reflections (highlights) result from single scattering and diffuse reflection from multiple scattering (Fig. 6.16). Theoretically, the facets should be oriented according to a Beckmann distribution

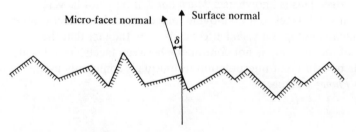

Figure 6.16   The Torrance–Cook surface model.

$$\frac{1}{m^2\cos^4\delta}\,e^{-\tan(\delta/m)}$$

where δ is the angle between the surface normal and the micro-facet normal and m is the r.m.s. slope of the facet. In practice, Gaussian and cosine distributions are frequently used. For small m, there is little difference between this model and Phong shading, but we have more control over the 'look' of the surface: we can make it appear plastic or metallic simply by changing parameters.

6.5.5 Ray-traced rendering

The above techniques all consider the effects of illumination *locally*: they take no consideration of the interplay of light from surfaces. One can do this by making the renderer trace the paths of rays of 'light', performing reflection and refraction at surfaces that are encountered. Since the paths of light waves are reversible (Fermat's principle), this is most conveniently done by tracing the rays *from* the eye into the scene and seeing what they encounter. The results are often impressive (Plate 3), since reflection, refraction, and shadows are automatically taken into account, but the technique is rather slow and, unless care is taken, the resulting image can suffer from severe sampling problems. Note that ray-tracing accounts for global specular illumination, but the diffuse component is still accounted for locally.

Ray-tracing does not involve projection onto a 2-D plane: all operations take place in the 3-D coordinate space in which the objects are positioned. For this reason, it is often termed an *object space technique*, while the methods described previously are *image space techniques*.

6.5.6 Radiosity

This is the state of the art in producing shaded surface realism for diffusely reflecting objects (Plate 4). Like ray-tracing, radiosity is an object space technique. One of the problems with ray-tracing is that the results are obtained from simple geometric optics: it is difficult to produce glows and diffuse reflections, for example. The radiosity approach is a little different. It can be thought of as tracing rays from the light source to every facet in the scene. The amount of light received by each facet is then calculated, and hence the amount re-emitted onto other facets is determined, so that each facet is given some illumination from each facet visible to it.

The problem reduces to one of solving an extremely large set of simultaneous equations, which is unfortunately very slow to execute; but the results are very impressive, and can be rendered using Gouraud shading. Of course, as soon as *any* object in the scene is moved, the radiosity calculation has strictly to be re-evaluated, so the technique is really only of use for still frames or for sequences where only the observer moves, not fully animated sequences. Research is in progress into ways of speeding up the technique and in using approximate methods for animated sequences.

6.6 Stochastic techniques

The techniques described so far are entirely deterministic. We can, in principle, describe any surface simply by producing a sufficiently complex model. For many objects, particularly natural ones, this is not very satisfactory. For example, when generating imagery of a field of daffodils, we would like to define the general shape once and let the computer generate slightly different instances in each case: we must include some randomness in the modelling and rendering processes. There are two popular techniques for achieving this: *fractals* and *particle systems*. Let us briefly consider each of these.

6.6.1 Fractals

Imagine trying to measure the length of a coastline. We could start by using a long pole. This would be approximating the true length by a series of straight-line segments and we would actually be determining the length of those segments. But we would be missing details smaller than the length of the pole. To obtain a more accurate measurement, we could make the pole (and hence the segments) smaller. However, we would still miss detail in the true coastline. This situation is true for any finite-length pole: there would still be detail smaller than the length of the pole being ignored. A curve such as the coastline is a fractal. Formally, we define a fractal as having a non-integer dimension: our coastline contains infinite variation but encloses a finite area. A second property of a fractal is that of *statistical self-similarity*: a coastline looks random when viewed from far away, and its details retain that property when viewed from nearby.

In computer graphics, fractals are usually calculated by a *random subdivision* algorithm. Consider an object made up of a series of planar triangular facets. Let us subdivide that facet into three by randomly selecting a point in its interior and randomly displacing it in the direction of its normal. Then, let us repeat the process on the three facets, then on the nine thus generated . . . and so on, until the facets are too small to see.

Objects generated with this recursive subdivision technique can be tailored to match a variety of natural phenomena, including clouds, waves and mountains (Plate 5). There are fractal techniques for other types of object, but a detailed description of them is beyond the scope of this work.

6.6.2 Particle systems

Another way of introducing randomness is by using a particle system. This is particularly good for simulating random motion in time, such as flames or the movement of leaves. For each frame in the animation, the following steps are performed:

1 Some particles are extinguished.

2 Some particles are created and given individual properties randomly perturbed about some mean values.

3 The remaining particles are moved, typically with some random modulation, according to their properties.

4 The resulting particle set is rendered.

This process is often thought of in the same way as time-lapse photographs of the evolution of a biological colony. Rendering particle systems accurately is a time-consuming process, since the particles may hide each other and may be transparent or cast shadows. Often, a simplified model is used in which each particle is self-luminous. However, the effects attainable with particle systems (Plate 6) cannot currently be achieved by any other means.

6.7 Summary

This chapter has provided an introduction into the fundamentals of image synthesis and indicated some recent developments in the simulation of natural phenomena. There are many applications of these techniques in relation to image processing, as the examples given here indicate. A specific application in telecommunications, the use of a head model for image coding, is described in detail in Chap. 12.

References

Blinn J.F. (1977) 'Models of light reflection for computer synthesized pictures', *Computer Graphics*, vol. 11, pp. 192–8.

Foley J.D., van Dam A., Feiner S. K. and Hughes J. F. (1990) *Computer Graphics: Principles and Practice*, 2nd edn, Addison-Wesley, Reading, Mass.

Hall R.A. (1988) *Colour and Illumination in Computer Graphics*, Springer-Verlag, New York.

Magnenet-Thalmann N. and Thalmann D. (1987) *Image Synthesis*, Springer-Verlag, Tokyo.

Newman W. M. and Sproull R.F. (1979) *Principles of Interactive Computer Graphics*, McGraw-Hill, New York.

Rogers D.F. (1985) *Procedural Elements for Computer Graphics*, McGraw-Hill, New York.

Torrance K.E. and Sparrow E.M. (1967) 'Theory of off-specular reflection from roughened surfaces', *Journal of the Optical Society of America*, vol. 57, pp. 1105–14.

PART 2

Implementation

The previous section dealt with a variety of concepts and theories about images and image processing. These theories are of little practical consequence, however, unless they lead to implementations. In the realm of image processing, implementation is far from being a trivial problem; indeed at times it can be a very considerable headache! The basic reason for this is the dimensionality of images: two of space and one of time. Sampling each dimension at the density appropriate for viewing produces huge 3-D arrays of numbers, fit to break the teeth of many a number-crunching computer. As the complexity of an algorithm grows, so it becomes more and more difficult to execute it in real time.

In Chap. 7, Tim Dennis shows how some of the theoretical ideas outlined in Chap. 2—particularly those in the multidimensional frequency domain—can be applied in practical experiments and measurements. By means of the interesting idea of the zone plate, the frequency-domain effects of sampling and filtering can be seen before one's eyes. Following this, in Chap. 8, Adrian Clark and Kirk Martinez give an introduction to image-processing architectures. Mention is made of the various common configurations of storage devices, buses, and processors that can help to speed up processing.

The interaction between hardware and software is of considerable interest. In Chap. 9 Tim Dennis reports on his considerable practical experience in designing software to work rapidly and efficiently in the execution of a variety of operations on images, such as, for example, convolution. Finally, in Chap. 10 there is an account by Adrian Clark, Kirk Martinez, and Bill Welsh of parallel architectures and neural networks for image processing, an area of current research that holds promise of achieving the very high computational speeds and special characteristics in some of the futuristic systems referred to earlier in the book.

7 Practical considerations in image processing

TIM DENNIS

7.1 Introduction

In this chapter we introduce some practical aspects of image processing and discuss their influence on the choice of such factors as sampling rates, pre- and post-filtering, and quantization. These practical considerations arise in the implementation of the corresponding theoretical concepts given in Chaps 1 and 2. Initially, the *zone plate* test pattern (Drewery, 1978) is discussed in some detail, as it provides instructive demonstrations of operations such as analogue filtering, directional digital filtering, and sampling, which are conveniently visualized in the frequency domain.

7.2 The zone plate

The zone plate has long been known as an optical test pattern for assessing the frequency-domain performance of lens systems. Its principle is similar to that of a swept-frequency generator in electronic engineering; the use of a such a generator is a straightforward way to give a direct plot of the frequency response of an electrical circuit, e.g. to check the response of an analogue low-pass filter. The vertical input of an oscilloscope is fed either with the raw output of the network under test, or a signal representing just its amplitude, while the horizontal deflection signal drives the voltage-controlled oscillator directly. The waveforms observed for a Butterworth low-pass filter will resemble those in Fig. 7.1 (irregularities in the upper trace are because of sampling deficiencies in the graphics software that generated the diagram).

The same test procedure can be used on sampled-data systems to check on aliasing effects. Suppose we have a sampled data system with an output recovery filter, but no input low-pass filter. Let the sampling frequency be F_s, and assume that we apply a swept frequency as before

Original sweep

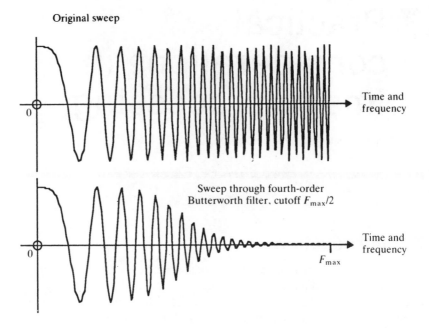

Figure 7.1 Swept-frequency response measurement.

and observe the output of the recovery filter. We also assume that the sweep rate is so slow that waveform distortion is negligible.

For low frequencies (those $\ll F_s/2$), the system is transparent and has no effect. However, as soon the input frequency, f_i, exceeds the Nyquist limit at $F_s/2$ aliasing occurs and the frequency of the output, f_o, begins to decrease in such a way that $f_o = F_s - f_i$. By the time $f_i = F_s$, $f_o = 0$ and the output is a fixed d.c. level dependent on the relative phases of F_s and f_i. As f_i continues to increase, f_o now increases again and the pattern repeats itself indefinitely. This effect is even more illuminating if it is assumed that after the sampler there is some frequency-dependent processing, e.g. an arbitrary low-pass response like that in Fig. 7.2(a). The envelope of the output sinusoid will now resemble Fig. 7.2(b)—a series of repetitions of the original low-pass response. The positions of the midpoints of the replications indicate the frequencies that will be aliased to d.c. in a sampled data system; the pattern also strongly resembles the amplitude part of the spectrum of any ideally sampled signal.

The zone plate is a 2-D spatial analogue of the (temporal) swept frequency generator discussed above. One version of it has instantaneous spatial frequency proportional to radial distance, r, from the centre of the pattern.

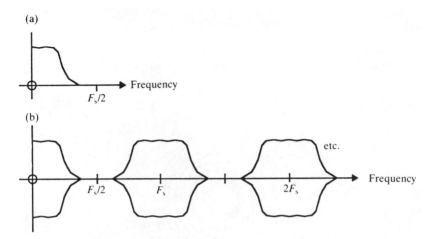

Figure 7.2   (a) Filter response and (b) swept-frequency envelope for sampled system.

Let the pattern amplitude be cos (ϕ); then we require:

$$\frac{d\phi}{dr} = \frac{k}{2\pi}\,r$$

where k is the constant of proportionality. Integrating both sides gives

$$\phi = \frac{k}{4\pi}\,r^2 + \phi_0$$

Since

$$\phi = \frac{k}{4\pi}\left(x^2 + y^2\right) + \phi_0$$

then taking partial derivatives with respect to x and y gives

$$\frac{\partial\phi}{\partial x} = \frac{k}{2\pi}\,x \quad \text{and} \quad \frac{\partial\phi}{\partial y} = \frac{k}{2\pi}\,y$$

which implies that for constant y, the horizontal spatial frequency is proportional to x and for constant x the vertical spatial frequency is proportional to y. This means that the video display itself becomes a 2-D plot of the spatial frequency response of any processing that has been done on its signal input, indicated by the amplitude (and phase) of the parts of the zone plate that survive processing.

Figure 7.3 is an off-screen photograph of a computer-generated zone plate pattern held in a picture store. The active display is 512×512 elements, and the constants are set so that the spatial frequency is exactly one cycle per two picture elements at left and right, and one cycle per two lines at top and bottom. Any imperfections in the original pattern as reproduced here are inherent in the recovery filter after the

Figure 7.3   Digitally synthesized zone plate test pattern.

digital-to-analogue (D/A) converter, the video display, and the
photographic reproduction chain. One defect that is not, of course,
visible in the still photograph is the effect of interlace on the high
vertical spatial frequencies: because adjacent lines on the display are
laid down on alternate fields, there is a strong frame rate flicker (25 Hz
in the United Kingdom) in these parts of the picture.

Figure 7.4 shows the same pattern after passing the video signal
feeding the display through an analogue low-pass filter cutting off at
approximately 2 MHz. All horizontal components whose electrical
frequency is greater than 2 MHz are removed, and the zone plate
pattern is visible only in a central vertical strip of the picture.

Figure 7.5(a) is the result of low-pass filtering the stored image by a
simple running average of width eight picture elements horizontally. It
will be recalled that the impulse response of such a filter is a rectangular
function, and hence its frequency response will be of $(\sin u)/u$ form,
where u is horizontal spatial frequency. This is exactly what we see on
the zone plate, with characteristic transmission side-lobes on each side
of the main low-pass peak; even the phase inversion caused by the first

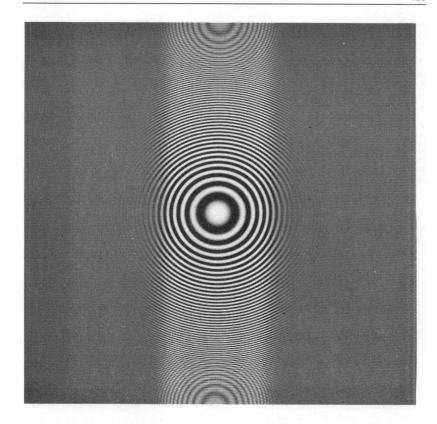

Figure 7.4   Zone plate through sharp-cut analogue low-pass filter, cutoff frequency 2 MHz.

(negative going) side-lobe of the sinc response is detectable by following one of the rings. In Fig. 7.5(b) the direction of the average is diagonal, running from lower left to upper right.

7.3 Sampling

Section 7.2 showed how a 1-D frequency sweep, after sampling, was converted by aliasing into a series of replications of the first part of the sweep, that between 0 and $F_s/2$. Exactly the same occurs with a 2-D zone plate, which is illustrated in Fig. 7.6. The original full resolution pattern of Fig. 7.3 has been subjected to a simulated subsampling process at a rate of 1 pel in 4. The sample values are passed through a low-pass digital filter that has the correct cutoff frequency of $F_s/8$, to give Fig. 7.6(a). Aliasing is manifested as a horizontal series of spatial replications of the low-frequency part of the zone plate; the vertical components are unaffected since every line is being processed. The 'eyes' of the replications indicate the positions of spatial frequencies on

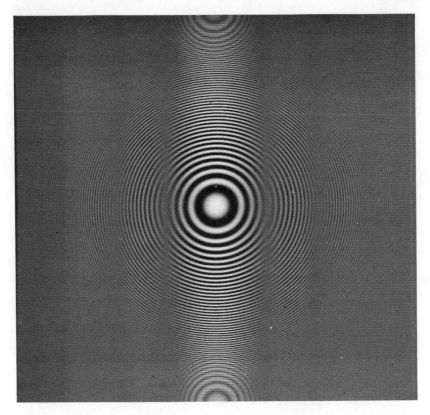

(a)

Figure 7.5(a) Digitally filtered zone plate, using average of eight picture elements horizontally.

the original pattern that are being aliased to zero frequency (d.c.). Clearly, if we wish to avoid such contamination it is necessary to adopt the usual practice and pre-filter any input signal to exclude potential sources of aliasing, which gives Fig. 7.6(b). Some residue of the aliasing remains as a result of imperfections in the software implementation of the filters.

The appearance of these effects on real pictures is shown in Fig. 7.7. Figure 7.7(a) is an original picture, at full 512×512 pel resolution, while Fig. 7.7(b) is the same after 4 : 1 horizontal subsampling and recovery. Figure 7.7(c) shows the same image with inclusion of the pre-filtering stage, which effectively eliminates the spatial artefacts. We include this example not as a realistic method of data compression (but see Chap. 11), rather as a way of making clearly visible the defects that occur if correct practice is not followed: the quality comparison that should be made is between the two *recovered* images.

In real systems, a Nyquist-bandwidth analogue low-pass filter should

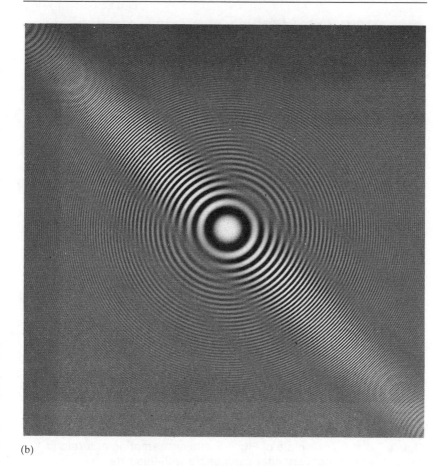

(b)

Figure 7.5(b)   Digitally filtered zone plate, using average of eight picture elements diagonally.

precede the analogue-to-digital (A/D) converter. Its effect is not so obviously beneficial as in Fig. 7.7, since picture sources rarely exploit fully the available bandwidth, but it often reduces the apparent noise level in the final picture since out-of-band noise is otherwise aliased into the passband of the system.

7.3.1 Sharp-cut filters

As noted in Chap. 2, as a filter approaches the ideal low-pass response, the greater is the amplitude of ringing generated on sharp transitions; in visual imaging systems this displays itself as a decaying sinusoidal artefact on each side of high-contrast vertical edges. It can be seen clearly in Fig. 7.7(c). It is especially severe in low-bandwidth systems, such as for videoconferencing, and it is often preferable to engineer an

(a)

Figure 7.6(a) Zone plate of Fig. 7.3 with subsampling at a rate of 1 pel in 4, with a recovery filter compatible with this rate.

extended transition from passband to stopband in order to minimize the effect. Subjectively, a small loss of resolution is often more acceptable than ringing.

7.3.2 Signal recovery

The signal recovery process in digital image systems is frequently treated with less respect than the earlier parts of the chain, with the output of the D/A converter fed directly to the display. There are disadvantages to this practice, caused principally by the frequency-domain characteristics of the converter output stage. In an ideal sampled-data system, the recovered signal is generated by weighted delta functions at a rate F_s fed to a low-pass filter with cutoff $F_s/2$. In a D/A converter, the digital input is latched and held for the duration of the sample; if the analogue settling time is short, this is a very good approximation to a sample and hold circuit, with impulse response:

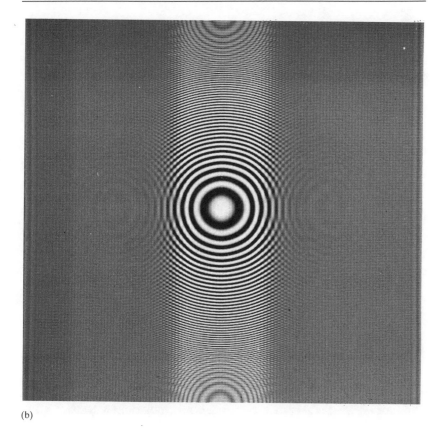

(b)

Figure 7.6(b) The zone plate has been correctly low-pass filtered *before* sampling as well as afterwards.

$$h(t) = \frac{1}{T} \operatorname{rect}\left(\frac{t}{T} - \frac{1}{2}\right)$$

which is illustrated in Fig. 7.8.

The Fourier transform of this impulse response is

$$H(f) = \operatorname{sinc}(fT) \exp(-j\pi fT)$$

where $T = 1/F_s$. The complex exponential corresponds to a phase shift caused by the asymmetry of the response about $t = 0$, while the sinc function $[= (\sin \pi fT)/(\pi fT)]$ is the amplitude part of the transform.

This is a rather poor approximation to an ideal low-pass response, in that it not only has significant residual amplitude at frequencies greater than $F_s/2$, but has roll-off within the passband which reduces the output at $F_s/2$ to sinc $0.5 = 0.636$, or about 4 dB lower relative to its value at zero frequency. The problem of non-zero response for $f > F_s/2$ is overcome by including the conventional analogue filter, while the

(a)

Figure 7.7(a)   Original natural image.

in-band losses can be eliminated either by resampling, or more simply by including a filter with a specially shaped rising response before ultimate cutoff at $F_s/2$. However, in most cases, and especially in very high resolution systems, the post-filter can be left out altogether without serious defects; the presence of a sharp-cut filter may even be a disadvantage, especially in graphics systems, where the ringing artefacts it introduces are probably more subjectively disturbing than the 'blocky' effects of discrete sampling.

7.4 Quantization

A fundamental feature of any digital signal-processing system is that the data are represented in discrete form, in both time (the samples) and amplitude. Sampling rates are chosen on the basis of a compromise between the 'cost' of data handling and distortions caused by aliasing; high sampling rates give good quality, but both the cost of the signal processing involved and the monetary cost of any transmission are also

(b)

Figure 7.7(b) 1 in 4 subsampling *without* pre-filter.

high. The selection of the number of discrete amplitude levels to be used also affects the ultimate serial data rate and the complexity of the signal processing and is thus subject to similar trade-offs. In the case of audio signals, quantization error manifests itself as an intrusive signal-dependent noise. In telephonic speech, the dynamic range of the signal is relatively well controlled and the user is tolerant of distortion, so 256 non-linearly spaced levels (8 bits/sample) are acceptable. With high-quality audio signals, such as written on compact discs, distortion at all times has to be below threshold and as many as 65 536 linearly spaced levels are used.

In the case of picture signals, the effect of·quantization distortion is powerfully graphic in nature, and appears as a series of stepped contours surrounding features in the image; Fig. 7.9 gives an example of eight-level quantization of an image containing both a natural picture and a test grey scale.

Linear quantization of digital video signals is universal for three principal reasons:

(c)

Figure 7.7(c)   1 in 4 subsampling *with* pre-filter.

1   Unlike such communication signals as audio, where the amplitude probability density function (PDF) peaks at zero and a quantizer with more closely spaced levels near zero is beneficial, the PDFs of picture signals have no particular structure, except if averaged over many frames when a uniform density may be expected.

2   The non-linearity in the display device, assumed still to be a cathode ray tube, is approximately complementary with human visual perception of the brightness of a luminous source.

3   Even if it were beneficial, a non-linearity on the analogue side of the A/D converter is difficult to implement reliably, and would in any case be simulated by a simple and readily available *linear* converter followed by a look-up table on the digital side.

Of these factors, the fortuitous physiological match between the eye and display tube has been discussed in Chap. 1.

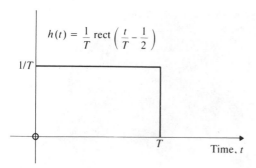

$$h(t) = \frac{1}{T} \text{rect}\left(\frac{t}{T} - \frac{1}{2}\right)$$

Figure 7.8 Impulse response of a sample-and-hold circuit.

7.4.1 Quantization and noise

In the case of many video image sources such as cameras and flying-spot scanners, it is inevitable that the output is contaminated by a certain amount of random noise. Perhaps unexpectedly, the effect of this interference is to relax the requirement for quantization accuracy. How this occurs can be seen from Fig. 7.10, where the process used to create Fig. 7.9(b) has been repeated, but with the addition of uniform PDF noise before eight-level quantization. The range of the noise is equal to

(a)

Figure 7.9(a) Original image with 256-level quantization.

(b)

Figure 7.9(b) Image with 8-level quantization.

the quantizer step size. The mean-squared error introduced by the
eight-level quantizer, output to input, is of course the same in both
cases, but what has changed is its spatial distribution. Transitions
between adjacent quantum levels now occur at random, in positions not
closely related to the spatial structure of the image. The eye is itself a
spatial low-pass filter, which makes it unresponsive to fine detail, and
tends to perceive instead the local average of any such region. The
coarsely quantized picture thus appears subjectively more acceptable
when a small amount of noise is added before quantization; this is even
more convincing on live signals, when there is the additional element of
physiological temporal averaging between adjacent frames.

The most demanding kind of video source in terms of the severity of
quantization effects is one with a low noise level and large areas of low
contrast (high-contrast edges tend to be less affected because of visual
masking). Using such sources, subjective tests can be carried out to
determine the minimum number of quantum levels required to give
satisfactory grey-scale rendition. The usual figure quoted is 256,
corresponding to 8 bits/sample. If the source is from a simple camera
with typical noise levels, as few as 6 bits/sample or 64 levels is often
sufficient. For very low noise inputs, or signals subjected to multiple

Figure 7.10 Eight-level quantization with uniform PDF random noise added *before* the quantizer. Compare with Fig. 7.9(b).

stages of digital processing, where rounding errors could otherwise accumulate, 9-bit quantization may be required.

The smoothing of quantization error by noise was exploited successfully in an early scheme for data compression of video signals, which used as few as 2 bits/sample. Pseudorandom noise with a power spectrum strongly weighted towards high spatial frequencies, and with an amplitude PDF uniform between quantum steps, was added to the incoming video signal (Thompson, 1968).

7.5 Summary

This chapter has discussed the factors that need to be considered in selecting the basic parameters of a digital imaging system, factors that if neglected result in impaired picture quality. The most important concerns the classical relationship between sampling rates, signal bandwidth, and aliasing, and how these affect the appearance of an image. This interaction has been illustrated by reference to a demanding test pattern, the zone plate, whose structure gives an immediate insight into the frequency domain performance of a sampled image system. Experiments on sampling the zone plate illustrate especially the importance of correct pre-filtering. At the same time there is a relative insensitivity to the presence or absence of a corresponding recovery filter (the system used to generate the illustrations works at a sample rate of approximately 15 MHz; no recovery low-pass filter, apart from the 'sample and hold' action of the D/A converter, was in circuit). The reader is referred to the early sections of Chap. 11, on data compression, for further discussion on the way the 2-D or 3-D nature of an image enables the designer to choose sampling patterns which, for the same basic sample rate, give greatly enhanced performance in terms of image quality for natural scenes.

The other major choice of the designer, the number of quantization levels, is discussed, together with the paradoxical effect on quantization distortion of noise on the analogue source signal.

References

Drewery J. O. (1978) 'The zone plate as a television test pattern', BBC Research Department Report no. 1978/23.

Thompson J. E. (1968) 'Reduction of perceptual redundancy for data compression of television signals', Ph.D. thesis, University of London (Imperial College).

8 Image-processing architectures

ADRIAN CLARK and KIRK MARTINEZ

8.1 Introduction

In this chapter we consider computing architectures for image processing, assuming that the image has been sampled and quantized as described in the previous chapter. The treatment is introductory, with more advanced architectures being considered in Chap. 10.

An immediate requirement of the architecture is to be able to handle the large datasets encountered. For example, images of near-broadcast quality are commonly digitized into 512×512 pixels (giving 0.25 Mbytes/frame at 8 bits/pixel). High-resolution television is about 1920×1150 pixels, while other sources produce even larger imagery; the French SPOT satellite, for instance, records a 6000-pixel-wide swath in its 'panchromatic' mode. Fortunately, many image-processing operations are rather simple, which makes the processing of large images tractable on modern computers. Since these comparatively simple operations are usually applied to every pixel of an image, great improvements in execution times can be achieved by hardware that is designed specifically for manipulating image data. Indeed, many novel computer architectures have been developed specifically for this purpose.

Execution time is an important factor. It depends on the number of instructions, the average number of clock cycles per instruction, and the clock speed. Consider a 512×512 image which requires 100 operations per pixel: if the task must be completed in 20 ms, each operation must be completed in under 0.8 ns, which is beyond the capabilities of current (serial) computer technology. (As a comparison, the speed of light *in vacuo* is about 1 foot/ns.) The same problem is encountered if a high-resolution image is to be processed in seconds or if the number of operations per pixel is very large.

There are several ways in which processing speeds can be improved. The most obvious approach is to reduce the cycle time of the computer, but the limits of technology are quickly met: the Cray-1 computer, for example, has a 10 ns clock and is constructed from emitter-coupled logic (ECL) circuitry. Experimental devices with a 2.5 ns cycle time have

Conventional		Pipelined		
fetch 1	fetch 1			
fetch 2	fetch 1	fetch 2		
add	fetch 1	fetch 2	add	
store	fetch 1	fetch 2	add	store
fetch 1		fetch 2	add	store
fetch 2			add	store
add				store
store				
fetch 1				
fetch 2				
add				
store				
fetch 1				
fetch 2				
add				
store				
fetch 1				
fetch 2				
add				
store				

Figure 8.1   Illustration of conventional and pipelined architectures.

been built using gallium arsenide technology, but at the time of writing these are prohibitively expensive. The finite value of the speed of light limits the overall size of the computer: a machine with a 2.5 ns clock may have no paths longer than about 1 foot, or propagation delays become an overriding factor. However, complex image-processing problems may need a thousand times this speed if today's big batch jobs are to be run in minutes or if real-time image coding is to be feasible.

Another approach is to make more efficient use of the computer's central processing unit. This is usually achieved by a technique known as *pipelining* which will be explained by a (somewhat simplistic) example (Fig. 8.1). Consider adding together two arrays (vectors) of numbers on a conventional computer. For each pair of elements in the two arrays, the addition proceeds by fetching the operands from memory, carrying out the addition, and writing the result back to memory. Although this may be one machine instruction, when the overhead of fetching and storing is taken into account, the instruction requires four clock cycles—so the unit performing the addition is only 25 per cent utilized. In a pipelined computer, however, more than one thing happens simultaneously: while the current pair of numbers are being added, the next pair are being read from memory and the previous result is being written back to memory. With a sufficiently careful design, almost 100 per cent processor utilization can be achieved when processing vectors of numbers. This pipelined approach is used in most large, general-purpose computers (e.g. the Cray machines and the Cyber 205).

Pipelining is also used to advantage in reduced instruction set computer (RISC) devices, such as the MIPS and SPARC chip-sets and in digital signal-processing (DSP) chips such as the TMS320 series.

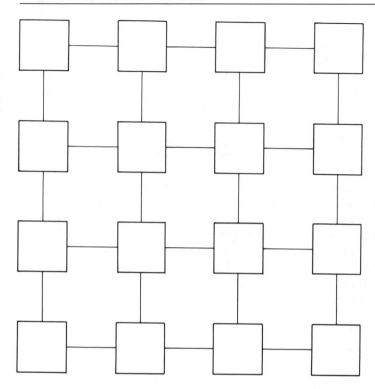

Figure 8.2 A processor array.

These processors are not microcoded (which is how conventional computers implement the fetch–add–store sequence as a single instruction) and simplify the instruction set so that most operations can be performed in one clock cycle. However, this places the onus on the programmer, so that complex optimizing compilers are required to make best use of these devices.

The other main approach to improving processing speeds is to build computers with more than one processor, allowing it to do more than one thing at once. There are many different ways of configuring such designs (Chap. 10 is devoted entirely to this topic), but the most common approach is to make use of rectangular arrays of processors (Fig. 8.2). Each processor has its own memory, so that an image is (ideally) mapped with one pixel per processor. All the processors perform the same operation on their datum in step. This approach is excellent for many image-processing problems, although complications do arise when the image is larger than the array. Owing to the large number of processors required to build a reasonably sized array (even a 64×64 array, small compared with some sources of imagery, requires 4096 processors), they are usually extremely simple and capable of operating only on single-bit data. Special parallel programming languages are also required for processor arrays, unlike pipelined machines. This has both advantages and disadvantages: operations that are intrinsically parallel are simpler to express in a parallel programming language, but some operations are inherently serial and rather difficult to program efficiently. Furthermore, such software is inherently tied to the machine for which it was written.

The aim of this chapter is not to make an exhaustive survey of all image-processing architectures; that would take up the entire book! Instead, a tutorial approach is taken: the simplest architectures are described and the problems associated with them are mentioned. The concepts given here serve as an introduction to Chap. 10, which discusses parallel architectures for image processing. Good introductions into modern computer architectures can be found in the books by Hockney and Jesshope (1983, 1987). Architectures developed specifically for image processing are described in the books by Kittler and Duff (1985), Duff (1983), and Fu and Ichikawa (1982), as well as in the original papers cited in the text.

8.2 Simple image-processing architectures

8.2.1 The framestore

Probably the simplest image-processing 'architecture' is a computer with an attached display device, usually a framestore. This is a block of memory, separate from the computer's own memory and large enough to hold an image, which is interfaced to the computer's peripheral bus (see Fig. 8.3). Image data, usually in the form of 8-bit bytes, are written into the framestore's memory under computer control, usually by direct memory access (DMA) transfers. The contents of the memory are continuously read out at video rate, passed through a digital-to-analogue (D/A) converter, and displayed on a monitor. The output stage, as shown in the figure, usually incorporates a colour map or look-up table to permit pseudocolouring: the 8-bit values read from memory are used as an index into a table which contains 8-bit values for each of the red, green, and blue guns of the monitor. This allows 256 colours to be displayed simultaneously from a 'palette' of about 16.5 million. Some framestores, designed for particular applications, have hard-wired colour maps, but most allow the map's contents to be set by the host computer.

The majority of commercially available framestores, even those for use on microcomputers, incorporate additional features, such as the ability to zoom regions of the image and to pan the zoomed region about the framestore's memory. Other widely available features include line-drawing and region-filling, usually implemented by firmware in the

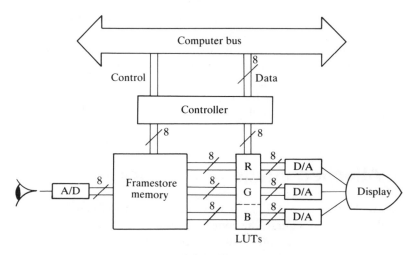

Figure 8.3 Architecture of a typical framestore.

framestore's controller, and a pointing device such as a mouse or graphics tablet. Most of the more modern devices allow images to be digitized into their memory (this is usually termed 'frame-grabbing'); some have enough memory to hold several images simultaneously, and hardware that allows different images to be displayed on the red, green, and blue channels of the monitor, thereby permitting true-colour displays.

8.2.2 The memory-mapped display

Conceptually, although not architecturally, the simplest way to view an image is to have a 'window' into the contents of the computer's main memory. The memory-mapped display does just this. This approach has a number of advantages over the attached framestore concept: the total electronics involved is reduced, thereby lowering the cost, and the display is modified simply by writing into the appropriate region of memory—there is no requirement for a device driver to interface between hardware and operating system. However, there are also disadvantages: since the memory must be continuously read for display, care must be taken when writing into it, unless dual-ported memory is used; 32-bit memory addressing is required for all practical systems; there is no support for line-drawing or region-filling, which has to be carried out by the processor; and so on. Generally, it is felt that the advantages are outweighed by the disadvantages, and the memory-mapped approach is usually adopted only in smaller systems with specific applications.

Modern workstations, many of which have image display capabilities, fall, in a sense, between the two categories: they have 'display controllers' that are separate from, but closely coupled to, the central processor. The screen display is then memory mapped to the display controller. This hybrid approach is, in many ways, better than using either method individually: display manipulations—e.g. moving windows on the screen using block-transfer instructions or displaying images—are very fast, while the display controller performs mundane tasks such as line-drawing without any interaction from the central processor.

8.3 Attached image processors

As yet, we have only looked at architectures for image display; but the real bottleneck is, of course, the computer itself. The obvious solution is to attach some processor, more suited to processing images, to the host. However, the nature of the task makes some demands on the attached processors. Firstly, the time taken, even with DMA transfers, to transfer an image from main memory (or from disk) to the attached processor is frequently comparable with the actual processing time. Hence, the attached device should have enough local memory to hold several images at once. (This requirement rules out many of the high-performance floating-point attached processors used for general scientific work on super-minicomputers.) Equally importantly, the attached processor must be able to display images locally; hence, these devices are usually designed as 'intelligent framestores', where fixed-point operations are performed on the contents of the local memory.

These devices can carry out a variety of image-processing operations locally (see Fig. 8.4). Many of these operations—histogram equalization, for example—make use of look-up tables (LUTs) within a feedback loop: a pixel is read from memory, used as the index into the LUT, and the value from the LUT written back into memory. To optimize processing, common operations such as these are pipelined, which effectively allows one pixel to be processed per clock cycle. Some of the other operations require hardware support to achieve near-real-time performance; real-space convolution is usually implemented in this way.

Many devices of this basic type have gained widespread use in various image-processing disciplines. Indeed, most commercial image processors are bus-structured, pipelined systems (see Fig. 8.1), with one microprocessor controlling various special-purpose subprocessors. Hence, image-processing equipment tends to be manufactured by specialist companies and produced in comparatively small numbers. For vision and general applications, the systems manufactured by the American companies Vicom and Datacube are very popular, while International Imaging Systems (I^2S) systems (also American) are

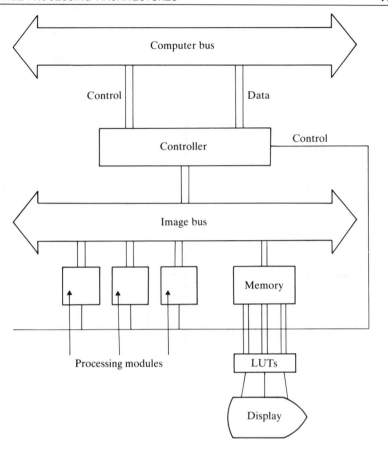

Figure 8.4 Architecture of a typical attached image processor.

ubiquitous in the remote sensing field. The general philosophy of these systems is to concentrate speed where it is needed, with subprocessors designed for certain tasks (such as those in Fig. 8.5). If, for example, a system is required for an industrial solution, only the necessary subprocessors are required. Each subprocessor has the advantages of dedicated systems, such as high performance/cost ratio.

In the Vicom system, one standard bus is used for general communication but three image buses are used for image data. A pipeline controller manages the flow of data between image memories and processors. A convolver and a point processor carry out various common image-processing operations very quickly. This structure means that special subprocessors can be included to carry out the time-critical parts of algorithms rather than aim for generality, with the attendant cost and speed tradeoffs. The MC68000 processor allows easy control in a high-level language (Pascal) as well as simplified addressing for irregular data accesses.

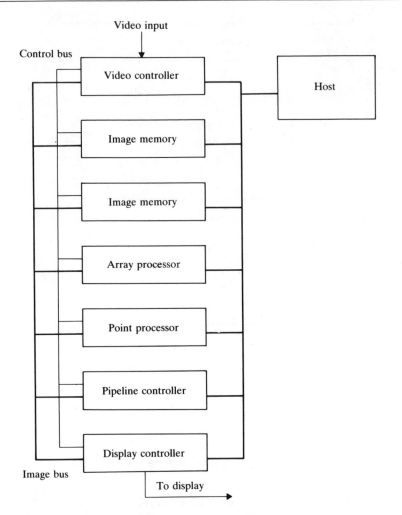

Figure 8.5 Use of subprocessors for specific tasks.

This approach is also taken in the more recent Datacube systems, which are based around a VME control bus and high-speed image buses. These use high-speed ribbon-cable image buses which are easily reconfigurable manually or via a switcher board. Image data flows at a high rate from board to board, to and from image stores. Vicom has flexible but comparatively slow pipelining whereas Datacube systems swap some flexibility for speed. Generally, whole frames are processed by dedicated boards carrying out convolution, histogramming, etc. However, 'region of interest' (ROI) boards allow small portions of images to be processed alone. For example, the APA512 board produces useful measurements on individual 'blobs' such as number of pixels, perimeter, orientation, sizes, and min/max coordinates, all in one frame period. This is a two-board coprocessor comprising around 180 integrated circuits. This approach seems ideally suited to robotics and industrial inspection systems, as well as giving useful primitives for research.

Many similar systems have been developed in the research community. For example, PICAP II (Kruse and Gudmundsson, 1982) was developed at the University of Linköping in Sweden and contains up to 15 sub-processors. This includes convolvers, LUTs, and display processors connected by a single time-shared bus. The Japanese Tospix system (Kiode, 1983) is a bus-based system with convolver, max/min/med, histogrammer, and labeller subprocessors.

With the continuing improvement in the cost/performance ratio, it is now feasible to produce affordable attached image processors with a significant floating-point capability. The Transcept (now part of Sun Microsystems) TAAC-1 (Fig. 8.6) is a good example of this: attached to the Sun workstation's bus, the device is addressed as 1024×2048 pixels, each being 32 bits. The device is closely integrated with the host's operating system, allowing the contents of the image memory to be displayed (as 8-bit colour mapped or 24-bit true colour) in windows on the workstation's screen. It is programmed in a high-level language (C), with hardware support for both integer and floating-point operations. A number of common image-processing operations, such as histogramming and convolution, are programmed in its assembly language and are available via a library. Hence, operations that are compute-intensive (e.g. fast Fourier transformation) or require floating-point arithmetic for accuracy (e.g. image rotation) can be performed in an interactive environment, well matched to the workstation's user interface.

The main advantage of devices such as the TAAC-1 is in their programmability: special-purpose hardware, although faster, is limited to the tasks for which it was designed, but a general-purpose device can be programmed to perform a much wider range of operations.

8.4 Recent developments

There are new devices which promise to make significant changes to image processing systems. One of these is the purpose-designed DSP chip—e.g. the Texas Instruments TMS320C30, the Motorola DSP56000, and the NEC μPD77230, which have the capability to perform some everyday image processing tasks at very high rates for comparatively little cost. The NEC device, in particular, appears to be well suited to image processing.

The advantage of signal-processing devices is that they usually have ALUs several times faster than microprocessors, most instructions requiring one clock cycle, with designs that match signal processing operations: for example, the TMS32010 pipelines sums of products

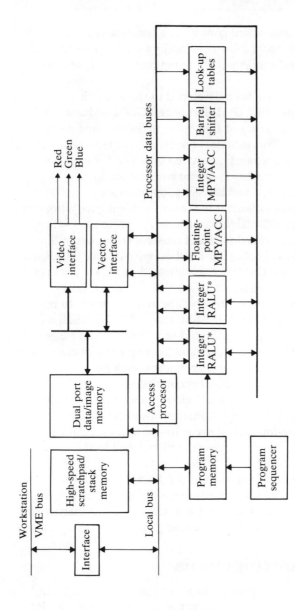

Figure 8.6 The Sun TAAC-1 applications accelerator.

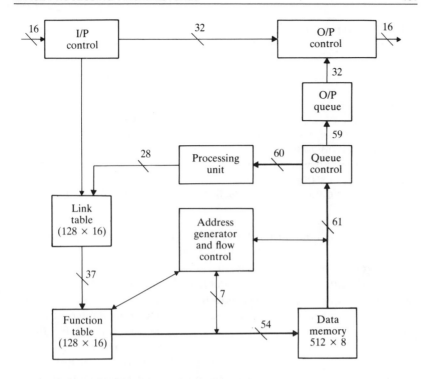

Figure 8.7 The NEC μPD7281 DSP chip.

efficiently. The Inmos IMSA100 is less general, but contains thirty-two 16×16 multiply-accumulators in a transversal filter structure and is capable of processing $2.5 \times 10^6 - 10^7$ samples/s.

The NEC μPD7281 has very wide data paths arranged in a loop, passing through various processors, as shown in Fig. 8.7. Data enter the input control section where they may be passed to the processing loop. In the loop, there is a conventional fast ALU (e.g., 16-bit multiplication in 200 ns) as well as a number of LUTs, in recognition that many non-linear operations are best carried out by LUTs. The wide datapaths, some up to 61 bits, allow tokens and data to be included. The tokens could indicate which operation to do, information about the data, and so on. By manipulating tokens, data may pass several times around the loop before being passed to the output queue controller. An address generator and flow controller unit can manipulate tokens and allow more control; it also controls refresh tokens, which are needed because the LUTs are dynamic RAMs.

For development, a computer would normally be used as host, or the chip could be integrated into an image-processing system. Typical processing times are given in Table 8.1

Another interesting device is the Inmos Transputer (see, for example, Hockney and Jesshope, 1987): this is a reasonably powerful processor in

Table 8.1   Typical processing times

Operation	One processor	Three processors in pipeline[*]
3 × 3 convolution of a 512 × 512, 8-bit image	3.0 s	1.1 s
Half-size shrink of binary image	80.0 ms	30.0 ms
Smoothing a binary image	1.1 s	0.4 s

[*] Up to 14 processors may be pipelined. Note the speed-up of around 2.7 when using three processors; this is a high efficiency (90 per cent).

its own right, with on-chip memory and (in the more recent versions) floating-point coprocessor. Its main advantage, of course, is that transputers can be connected together to form parallel computers. At the time of writing, there are no commercial image-processing systems based on transputer technology, but these are sure to emerge. However, it is likely that such systems will have their applications limited to those problems that require a good number-crunching performance, but little communication between processors, since the throughput of the processor is somewhat greater than that of the interprocessor links. Restoration applications, particularly in the medical imaging field, are likely to be the most affected.

Vision-type image-processing problems, on the other hand, are characterized by fairly simple operations but a significant communication of a pixel's information to its neighbours. A typical example is John Canny's edge detector (Canny, 1983), which consists essentially of a number of local operations (such as convolution with a mask) and some neighbourhood operations. Algorithms of this type require the speed of communication between processors to be comparable with that of the processors. Hence, vision applications usually gain more from a large array of quite simple processors than from a few, powerful processors.

8.5 Software packages for image-processing systems

A particular piece of processing hardware can rarely provide a complete solution to any problem—there is almost invariably some element of software. Let us now consider the software aspects of image-processing architectures. The detailed implementation of image-processing algorithms in software is considered in the next chapter.

It is widely accepted that developing software for any application is very time-consuming. This is especially true for image processing, where 'hardware assist' pays such dividends; the facilities available, methods of communication, and even image representation vary greatly from device to device, so developing reusable software is very difficult.

For conventional computers, several products are in widespread use. Image display can be coded in software via calls to GKS, the international standard for computer graphics, or, on workstations, via X-Windows; however, neither of these provides an ideal solution.

Software to perform the actual processing usually takes the form of libraries of routines; this approach provides a degree of system independence and simplifies the development of new applications software. The best known of these is SPIDER (Tamura *et al.*, 1983), which provides FORTRAN 'subroutines' for a variety of common operations, including transformation, enhancement, and coding. A number of similar products are available or under development.

In the Unix environment, the HIPS package (Landy *et al.*, 1984) is fairly popular. This comprises a number of 'filter' programs, which can be connected using the Unix 'pipe' mechanism to achieve a particular effect. The advantages of this approach are that the Unix command interpreter provides a simple programming language, while the machine-specific code (e.g. to display images) is isolated into a few programs, making it quite simple to interface new devices. HIPS supports a number of image representations. Although generally desirable, this does introduce some problems, since not all programs support all representations; it is frequently necessary to pass images through programs that simply convert the representation.

A different approach was adopted in the SEMPER package (Saxton *et al.*, 1979), which is almost totally machine and device independent. SEMPER has its own command language, closely integrated into the processing software. While HIPS is a collection of tools, SEMPER is a complete system, providing the same user interface on all machines. The only real disadvantage of SEMPER is that it uses a fully complex image representation throughout: this provides a certain degree of consistency, but makes processing 8-bit imagery, almost ubiquitous throughout the discipline, rather slow. Hence, SEMPER is usually adopted in environments where Fourier-space operations are heavily used, e.g. in image restoration.

Systems that incorporate special-purpose hardware are generally regarded as being quite distinct from general-purpose packages such as those described above. (SEMPER has been extended fairly simply to drive custom processing hardware; so can HIPS, but only by dispensing with the 'pipe' feature of commands.) Manufacturers of commercial attached image processors (e.g., I^2S) usually supply libraries, running on the host computer, that interface to their hardware. Providing the library contains all required operations, this is quite satisfactory; however, if something not catered for should be required, problems arise. One is faced with the prospect of developing additional routines in a low-level language on a machine with little or no debugging support. In many cases, even this is not feasible, since attached image processors generally have a limited arithmetic capability and (as they are usually pipelined) cannot random-access the pixels in an image. It is then necessary to read the image back onto the host and manipulate it there. This has a twofold penalty on throughput: in addition to processing the image on the host, it has to be read in from the attached processor and possibly written back. Indeed, one not infrequently finds that, for sophisticated algorithms, these overheads are so great that there is little gain in overall throughput, despite the increased hardware cost. This is the main reason why high-speed, programmable devices, such as the TAAC-1 mentioned above, are so interesting.

For parallel image processors, such as those discussed in Chap. 10, parallel languages are usually designed (Duff and Levialdi, 1981). These treat an entire image as a single datum (providing, of course, the number of processors is at least as large as the number of pixels) and can hence perform simple operations on all pixels at high speed. From a software viewpoint, operations that access all pixels independently of each other are very efficient, but when processing is context sensitive and therefore cannot be made parallel, the speed advantage is lost.

8.6 Summary

This chapter has presented a simple introduction to the design of 'conventional' computer architectures for image-processing applications. The various approaches used to process image data quickly (pipelining and parallelism) were discussed. The design of the conventional framestore was considered. Characteristics of commercial image-processing systems, most of which are based around a high-speed image data bus and incorporate special-purpose hardware for common operations, were discussed. The trend towards modern, high-performance systems attached to workstations was mentioned. Recent developments, such as DSP chips and parallel systems, were elucidated. Indeed, most research into image-processing architectures is directed towards parallel processors and neural networks, which are considered in Chap. 10.

Software systems for image processing were briefly considered. A number of software packages exist for general-purpose computers, available as libraries or bundled systems; these are especially useful when developing novel applications. For high-speed processing with some hardware assist, one has to use the manufacturer's software or write one's own. Since attached image processors usually have rather simple processors, they are frequently incapable of performing the more sophisticated processing operations—which must then be carried out on the host, with the consequent speed penalty. General-purpose applications accelerators, programmable in a high-level language, promise significant improvements. For a very high speed, parallel processors offer the best throughput. However, the individual processors on such systems are very simple, so the range of operations that can be performed is quite restrictive.

References

Canny J. (1983) 'Finding edges and lines in images', MSc thesis, MIT AI Laboratory.

Duff M. J. B. (1983) *Computing Structures for Image Processing*, Academic Press, London.

Duff M. J. B. and Levialdi S. (1984) 'Languages and Architectures for Image Processing', Academic Press, London.

Fu K. S. and Ichikawa T. (1982) *Special Computer Architectures for Pattern Processing*, CRC Press, Boca Raton, Fl.

Hockney R. W. and Jesshope C. R. (1983) *Parallel Computers*, Adam Hilger, Bristol.

Hockney R. W. and Jesshope C. R. (1987) *Parallel Computers 2*, Adam Hilger, Bristol.

Kiode M. (1983) 'Image processing machines in Japan', *IEEE Computer*, vol. 16, no. 1, pp. 68–79.

Kittler J. and Duff M. J. B. (1985) *Image Processing System Architectures*, Research Studies Press, Letchworth.

Kruse B. and Gudmundsson B. (1982) 'Parallelism in PICAP', in *Multicomputers and Image Processing*, Preston K. and Uhr L. (eds), Academic Press, New York.

Landy M. S., Cohen Y. and Sperling G. (1984) 'HIPS: A Unix-based image processing system', *Computer Vision, Graphics and Image Processing*, vol. 25, pp. 331–47.

Saxton W. O., Pitt T. J. and Horner M. (1979) 'Digital image processing: the SEMPER system', *Ultramicroscopy*, vol. 4, pp. 343–54.

Tamura H., Shigeyuki S., Tomita F. and Yokoya N. (1983) 'Design and implementation of SPIDER—a transportable image processing software package', *Computer Vision, Graphics and Image Processing*, vol. 23, pp. 273–94.

9 Software techniques

TIM DENNIS

9.1 Introduction

In this chapter we give information based on a number of years' experience of image-processing software development gained by the members of an image-processing research group. This has ranged from relatively simple control tasks on a real-time hardware-coding simulation system (Brown *et al.*, 1977) through testing of industrial inspection processes (Dennis and Clark, 1985; Dennis *et al.*, 1988) to all-software simulations of complex hybrid digital video coding schemes (Ghanbari and Pearson, 1988).

Historically, most prepackaged image-processing software has been written, and much continues to be written, in FORTRAN; after experience with this and other programming languages, C has been the preferred choice of most members of our laboratory since 1978 for nearly all picture hardware control and processing tasks. If we equate efficiency with maximum speed, it has proved ideally suited to the operations that may have to be performed on large 2-D or 3-D arrays of data. This is principally because of its modular structure, its handling of large arrays and complex data structures, and in the way it is usually possible to write code that is able to exploit the known properties of a target CPU (such as a 68000). This is not a trivial factor, since the aim, in the case of a research laboratory at least, is usually to test and then to optimize techniques that perform some desired task; the researcher wants to see the results of a change to an input parameter as rapidly as possible, both to get an immediate 'feel' for the effect the variable is having on the system and to make best use of his or her own time. In the case of a software-based industrial system, the need for fast processing is obvious if it is to achieve a desired throughput and if the development cost of dedicated hardware can thereby be avoided.

Where examples of programs are given, we give them directly in C and have to assume at least a passing familiarity with the language. For further information see Kernighan and Ritchie (1978).

Portability is often a concern of programmers, but there is always the danger of sacrificing efficiency. However, our experience has been that even when the hardware on two systems is not identical and has very different access modes, the system-specific changes required are straightforward to implement. This is especially the case if maximum use is made of the modular structure of the language to separate distinct tasks.

9.2 Architecture and software

Chapters 8 and 10 discuss a number of possible hardware architectures for software-based picture manipulation tasks. In this section we consider more closely the ways in which the image store can appear to the user, from the point of view especially of the smaller image-processing system. In all the discussions it is assumed that the real-time video display function is proceeding independently of the computer access function; how exactly the two interleave is a matter for the store designer. In a simple case the computer steals a memory access cycle to insert its own address and carry out a read or write as required; the resulting interference with the display is not always a serious problem. By providing two access slots within a cycle the interference can be avoided.

There are several ways to manage software access to image memory, which can be broadly classified as direct or indirect methods. In the indirect methods control is exercised by means of a small set of memory-mapped registers, including address pointers that identify a picture element (pel) of interest. Direct access corresponds to full memory mapping, where the picture store appears complete in the address space of the system. There are variations between these extremes which include forms of windowing where a small section of image memory is directly mapped, say 64 kbytes, and the hardware address pointers hold values that are combined with the processor-supplied address to locate the physical region in the image store. The trade-off is between use of address space and program complexity: generally, the larger the area of memory that is directly mapped, the more straightforward is the task of the programmer. We give some simple examples to illustrate these points.

9.2.1 Indirect addressing

Figure 9.1 shows a simple diagram of the way a processor can access an image store (which may be larger than the machine's own directly addressable range) by means of externally accessible registers Y and X, while Table 9.1 is a more detailed list of the memory-mapped registers which would be required. The example assumes a 0.25 Mbyte picture store, organized as 512 lines of 512 elements each. Splitting the address into two 9-bit segments is sensible in this case, as the segments will automatically correspond to the X and Y coordinates of a picture

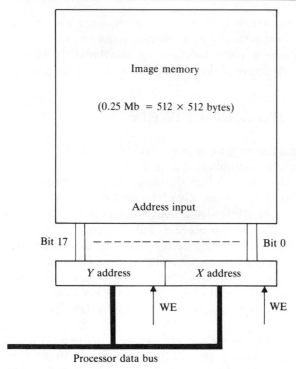

Figure 9.1 Indirect addressing to image store. WE is write enable.

element. The addressing required for continuous *video* display is not shown: in the elementary case, counting circuits would generate the *X* and *Y* addresses at a rate derived from the particular television display standard. Computer access would 'take over' the address lines for the time required to perform its transaction. This method is really the only practical one for 8-bit processors with limited address space, such as the 6809.

Assuming the user is allowed by any resident operating system to address absolute memory locations and that the registers occupy consecutive addresses, the arrangement in Table 9.1 is best handled in C by means of a structure definition:

```
struct imstore_type {
    unsigned int xaddr, yaddr;
    unsigned char data;
    unsigned int status, control;
    };
```

The unequal size of the structure members is handled automatically by the compiler, but note that it would fail with a processor where a word-sized object has to begin on an *even* address, since in such a case the compiler would automatically assume the existence of a 1-byte 'hole' after the definition of the data structure member.

Table 9.1

Register name	Size (bits)	Address offset	Function
X address	16 (9 used)	0	X direction access coordinate
Y address	16 (9 used)	2	Y direction access coordinate
Data	8	4	read: data read from picture at coordinates (X,Y) write: data inserted into picture at (X,Y)
Status	16	5	(read only) image store state, e.g. line and field timing information; interrupt flag bits
Control	16	7	(write only) e.g. snatch enable; access mode; interrupt enable

A simple function `get_pel` to read and return the value of a single pel from a specified location (`xpos, ypos`) in a system with a single store using indirect access would be:

```
unsigned int get_pel(xpos, ypos)
    unsigned short xpos, ypos;
    {
    extern struct imstore_type *im_ptr;
    im_ptr->x = xpos;
    im_ptr->y = ypos;
    return(im_ptr->data);
    }
```

Here we assume that there is a global pointer variable `im_ptr` which has been initialized elsewhere to point to the base address of the store's memory-mapped register set. The function returns an `int` value, even though the data being read from the store are only 8 bits wide; it is helpful to declare everything `unsigned` to ensure that the system does not attempt to do a sign extension and return negative numbers for all values greater than 127. Note that `int` may be 16 or 32 bits wide, depending on the processor. It will usually be 16 bits on an 8-bit machine.

The use of structures is especially powerful when the system has more than one image store, as it has when colour is being handled. Suppose the colour stores are numbered 0–2 and that their register sets occupy consecutive memory locations; it is then possible to treat the set as an array of structures. A function `put_grb()` to write a pel to all three stores would look like this, where variable `src` is a pointer to an array of 3 bytes holding the green, red, and blue values:

```
put_grb(xpos, ypos, src)
    unsigned int xpos, ypos;
    unsigned char *src;
    {
/*
Global pointer to base address of store 0
*/
    extern struct image_type *im_ptr;
/*
Local pointer
*/
    struct image_type *loc_ptr;
    int count;
    loc_ptr = im_ptr;
    count = 3;
    while (count--){
        loc_ptr->x = xpos;
        loc_ptr->y = ypos;
        loc_ptr->data = *src++;
        loc_ptr++;
}
    return(0);
    }
```

It is clear from these examples that the price paid for economy of addressing is a significant software overhead, especially for random access into the picture memory. Fortunately, many image-processing operations involve simple stepping actions horizontally along scan lines or vertically across them. To help in these cases, it is possible to redesign the hardware of the stores and replace the physical X and Y address registers by up–down counters. Then using some bits of the control register, modes can be selected in which either or both of the counters increment or decrement whenever the 'data' register is addressed, thus implementing an automatic stepping function in any of eight directions.

Assuming an autoincrement mode has been selected that causes horizontal stepping, the code to copy 512 bytes, or one line, of the contents of a `char` buffer `src` to the store would be:

```
count = 512;
sp = src;              /* sp is a character pointer */
loc_ptr->xpos = 0;   /* start X-register at zero */
while (count--)
    loc_ptr->data = *sp++;
```

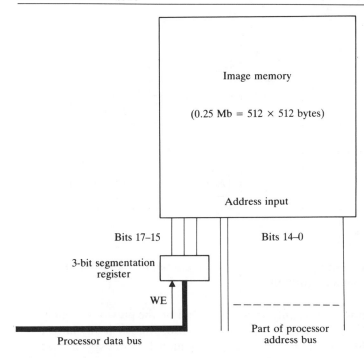

Figure 9.2   Partial direct image store addressing.

This is a considerable improvement over the situation without autoincrement where the X register would have to be updated for each element within the `while` loop.

9.2.2 Partial direct addressing

In this arrangement the hardware provides limited direct access to contiguous areas of the picture, either in the form of a rectangular window or more simply a strip equal to its maximum width. The window may be positioned at a fixed set of locations or more usefully at any position within the actual image; its size may be varied up to its maximum area limit.

The example of Fig. 9.2 shows a possible 32 kbyte fixed-strip arrangement for the example 512 × 512 picture store. The low 15 bits of the processor address bus are extended directly to the image memory, together with a control line (not shown) which decodes the remaining address bits to indicate when the 32 kbyte section that is to be mapped into the image memory is being accessed. The top three bits of the image address come from a memory-mapped segmentation register which can be manipulated via normal programmed write operations.

The computer thus has access to one of eight strips of the image, each 64 lines high. Values 0–7 in the segmentation register control which physical strip of the image is available.

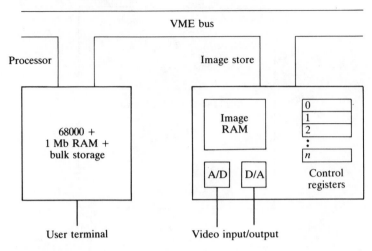

Figure 9.3 Example architecture for a simple memory-mapped image-processing system.

This method is certainly an improvement on the previous single-pel access technique in terms of speed, but the software is, if anything, even less straightforward: the author has encountered a store system that worked on a fixed-strip technique of the kind above. Single line access was not difficult, but such tasks as addressing an arbitrary vertical column required calculation of which strip the first pel lay in, and where, followed by some number of whole strips, ending with a number 'left over' in the last strip.

9.2.3 Full memory mapping

The most satisfactory way to access a picture store is undoubtedly to extend the 'partial direct' concept until the window encompasses an area at least the size of the largest picture that can be displayed; 512×512 is often convenient. If the addressable area is actually larger than can be displayed, then so much the better: the hardware usually allows a display window to be scanned over the full space. The program examples that follow can, of course, be used wherever it is possible to read for processing a complete image, from a file or indirect access store, into memory arrays declared (or obtained via malloc() under Unix) by the programmer.

In the following discussion we use as an example of a simple, directly addressable stand-alone image processing system the arrangement shown in Fig. 9.3, which consists of a 68000-series single-card processor on a VME bus with 1 Mbyte or so of its own RAM. Also on the VME bus is a set of one or more fully mapped picture stores, each capable of displaying 512 8-bit pels per line by 512 lines, interlaced. The addressing is such that consecutive locations lie left to right along video scan lines and top to bottom, and there is no separation in the hardware between X and Y components. We assume that there is access to auxiliary bulk storage in the form of floppy or hard disks, and that there is a resident operating system, such as OS9 or Unix, which allows absolute addressing in some form. There will, of course, still be a small set of control registers for each store which can be handled by a structure definition.

For live picture input and display output each of the stores has A/D and D/A converters. Picture acquisition is under software control by manipulation of control or status registers in the hardware: it is reasonable to expect a processor to be able to react to events at video frame or field rate without difficulty, possibly under interrupt. The blanking interval in the 625-line 50 field/s standard is approximately 1.6 ms, and any gross disturbance to the settings of the system (such as moving a display window) should be done during this time to avoid objectionable effects on the picture. Events at line or pel rates would not normally be amenable to software control.

Store manipulation

We give a simple example of an area access procedure which fills a rectangular region of the store at position xpos, ypos, size xsize, ysize, with a constant amplitude, amp. Variable base_addr is assumed to be defined elsewhere and to point to the address of the top left-hand pel in the image store.

```
fill(amp, xpos, ypos, xsize, ysize)
    unsigned int amp, xpos, ypos, xsize, ysize;
    {
    register unsigned int count1, count2;
    register unsigned char val, *sp;
    val = amp;
    count1 = ysize;
    sp = base_addr + (512 * ypos + xpos);
    while (count1--){
        count2 = xsize;
        while (count2--) *sp++ = val;
        sp += (512 - xsize);
        }
    return(0);
    }
```

The program uses two nested loops, the innermost one stepping along a line as this is the fastest access mode. Pointers are used wherever possible in preference to array constructions of the kind array[index++]=val. All the local variables are of type register, which means that they reside in one of the machine's fast registers: data, or address if a pointer; unnecessary memory references are thereby avoided. If there are more local variables than the processor has available registers, they should be reserved for those that change most rapidly, usually within the innermost of sets of nested loops.

We have found that knowledge of the way a particular compiler generates assembler code is often a useful guide on the best way to encode an operation in C for maximum speed. As an example, we include the output of a particular 68000 C compiler for the `fill` routine above, with comments made from the line of C that generated the adjacent instructions. `L1, L2...` are labels, while arguments are all passed on the stack as 4-byte quantities.

```
_fill:
     link      a6, #0
     movem.l   d5/d4/d3/d0/a5,-(sp)  * (Save working registers)
     move.l    8(a6),d3              * val = amp;
     move.l    24(a6),d5             * count1 = ysize;
     move.l    16(a6),(sp)           * sp = base_addr +
     pea       512                   * (512 * ypos + xpos);
     jsr       a.lmul
     move.l    (sp),d7
     add.l     12(a6),d7
     add.l     base_add,d7
     move.l    d7,a5
L1:
     move.l    d5,d7                 * while (count1--)
     subq.l    #1,d5
     tst.l     d7
     beq.s     L3
     move.l    20(a6),d4             * count2 = xsize;
L5:
     move.l    d4,d7                 * while (count2--)
     subq.l    #1,d4
     tst.l     d7
     beq.s     L7
     move.b    d3,(a5)+              * *sp++ = val;
     bra.s     L5
L3:
     clr.l     d7                    * return(0);
     movem.l   (sp)+,d5/d4/d3/d0/a5  * (recover registers)
     unlk      a6
     rts
L7:
     move.l    #512,d7               * sp += (512-xsize);
     sub.l     20(a6),d7
     add.l     d7,a5
     bra.s     L1
```

The instructions in the innermost `while` loop are the most critical, as they get performed ($xsize$ * $ysize$) times. The use of register variables and the post-increment pointer mechanism means that the compiler is able to do the actual write operation with a single machine instruction. This would not have been the case had we used post-decrement, as there is no corresponding mode in the 68000.

An unexpected gain occurs (with the same compiler) if

```
while (count2--) *sp++ = val;
```

is replaced by the apparently more complex

```
do *sp++ = val; while(--count2 > 0);  when it generates:
```

```
L5:
    move.b   d3,(a5)+
    subq.l   #1,d4
    bne.s    L5
```

which has just two loop-control instructions compared with the five in
the first case, and corresponds exactly to the code an assembly language
programmer would use for the same operation.

Further enhancements

In a simple operation like `fill`, and if permitted by the VME-bus
hardware, use can be made of word or long-word access to perform the
bulk of the transfers, with suitable padding at each end of the line to
comply with 4-byte address boundaries. Thus, to fill a line of length 403
pels, starting at pel 0 on the line, requires 100 4-byte transfers, followed
by three of size `char`. Of course, the same data have to be copied to
all 4 bytes of the longer-sized source variable before the transfer begins.
It is more usual to resort to this method when a full picture is being
handled and is known to have a size that is exactly divisible by 4.

9.3 Programming examples

9.3.1 General software considerations

- *Language* Work in a programming language that allows direct
  exploitation of machine properties and does not attempt to conceal
  the hardware from the user in the way associated with, for example,
  some implementations of PASCAL.
- *Loop control* Examine the way loop control is handled, and use that
  which is most efficient at the assembler level.
- *Variables* Make maximum use of (fast) register variables, but save
  them for the innermost loop of a nested set. Avoid floating point. To
  maintain precision, instead use long integers and defer rounding until
  the last possible stage. If fractional quantities have to be represented,
  approximate as a vulgar fraction whose denominator is a power of 2.
- *Subroutines* Avoid subroutines that do very little (such as a
  `get_pel(xpos, ypos)` function in a directly addressed
  store) since the overhead in argument passing and stack activity is
  often considerable.

9.3.2 Convolution

In Chapter 7 we used a number of filtering operations in the discussion on sampling. These were implemented by direct convolution of a mask representing the desired impulse response with the source picture. The mask is positioned at all possible locations in the source and a sum of products of mask elements and associated pels computed. The direct method is only really practical if the mask size is restricted to less than about 100 pels, otherwise computation time becomes excessive. However, large area operators *can* be handled efficiently if they have many zero-valued elements. Another method is to cascade two or more 'small' convolutions in order to obtain the effect of a large one.

A way of exploiting a sparse impulse response is to generate from the full mask an array of structures representing only non-zero mask elements and containing their associated offsets *in the image store* relative to the position of the central mask element. Suppose we have an original impulse response:

$$
\begin{array}{ccccc}
0 & -2 & 0 & 0 & 0 \\
1 & 3 & 4 & -3 & 1 \\
0 & 0 & 0 & 2 & 0
\end{array}
$$

then for a 512×512 element store the table of (multiplier, offset) pairs is:

$$(-2, -513)\ (1, -2)\ (3, -1)\ (4, 0)\ (-3, 1)\ (1, 2)\ (2, 513)$$

The table elements are best described by an array of structures of this kind:

```
struct mask_type{
  int mult, offset;
  };
```

The convolution summation itself is then a compact loop:

```
count = nz_elements;
sum = 0;
mask_ptr = mask_elements;
while (count--){
    sum += mask_ptr->mult * *(sp + mask_ptr->offset);
    }
```

Variable sum accumulates the result of each process; nz_elements is the number of non-zero elements in the original mask; mask_ptr is initialized to point to the array of structures; sp is a pointer to the current centre pel in the source image. This is another case where detailed investigation of the assembler code generated by the compiler is worthwhile, when the programmer may decide to implement this critical part of the process as an assembler subroutine.

The technique of specifying an area operator by means of multiplier/offset elements is capable of generalization. The set of offsets can describe *any* pattern of pels, geometrical or otherwise, which we wish to consider, in any order. There is no requirement either that the other element be a multiplier (it could be a code for some logical operation) or that there should be just one component associated with each offset.

9.3.3 Look-up tables

Look-up tables are essential tools in image-processing software and hardware, usually to increase speed. They should be used whenever the range of a variable is known in advance and where repetitive or complex calculation would otherwise be required, such as the trigonometric functions and power laws. It is sometimes even worthwhile to replace multiplication by a constant by a look-up table; this is especially the case if the system is not equipped with fast arithmetic hardware.

A good example is where it is required to perform the conversion of red, green, and blue primary colour components to luminance and colour difference. The equation that relates luminance to R, G and B is (in the NTSC system):

$$Y = 0.299R + 0.587G + 0.114B$$

On the assumption that the result is required in integer form and that integer multiplication will be used, we do an approximate calculation by scaling everything by a convenient power of 2, for example 1024, to allow the final integer division to be done by a simple right shift:

$$Y = (306R + 601G + 117B)/1024.$$

The multiplications are eliminated by constructing three integer look-up tables that contain all products of 306, 601, and 117 with integers between 0 and 255. The C code to calculate luminance, scaled 0–255, then becomes

```
lum = (R_lut[*rp++] + G_lut[*gp++] + B_lut[*bp++] + 512) >> 10;
```

where rp, gp, and bp are pointers to the individual colour stores. The addition of 512 before the right shift (division by 1024) is to minimize rounding error.

Binary convolution

Suppose we wish to perform a low-pass filtering operation on a two-level picture, with a mask of size 4×4 elements, to generate a grey-scale output (this might be needed in a caption generator to give natural-looking outlines). There are 2^{16} possible combinations of inputs that will be run through the actual convolution mask at leisure to create the 65 536 element look-up table which then operates on real pictures. Again, the look-up table is completely general in that its output can be *any* function of its inputs.

9.4 Summary

We have discussed ways of performing image processing on small picture store/computer hardware combinations, and how this is affected by the design of the hardware, in particular the way the picture memory is accessed. A basic design of a stand-alone system has been given, derived from practical experience in the use of such apparatus for research and near-real-time industrial purposes. We have concentrated on software design that produces programs that run fast, by using the C language and access methods that do tend to be expensive in memory space. We suggest that some knowledge of the mechanics of compiler action is valuable to enable the programmer to write code at the C level in a way that makes efficient use of a CPU's instruction set.

References

Brown M. A., Dennis T. J. and Pearson D. E. (1977) 'Interframe predictive coding of television signals with computer control', *Proceedings of the IERE Conference on Digital Processing of Signals in Communications*, University of Loughborough, IERE Conference Proceedings no. 37, pp. 237–44.

Dennis T. J. and Clark L. J. (1985) 'Real-time detection of spot-type defects', *2nd International Technical Symposium on Optical and Electro-optical Science and Engineering*, Cannes, France, SPIE Conference Proceedings 596, paper 26.

Dennis T. J., Clark L. J. and Gunawardena C. A. (1988) 'Computer controlled sizing and quality inspection system for agricultural produce', *International Conference on Computers in Agricultural Extension Programs*, Florida.

Ghanbari M. and Pearson D. E. (1988) 'Statistical behaviour of VBR-coded television pictures', Paper D3, *International Workshop on Packet Video*, Torino.

Kernighan B. W. and Ritchie D. M. (1978) *The C Programming Language*. Prentice-Hall, Englewood Cliffs, NJ.

10 Parallel architectures for image processing

ADRIAN CLARK, KIRK MARTINEZ and BILL WELSH

10.1 Introduction

We saw in Chaps 8 and 9 that equipment generally available for image processing is conventionally attached to the bus of a general-purpose host computer. Such hardware normally utilizes a single processor for manipulation of the image data and, as all data pass through it, it determines the throughput of the system. Pipelined systems (see Chap. 8) provide only a partial solution to the problem. There is, however, an alternative approach: instead of developing a single, powerful processor, a large number of simpler processors (ideally one per pixel) may be employed. With the great advances in the packing densities of components on integrated circuits, this is a very attractive approach. Many such parallel processors have been developed for image-processing applications. These parallel processors are, however, really designed for 'conventional' image processing applications: thresholding, transforming, filtering, etc. There are a great many problems, particularly in pattern recognition and vision, where the technique cannot be conveniently expressed in a programming language. For applications such as these, a somewhat different approach to parallel processing, a neural network, is often the most suitable.

In this chapter, the reader will be given an introduction to both conventional parallel processors and neural networks. A number of specific architectures will be examined in detail. In addition to the books listed in Chap. 8, parallel architectures for image processing are considered in Duff and Levialdi (1981), Fountain (1985), Uhr (1987), and Levialdi (1988).

10.2 The assessment of parallelism

A conventional serial computer stores its program and data in the same memory, fetching instructions and operands as necessary. Such an arrangement is termed a von Neumann computer. The maximum throughput that can be achieved is thus determined by the speed at which instructions and data can be read from memory.

An obvious way to improve performance is to use separate memories for instructions and data, fetching both simultaneously; this is known as the Harvard architecture. If this is coupled with a high-speed cache memory, so that blocks of instructions or data can be pre-fetched, it is possible to obtain a significantly higher throughput than with a von Neumann machine. This concept of partitioning memory is used in most of today's high-speed computers (e.g. the Cray machines and in some DSP chips) since the processor is capable of much faster operation than its memory.

The way in which the stream of instructions and data are treated allows a convenient categorization (due to Flynn, 1972):

- *Single instruction, single datastream (SISD)*   This is a von Neumann computer, in which a single instruction and datum are fetched from memory, processed, and the result written back.
- *Single instruction, multiple datastream (SIMD)*   Most parallel image processors fall into this category. Multiple streams of data are processed concurrently by multiple processors, but each processor executes the same instruction.
- *Multiple instruction, single datastream (MISD)*   This category consists of machines in which a set of processors operate on a single stream of data. A pipelined image processor is a good example of this type of system.
- *Multiple instruction, multiple datastream (MIMD)*   This is the most general category, in which many processors operate concurrently on their own data. Transputer-based systems, discussed below, are capable of MIMD operation.

We note, in passing, that Flynn's classification is by no means the only one (although it is the most popular). Furthermore, it has some serious limitations, since it makes no statement as to whether operations are actually performed simultaneously. Another problem is that some architectures do not fall neatly into any category. A good example of this is a data-driven system, which consists primarily of a stream of data, instructions being indicated by tokens embedded in the data. Neural networks do not fit well into this scheme either, but are occasionally classified as MIMD.

For image-processing applications, it is essential that the architecture is matched to the problem. For example, consider the processing of a 5×5 region of an image. A conventional SISD computer would require at least 25 cycles to access the data; but dedicated hardware could do the same task in a single cycle. On the other hand, this dedicated processor would be of little use in processing random points in an image (e.g. all those pixels that have a grey level greater than a particular value). For this reason, parallel image processors have been designed to address specific problems; furthermore, as indicated above, different types of architecture are more suitable for different types of problem.

10.3 Typical architectures

Although no two systems are identical, they often have similar characteristics, enabling us to think of them as belonging to separate classes. As for the simpler devices described in Chap. 8, this is usually achieved by considering the way in which they communicate. In the following subsections, we consider the main types and illustrate them with examples.

10.3.1 Bus-structured systems

This type of architecture is, in a sense, a development of the multifunction attached processors described in Chap. 8. The essential feature is that the various processors and regions of memory that comprise the system communicate via a high-speed bus. The host computer is usually attached to this bus. The greatest problem with this architecture is bus contention, i.e. two or more processors attempting to access the bus simultaneously. The same problem occurs, of course, with the peripheral buses of conventional computers. The various arbitration schemes adopted in that case are not always appropriate to the high-speed synchronous buses required for image data transfer. Instead, systems frequently have multiple image data buses.

The POLYP system (Maenner, 1984) is a good example of this (Fig. 10.1). POLYP is a multi-microprocessor system developed at the University of Heidelberg for medical applications, particularly the analysis of microscope slides. The major feature of the system is a multiple bus, the POLYBUS, connected to which are processors and memory modules. This is a 32-bit bus with arbitration, allowing any processor access to any memory module. Since it is a multiple bus, several transfers may take place concurrently; only if all data paths are in use is it necessary for a processor to wait. There is also a separate synchronization bus, which is used to assign tasks, and so on. Since the processors are capable of running separate tasks, POLYP is a MIMD machine.

Each of the thirty or so processor boards originally built contained a Motorola MC68000 system with local memory, although some processors were designed specifically to handle input/output. POLYP is

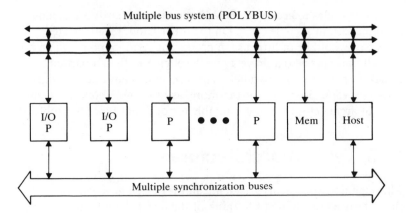

Figure 10.1   The POLYP system.

hosted by a conventional 68000-based computer running the Unix operating system. Program development is carried out on the host, where a library of functions is used to implement features such as message-passing between processors and synchronization. This makes programming a fairly straightforward task.

Despite the great flexibility inherent in systems such as POLYP, they suffer from a number of problems. The most significant of these is the decomposition of the overall processing into separate tasks for the individual processors. There are currently no formal methods for performing this kind of decomposition. A consequence of this is exhibited in the requirements for message passing and synchronization: if the overall processing is badly decomposed into separate tasks, frequent messages have to be passed between processors; this is wasteful of both processor time and bus bandwidth and can lead to a significant degradation in performance.

10.3.2 Pipelined systems

The basic principles of pipelined systems were discussed in Chap. 8. Essentially, a pipelined system simply consists of a series of connected processors; the output of one processor forms the input of the next, possibly with intermediate buffering. This means that pipelined processors fall into the MISD category. The overall throughput is hence determined by the slowest operation, so it is essential that they all operate at the same speed for the arrangement to be successful. Pipelined systems operate at peak efficiency only when all parts of the pipeline are in use; the time taken to fill the pipe (the set-up time or latency) is therefore an important characteristic which, for short data sequences such as small regions of an image, may form a significant overhead. Another problem with pipelined systems is that it is difficult

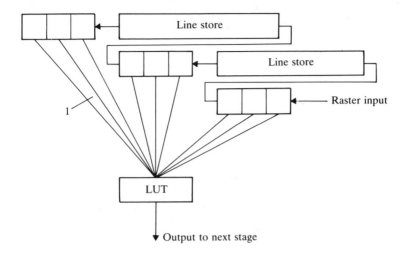

Figure 10.2 The Cytocomputer.

to access intermediate results. Nevertheless, for low-level image-processing problems, pipelined systems are more cost-effective than bus-structured systems.

A number of pipelined systems have been developed. These are usually data-driven and make extensive use of look-up tables (LUTs). The best-known is the Cytocomputer (Sternberg, 1983), again developed for medical applications (Fig. 10.2). This consists of a 3×3 window, scanned across the image by means of delay sections, which yields nine binary outputs for each window position on the image. These outputs are combined to form 9-bit indices into a 512-element LUT. The values read from the LUT may be output or used as input to another window scanner. Up to 80 stages may be cascaded in this way.

The PETAL system (Martinez and Pearson, 1985) was developed along very similar lines. This has a slightly more complex LUT arrangement (Fig. 10.3): the two-level pipeline of LUTs is designed to match 3×3 logical operators, which are developments from the elementary operators described in Chap. 2. The first stage pairs the central pixel of a region with all eight neighbours in turn, producing eight binary outputs which are combined into the index of the LUT. PETAL was developed as part of a research project into the coding of facial imagery.

The VAP (Keller *et al.*, 1983) is another similar system. This again comprises a cascade of LUTs, this time with 6-bit outputs (Fig. 10.4). Here, a programmable window scanner provides a neighbourhood of up to 16 pixels from a 64×7 region of an image. The wider data paths permit more general (grey-level) processing to be performed. The system is controlled by a PDP-11/34 host which allows the definition of the contents of the LUTs using a Pascal-like syntax.

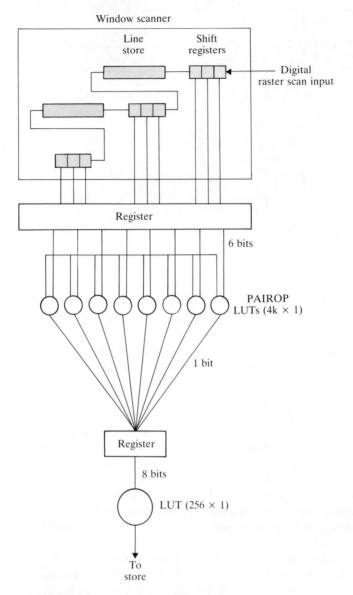

Figure 10.3   The PETAL system.

10.3.3 Processor arrays

This is a very general classification, but usually implies a system
configured as a 2-D array, with each processing element (PE) connected
to some or all of its neighbours. (Networks of processors interconnected
in other arrangements are considered later in this chapter.) Several PEs
are generally integrated on a single VLSI device. Ideally, one would

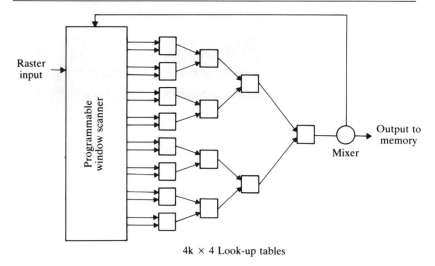

4k × 4 Look-up tables

Figure 10.4   The VAP system.

have a PE for each pixel of the image; this would, however, be
prohibitively expensive, even for moderately sized images. Hence, there
is a practical trade-off between the size of the array (i.e. the number of
processors), chip complexity, and cost. Due to size and cost constraints,
most PEs are capable of 1-bit operations only and have a very simple
instruction set. There is generally memory associated with each PE.
Arrays are normally configured as SIMD devices, with every processor
operating on its own datum simultaneously, under the control of a unit
that broadcasts instructions to the PEs.

   This architecture has both advantages and disadvantages over other
approaches. Its main advantage is that, as each PE is operating on data
held in its own memory, there are no bus contention or memory access
problems. Since every instruction takes place on every PE
simultaneously, the entire image is affected in a single operation. PEs
invariably have instructions to pass data to their nearest neighbours,
making neighbourhood operations such as convolution with a mask
very efficient (although one must take care at the edges of the array).
Since the processors are usually 1 bit, multibit manipulations such as
addition are carried out by assembly language subroutines. This allows
the precision of the processing to match that of the data, so one can
manipulate say 12-bit data using 12-bit operations.

   There are, however, a number of difficulties. Most image-processing
algorithms involve non-image operations; due to the primitive nature of
the PEs, such operations are very slow. As a consequence, programs for
processor arrays try to avoid such operations. This results in algorithms
that are very different from those encountered on conventional
computers (e.g. Fig. 10.5). A second problem concerns the match
between image and array sizes: when the image is smaller than the

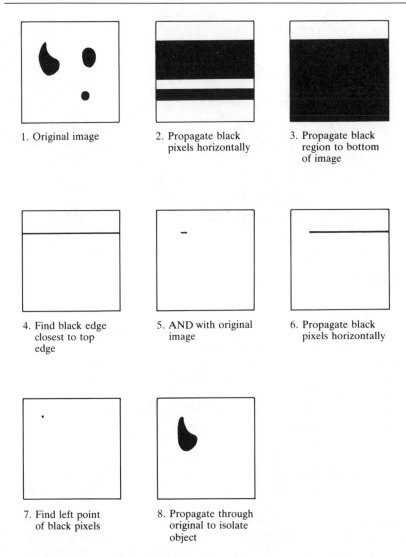

1. Original image

2. Propagate black
   pixels horizontally

3. Propagate black
   region to bottom
   of image

4. Find black edge
   closest to top
   edge

5. AND with original
   image

6. Propagate black
   pixels horizontally

7. Find left point
   of black pixels

8. Propagate through
   original to isolate
   object

Figure 10.5 To isolate an object in an image on a processor array, an unusual method may be used.

array, one is effectively wasting processor power; but when the image is larger than the array, one has to either store the image as a series of blocks in the PEs' memories ('block-mapping'), or with a set of adjacent pixels assigned to each PE ('crinkle-mapping'), as illustrated in Fig. 10.6. The final difficulty with processor arrays concerns the input and output of image data. Ideally, one would present a datum to all processors simultaneously; in practice, this would again be prohibitively expensive, so the approach usually adopted is to input data to each row

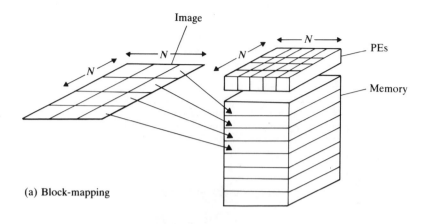

(a) Block-mapping

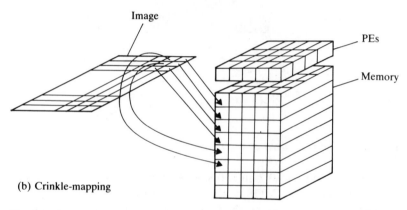

(b) Crinkle-mapping

Figure 10.6 Mappings of image larger than array size into memory.

of PEs, using their ability to perform nearest-neighbour shifts to pass
the data along the rows.

The best-known processor arrays are the CLIP (cellular logic image
processor) series, developed at University College London and based on
studies of retina-like structures embodying propagation (Duff, 1973,
1978). The most successful of these was the CLIP4, of which a number
were built for research use; commercial CLIP4 systems are now also
available (Stonefield, 1987). CLIP systems have been applied to a
number of image processing problems, usually concerning pattern
recognition, e.g. microscope slide analysis.

CLIP4 consists of up to 128×128 1-bit processors (the UCL
prototype system was only 96×96 due to production difficulties), each
with 32 bits of memory and connections to all eight nearest neighbours
as well as to a control bus, which connects to the host machine (a Sun

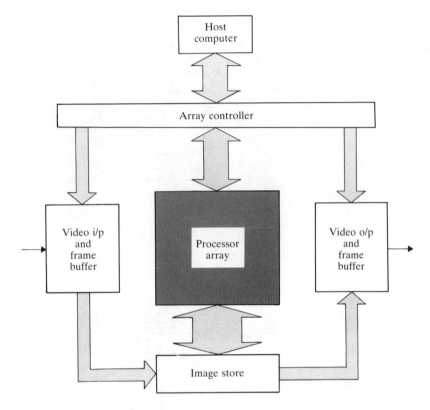

Figure 10.7 Overall view of the CLIP4 system.

workstation)—see Figs 10.7 and 10.8. The original system was constructed in custom NMOS, with eight processors per chip.

A subsequent development, the CLIP4S, was a 512×1 array, built from the same processors, which appeared as a 512×512 array to the programmer. This was a cheaper option that allowed larger images to be processed easily, although at a reduced speed.

In the CLIP4, an image is input from a separate image buffer, which converts it into 96 lines, one bit at a time, and passes it into the main register (A) and thence to the bit-planes. Each PE has two 1-bit ALUs, one to produce a result for propagation to neighbours (N) and the other for results to be stored in memory. Each ALU has 4-bit control, so a total of 256 operations are possible, although not all are meaningful. Two basic registers for operands (A and B) and a carry register (C) allow full addition to be performed, in addition to logical operations. A system register, connected to a parallel tree of adders, is provided; this allows the number of set bits in a bit-plane to be determined quickly and is useful for measuring areas and perimeters, for example.

The CLIP4 is programmed via the host computer using IPC ('image processing C'), a C-like language implemented under Unix. This permits

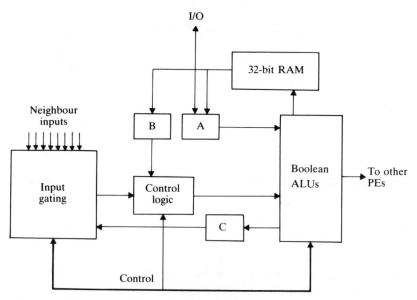

Figure 10.8 One CLIP4 processing element (A, B, and C are 1-bit registers).

manipulation of image data on the CLIP hardware to be expressed in a manner very similar to a conventional programming language.

The most recent development in the CLIP series is the CLIP7 (Fountain *et al.*, 1988). This is a 256 × 1 array, with each of the 16-bit, 5 MHz PEs having 64 kbytes of memory and 8–bit external data paths. As with the CLIP4S, the CLIP7 can be programmed as if it were a square array.

Another processor array, the distributed array processor (DAP), was developed by International Computers Limited in the 1970s as an attached processor for numeric applications. However, it was quickly realized that image processing tasks could be executed efficiently and a variety of such applications have been tackled using DAPs (Flanders *et al.*, 1977). These are normally more numeric-intensive than CLIP applications, e.g. FFT-based speckle image reconstruction algorithms or multi-spectral compression using the Karhunen–Loève transform.

The original DAPs comprised 64 × 64 PEs, each with 4 kbits or 16 kbits of memory and connected to their four nearest neighbours. These DAPs appeared as memory modules to their host ICL 2980 series computers, making data transfer particularly simple (although the storage schemes on host and DAP were different, so that DAP programs had to reorder binary data before and after processing, using standard subroutine calls). DAP PEs are again 1-bit processors, with three registers (Fig. 10.9). One of these registers, the A (activity) register, could be used to enable or disable individual PEs, a particularly useful feature. A FORTRAN-like parallel programming

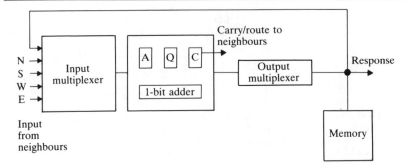

Figure 10.9   Schematic diagram of a single DAP processing element.

language, DAP-FORTRAN, was developed for the machine to permit easy programming.

Subsequent DAP developments have been carried out by Active Memory Technologies. The most recent DAP PEs are constructed from custom VLSI devices with a 10 MHz clock and have up to 128 kbits of memory. Arrays of up to 128 × 128 can be obtained. At the time of writing, DAP systems form one of the major parallel processing resources to the scientific and engineering communities in the United Kingdom.

Image-processing systems based around the Inmos 'transputer' are a comparatively recent development. The transputer is a microprocessor designed to allow easy integration into a parallel system (see, for example, Hockney and Jesshope, 1988). They are reasonably powerful devices in their own right, the most recent having a 32-bit architecture, and can add integers in about 33 ns or multiply two 64-bit floating-point numbers in under 700 ns. Each device incorporates four serial channels, capable of operating at 20 Mbits/s in both directions, greatly simplifying the construction of parallel networks. The Pascal-like programming language OCCAM was developed for the transputer; it includes the concepts of 'process' and 'channel' and so is well suited to a MIMD processor. A number of more conventional programming languages, such as 'parallel C' and 'parallel Lisp' have been developed by third parties. A system containing some 42 T414 transputers has been built for vision applications (Page, 1988), and a system comprising 36 T414s has been used for vector quantization (Kanayama *et al.*, 1988).

The greatest problem in the use of transputer systems for image processing is, as we might expect, the input and output of image data, since the serial interdevice communication is too slow. One interesting development in this area is a prototype system at Sheffield University, in which a 16 × 16 array of transputers has been interfaced to duplicate framestores which contain overlapping regions of a full image (Brown, 1989).

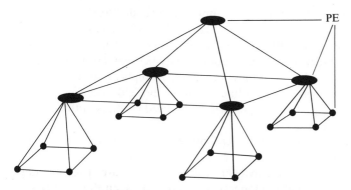

Figure 10.10 Three-layer pyramidal architecture.

10.3.4 Novel architectures

A number of other architectures are applicable to image-processing problems.

Systolic arrays are composed of a regular structure of similar elements. These differ from processor arrays in that the elements are generally dedicated ('hard-wired') to perform a particular function; hence there is typically little or no local memory and the device cannot be programmed. (These features are not fundamental to the systolic concept; general-purpose systolic machines are quite feasible and, indeed, have been built.) The throughput is determined by the rate at which data are clocked through the system. Systolic arrays are thus only suitable for specific tasks, frequently numeric-intensive ones which do not map well onto a conventional processor. For example, systolic architectures have been suggested for the eigen decomposition of covariance matrices, which is the rate-determining step in parallel implementation of both the Karhunen–Loève transform and the MUSIC direction-finding technique used in sonar and radar processing.

Over recent years, a number of algorithms have been developed, often modelling the processes of visual perception, which make use of respresentations of the image at different scales. A pyramidal arrangement of processors maps well onto this type of algorithm. At the lowest level, the base of the pyramid, a set of operations are performed on a number of regions of an image. Results from these are passed up the pyramid, where another layer combines several results and passes that up the pyramid, and so on. Building such a structure in hardware is an obvious development of the processor array concept, since it comprises effectively a series of layers of PEs, with inter-layer, as well as intra-layer, connections (Fig. 10.10).

A number of systems of this type are under development. This includes the GAM pyramid (Schaefer *et al.*, 1987) which has a 16×16 base, and is constructed from chips originally designed for a processor array, and the PAPIA system (Cantoni and Levialdi, 1987), which uses custom NMOS devices with a base size of 128×128. Each NMOS chip contains five PEs, each PE having 256 bits of memory. Current systems are SIMD in nature, with limited connectivity between layers; proposed systems aim to remove both these restrictions. Applications of pyramidal processors are most likely to be in the field of computer vision, since they promise to perform high-speed multiresolution processing of images.

The final architecture worth mentioning is the hypercube, an N-dimensional generalization of the 3-D cube. This is a fairly old concept that has only recently been realized in hardware. The advantage of the hypercube is that the longest connection between PEs is only $\log_2 N$ steps for a system of size 2^N (actually, this is also true for a pyramid).

The Connection Machine, developed at MIT (Hillis, 1985), is a hypercube built from 64-kbyte PEs, each PE having 4 kbytes of memory and running at 4 MHz. This system was developed for artificial intelligence research in vision and other problems; it executes code written in Lisp. The greatest problem with such a system is, of course, programming it effectively, since it is very difficult to visualize the flow of information. Another significant problem is that of collisions: many of the data paths intersect, so there must be a mechanism for stopping the collision of several pieces of data; this is achieved by stacking the data at the nodes where paths cross.

10.4 Neural networks

The attempts to produce automatic vision systems have absorbed a considerable amount of research effort over the past thirty years. However, results have not met expectations, and not many examples of automatic vision systems are found outside the laboratory. This may be because the variety of machines that exists today are special-purpose devices limited to performing a few visual inspection tasks. Making these systems reliable enough to be useful necessitates making them too inflexible for general-purpose usage. It may be difficult to improve the performance of these devices because of the constraints of serial processing by a single processing unit.

In the early days of automatic vision it was commonly believed that image recognition could be performed easily by computers if suitable programs were written. After all, human beings were able to do this easily and computers were seen to perform arithmetic and data sorting tasks much more efficiently than we could. That view was soon proved wrong and the realization dawned that the problem domain was unsuitable for computers.

It was partially due to these initial failures that computer researchers became interested in the way that brains process information. The existing knowledge of the brain was employed by people such as McCulloch and Pitts in order to produce theoretical models of neural units that could be used in artificial intelligence machines. During the last decade there has been a resurgence of interest in artificial neural networks.

The architecture of the brain is based on an enormous set of massively interconnected processing units called neurons. It is believed that the information stored in the brain and the sort of global processing it carries out are determined by the pattern of connectivity between the neurons. The brain has a significant advantage compared with computers when dealing with images. The enormous amount of information in an image is processed using the massive parallelism inherent in the brain; in a conventional computer it is necessary to channel this data through a single processor.

The basic structure of a neuron is of a cell with many input fibres (up to 10 000) called the dendrites but only a single output fibre, the axon, which may branch out to connect with the dendrites of hundreds or thousands of other neurons. Each neuron can generate a signal by rapid polarization and depolarization across its cell membrane, in a process called cell firing. Bursts of changing potential are propagated down the axon and produce chemical changes at the connections between the axons and the dendrites of other cells. These connections, the synapses, do not transmit the signal directly but indirectly by altering the state of the neuron being input to.

The way in which the states of the neurons are changed is very complex and still not well understood. Approximately speaking, a neuron can be said to respond to a conjunction of signals at its inputs—some combinations may cause the cell to fire, whilst others may inhibit the cell from firing. A neuron may be regarded as a feature detector that is sensitive to the activity of certain inputs. The ability of the brain to learn information seems to be due to changes taking place in the synapses which may block or enhance the transmission of signals.

10.4.1 WISARD

An early attempt to build hardware that emulates the architecture of the brain and appears to do a useful job is the WISARD machine of Wilkie, Stonham and Aleksander (Aleksander and Burnett, 1983). In this machine, neurons are modelled using 256×1 bit RAMs. The machine is a pattern-recognition device and when used for visual recognition, a frame store is required to hold a digitized image of the scene to be analysed. The digitized image is first thresholded to produce two levels only, corresponding to black and white, or 0 and 1. The heart of WISARD is a collection of 256×1 bit RAMs, the address lines of which are connected to random sets of eight thresholded pixel values as

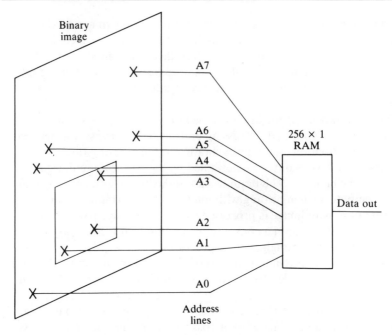

Figure 10.11 WISARD—sets of 8 pixels in a binary image connect to the address lines of a large number of 256 × 1 bit RAMs.

in Fig. 10.11. To clarify this, assume that a 512 × 512 pixel image is to be processed; this has 262 144 pixels and 32 768 RAMs are required. When the system is trained to recognize an object, the RAMs are set to read data and 1's are fed into all the data-in lines (the RAMs are cleared before training starts). This means that the locations that are addressed have a 1 written into them. In Fig. 10.11, the system is looking at a black square and some of the pixels in the square are connected to the address lines of one of the RAMs. If black corresponds to a 0 and white to a 1, then the location addressed is 11110001 and this will be set to 1. Similarly, locations in all the other RAMs are set. If the RAMs are now set to read data out and the system is shown the same object in exactly the same position, all the RAMs output 1's. Recognition is determined by counting the number of RAMs that output a 1; in this case all the RAMs output 1's so recognition is perfect.

It is clear that, due to the nature of the connectivity, if the object is moved slightly or if some noise is introduced, a large number of RAMs still respond and the device can achieve recognition if a threshold is set on the number of RAMs that are activated. Another technique that is used to achieve some translation and rotation independence is to train the device on a sequence of frames of the image in slightly different positions. This may cause more than one location to be set in each RAM so that the RAM may now respond to different conjunctions of its inputs. This process can only be carried on to a limited extent, since if all the locations of every RAM are set, then no further discrimination is possible.

From the above, WISARD is seen to be a rather crude neural net that consists of a totally independent set of neurons (the RAMs) in a single layer. Learning is not carried out by any analogue of synaptic modification but by making each RAM respond to definite conjunction of its inputs. Despite this apparent simplicity, WISARD has demonstrated a remarkable ability to recognize objects and is especially good at discriminating between human faces. It can even distinguish between different expressions on the same face.

10.4.2 Multi-layer perceptron

Another type of artificial neural network that has become popular in recent years is the multi-layer perceptron (MLP) using the back-propagation learning algorithm (Rumelhart and McClelland, 1986). Unlike WISARD, the basic unit of the MLP is a neuron with analogue inputs and outputs. This is one of the reasons why the net has mainly been simulated using conventional computers rather than realized in hardware. The basic architecture of the network is shown in Fig. 10.12. The network performs an association between a set of input patterns and a set of output patterns and can be used to classify input patterns into a set of categories. Although the MLP has analogue units, it is very often used with binary inputs. If the MLP has only one output unit, it can be used to make a yes/no decision concerning its input data. As the output of each unit can vary continuously between 0 and 1, it is necessary to set two thresholds during training in order to decide if the output is effectively in a 0 or 1 state. These are commonly set to 0.1 and 0.9. Having more than one output increases the number of categories that a pattern can be classifed into. Each unit produces an output by multiplying each of its inputs by a parameter called the weight and then applying a non-linear function to the sum of these products. This function is usually of a sigmoidal type that squashes the output level so that it is constrained to lie between 0 and 1. The signals are propagated through the network by feedforward to the units in the top layer. The outputs of these top layer units are the MLP's outputs to the external world. Before the MLP is trained, the weight parameters are set to small random values. The pattern association is learned by sequentially presenting possible patterns to the inputs of the MLP while simultaneously presenting the required associated pattern. This process, in which the input–output mappings are predefined, is called supervised learning. The required output patterns are presented to the net using extra inputs on each of the output nodes.

The output produced by the MLP due to feedforward from the inputs is compared to the desired output and the differences are used to change

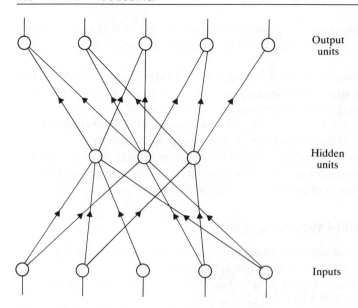

Figure 10.12 Basic structure of a two-layer perceptron.

the weights on the inputs to the top layer units. The changes are made so that the new output is closer to the desired output. The changes to the weights of these input lines are used to change the weights of units further down in the network; hence the reason why the algorithm is called back-propagation. This is illustrated in Fig. 10.13. This cycle of presenting an input pattern, feeding the signals through to the top layer, comparing the actual output with the required output, and back-propagating the errors is repeated for each pattern in the training set. It is usually necessary to present the training set many times before the mapping is learnt. This can be in the order of 10 000 times for some cases.

In order to use the MLP for image processing it is necessary to order the input units into a 2-D array and to compress the range of grey levels to a value between 0 and 1. Alternatively, a binary image can be used. There is interest in using the MLP to locate features in facial images, such as eyes. This type of feature can vary considerably between people and yet have some common structure. A template matching approach would consist in applying a set of templates of different eyes sequentially to the image in order to find a good match and this requires a large amount of processing time. In contrast, after training has taken place, the MLP would produce a response that is limited only by the time required for the input signal to propagate to the outputs. It is believed that the MLP, in common with other neural nets, may be able to extract common features from a set of data. The intention is to train the MLP on eye image data and test it on different eyes in order to ascertain whether any such generalization has taken place.

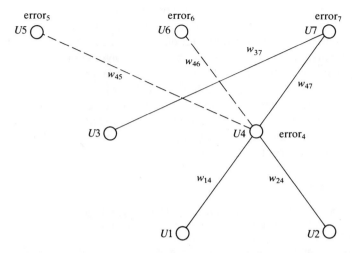

Figure 10.13 The back-propagation algorithm—error$_7$ depends on the difference between the target output and the actual output. The weights w_{37} and w_{47} are changed by an amount that depends on error$_7$. The value w_{14} of error w_{24} depends on the values of w_{45}, w_{46}, and w_{47}. As above, w_{14} and w_{24} will be changed by an amount that depends on error$_4$.

10.4.3 Other networks

Many other neural net architectures have been investigated. A few general remarks can be made concerning these networks. Like the MLP, most of them require many iterations through the training data in order for learning to take place. Although this is analogous to certain types of learning in biological systems such as reinforcement learning, there do not seem to be any models that exhibit learning on one presentation of the data. The need to iterate thousands of times involves hours of computing time when these nets are simulated. Unless real time hardware implementations of neural nets are built, it is difficult to perform experiments on anything other than simple problems.

10.5 Summary

The development of parallel image processors is one of the most active research areas of computer design. Advances in VLSI technology have made possible the development of affordable parallel image processors; many such devices are likely to appear in the near future, often based on transputers. Future developments are likely to be in pyramidal and other hierarchical architectures for vision applications, since there is good evidence that the human brain performs the kind of multiresolution processing for which these systems are designed.

Conventional computer architectures are not appropriate for some pattern recognition applications. Studies of the mechanisms in the brain have led to the development of simple but effective systems like WISARD, and also to neuron-like structures with a high degree of connectivity which may be configured in one or many layers. These neural networks have been used to address a number of practical pattern recognition problems, with a limited degree of success. There is much research under way into architectures of this type and it is possible that some significant advances in pattern recognition will be made by following this route.

References

Aleksander I. and Burnett P. (1983) *Reinventing Man*, Kogan Page, London.

Brown C. (1989) 'MARVIN: a multi-processor architecture for vision', *Proc. 10th OCCAM User Group Meeting*, Holland.

Cantoni V. and Levialdi S. (1987) 'PAPIA: a case history', in *Parallel Computer Vision*, Uhr L. (ed.), Academic Press, London.

Duff M. J. B. (1973) 'A Cellular Logic Array for Image Processing', *Pattern Recognition*, vol. 5, pp. 229–47.

Duff M. J. B. (1978) 'Review of the CLIP image processing system', *Proc. 6th National Computer Conference*, pp. 1055–60.

Duff M. J. B. and Levialdi S. (1981) *Languages and Architectures for Image Processing*, Academic Press, London.

Flanders P. M., Hunt D. J., Reddaway S. F. and Parkinson D. (1977) 'Efficient high-speed computing with the distributed array processor', in *High-speed Computer and Algorithm Organisation*, Kuck D. (ed.), Academic Press, New York.

Flynn J. (1972) 'Some computer organisations and their effectiveness', *IEEE Transactions on Computers*, vol. C-21, pp. 948–60.

Fountain T. J. (1985) 'A review of SIMD architectures', in *Image Processing System Architectures*, Kittler J. and Duff M. J. B. (eds), Research Studies Press, Letchworth.

Fountain T. J., Matthews K. N. and Duff M. J. B. (1988) 'The CLIP7 image processor', *IEEE Transactions on Pattern Analysis and Machine Intelligence*, vol. 10, no. 1, pp. 311–19.

Hillis W. B. (1985) *The Connection Machine*, MIT Press, Cambridge, Mass.

Hockney R. W. and Jesshope C. R. (1988) *Parallel Computers 2*, Adam Hilger, Bristol.

Kanayama Y., Fujii T., Ohta N. and Ono S. (1988) 'Architecture and performance of a multicomputer type digital signal processing system (NOVI)', *Proc. IEEE International Conference on Acoustics, Speech and Signal Processing*, vol. IV, pp. 2104–7.

Keller J., Comazzi A. and Favre A. (1983) 'VAP—an array processor architecture using cascaded look-up tables', in *Computing Structures for Image Processing*, Duff M. J. B. (ed.), Academic Press, London.

Levialdi S. (1988) *Multicomputer Vision*, Academic Press, London.

Maenner R. (1984) 'Hardware task/processor scheduling in a polyprocessor environment', *IEEE Transactions on Computers*, vol. C-33, no. 7, pp. 626–36.

Martinez K. and Pearson D. E. (1985) 'PETAL: a parallel processor for real-time primitive extraction', *Proc. SPIE Symposium on Architectures and Algorithms for Digital Image Processing*, vol. 596.

Page I. (1988) 'The Disputer: a dual-paradigm parallel processor for graphics and vision', in *Parallel Architectures for Computer Vision*, Page I. (ed.), Oxford University Press, Oxford.

Rumelhart D. E. and McClelland J. L. (eds) (1986) *Parallel Distributed Processing*, MIT Press, Cambridge, Mass.

Schaefer D. H., Ho P., Boyd J. and Vallejos C. (1987) 'The GAM pyramid', in *Parallel Computer Vision*, Uhr L. (ed.), Academic Press, London.

Sternberg S. R. (1983) 'Biomedical image processing', *IEEE Computer*, vol. 6, no. 1, pp. 22–34.

Stonefield, (1987) 'CLIP product description', Omnicrom Electronics Ltd, Horesham.

Uhr L. (1987) *Parallel Computer Vision*, Academic Press, London.

PART 3

Coding

The three chapters in this section are designed to give the reader an idea of current work in the area of image coding. Coding is concerned with the transmission and storage of images; in either case the desire is to represent the image with as few bits as possible without sacrificing too much in the way of quality.

In Chap. 11, Tim Dennis and Mohammed Ghanbari survey the main compression techniques that have been developed since work first started in this area about forty years ago. They describe ideas such as DPCM, transform coding, conditional replenishment, and vector quantization, which have stood the tests of time and competition and work extremely well in practice (often in combination with one another).

The following two chapters give accounts of more recent investigations and a view of possible future developments. In Chap. 12 Bill Welsh describes progress in model-based coding, in which a scene is coded by setting up a computer-graphics model of it. Information about motion can be transmitted at very low bit rates in the form of animation data for the model. Finally, in Chap. 13, Mohammed Ghanbari reports on coding for packet networks, which can accept bits at a variable rate; such coding offers the possibility of high compression ratios without the quality degradations that normally occur at motion peaks.

11 Data compression

TIM DENNIS and MOHAMMED GHANBARI

11.1 Introduction

The need for reduced-data representations of digital television pictures is obvious as soon as the raw figures that result from straight pulse code modulation are calculated. Methods have been devised that exploit both the inherent local statistical self-dependence of most picture material and the properties of human vision. As has been noted earlier in the book, human factors constitute a strong component in the selection of the basic parameters of a television system: the frame rate, the number of scan lines, and so on. Other physiological factors in vision such as spatial masking are also exploited in data compression methods.

In this chapter we cover the following topics: subsampling as a simple data compression technique; the reversible statistical methods that lead on to the irreversible differential pulse code modulation (DPCM); transform coding in its various forms, where the picture is divided into blocks and the attempt is made to form a representation from a series of orthogonal basis functions; vector quantization, a block method in which $M \times N$ sized blocks of elements are treated as vectors in an MN dimensional space; and sub-band coding, which is a frequency domain process where the multidimensional video spectrum is partitioned and the partitions subsampled in a reversible way. Finally we give a description of interframe methods which exploit the further local dependencies between adjacent frames of a moving picture source. In practice, image-coding schemes may exploit many of these techniques simultaneously (in so-called *hybrid* coding) to obtain very high compression factors.

11.2 Subsampling

The basic data rate required by a digital television signal depends on the bandwidth of the source and the number of quantum levels allocated to each sample. The number of amplitude resolution steps is usually 2^8 or 256, but as we have seen in Chap. 7, in many cases 128 or even 64 levels are adequate, depending on the level of noise that contaminates the signal. The figure 256 has as much to do with convenience in digital hardware and software, where the 8-bit byte is standard, as it does with subjective requirements.

Potentially the least difficult method of reducing the final data requirement is to ask if the simple-minded approach of using a sampling rate two or more times the analogue bandwidth, as dictated by Nyquist, is really necessary for television, and whether some saving is possible.

In the discussion on sampling in Chap. 7, we used deliberate undersampling to coarsen and thereby exaggerate for demonstration purposes the visual artefacts that are associated with aliasing in the sampling of picture signals. Undersampling a zone plate pattern by a factor of 4 : 1 in the horizontal direction revealed the set of frequencies which would be aliased to zero frequency, and which would thus be expected to cause most interference. Applying a low-pass pre-filter at half the reduced sampling rate was able to eliminate the interference, but did not, of course, produce a picture of usable quality, so undersampling in this form is not a viable method of data reduction.

A better approach is to return to the nature of the picture signal itself. The fact that a television signal is usually delivered as an apparently 1-D time-varying signal, from a camera or whatever source, obscures its actual origin as the scan of a 2-D image surface where light intensity is a function of position. Of course, if the scene is in motion, there is the third independent dimension of time. The appearance of addressable image storage, where a picture can be represented as a static array of samples, did much to clarify the multidimensional nature of the television signal, and the need to devise appropriate sampling strategies. It is obvious that a sampling process represents its target with an accuracy that increases with the density of samples per unit time, or per unit area.

It is interesting here to speculate what happens if we rearrange the 4 : 1 sampling process in the demonstration so that the samples are more evenly spread over the surface, rather than lying in vertical columns. We are constrained here by the technology to use a pattern derived from an orthogonal grid, spacing d, so one possibility is that shown in Fig. 11.1(a), where the sampling pattern is offset by $2d$ on alternate lines. Compared with the similar figure in Chap. 4, where each sample has four nearest neighbours, two each at 1 and 4 pels, every sample now has six immediate neighbours, two spaced at $2d$, and four at $d\sqrt{5}$ or about 2.24 original pel spacings.

Figure 11.2 shows the results of sampling the zone plate with the pattern of Fig. 11.1(a), where it can be seen that the frequencies likely to cause most difficulty now lie towards the periphery of the image. The source-distribution of major alias components can be predicted by examining the major axes of symmetry in the subsample pattern, which are superimposed on Fig. 11.1(a). Aliasing to d.c. will occur when a spatial sinusoid has a frequency in which there are an integral number of cycles between adjacent lines of symmetry. Thus the vertical columns

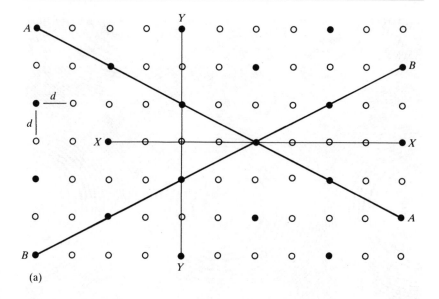

(a)

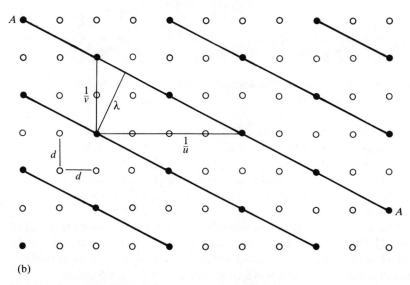

(b)

Figure 11.1 (a) Non-orthogonal subsampling pattern, showing major lines of symmetry. Black circles represent samples retained from an original orthogonal grid. (b) Diagonal sampling lattice symmetry, showing orientation and frequency of a spatial component that will alias to zero.

Figure 11.2 Result of subsampling the zone plate with the 4 : 1 pattern of Fig. 11.1(a).

of retained samples, such as YY, are spaced at $2d$, and should cause a vertically aligned component with horizontal wavelength $2d$ to alias to d.c., which indeed occurs on the zone plate. The horizontal lines, such as XX, are spaced at d, and since a component of this wavelength cannot exist in the pattern, no aliasing occurs on the vertical spatial frequency axis.

One of the major diagonal symmetries, AA, is shown in more detail in Fig. 11.1(b), where it can be seen that the first component that aliases to zero has horizontal and vertical wavelengths of $4d$ and $2d$ respectively, which combine to give a wavefront with $\lambda = 4d/\sqrt{5}$, angled at $\tan^{-1}(1/2)$ ($\approx 26°$) to the horizontal. Again, the edges of this alias and its analogues in the other quadrants of the zone plate are present.

The low-pass filter is designed by inspection to exclude the potential aliases as usual, and a simple possibility is a square with width and height both one-half the zone plate, or quarter the sampling frequency in both directions. This has doubled the horizontal bandwidth compared with that needed for orthogonal 4 : 1 subsampling, but the vertical resolution has been halved. However, the equal distribution of

Figure 11.3 A 4 : 1 subsampled natural image using the pattern of Fig. 11.1(a) and the appropriate 2-D pre-filter. Compare with Fig. 7.7(c).

band limitation between the horizontal and vertical spatial frequencies suggests that picture quality will be improved.

Figure 11.3 shows the effects on a real image of such a 2-D filter, implemented by cascaded horizontal and vertical low-pass stages. It should be compared with Fig. 7.7(c), from which it is clear that there is significant improvement, especially bearing in mind that the basic sampling rates are the same: all that *has* changed is that the pattern of samples is now more smoothly distributed over the original picture. This subsampling technique has real application for moderate data reductions where loss of resolution is acceptable, e.g. when a broadcast-quality picture source is the feed for a low-resolution videoconference system (Chiariglione *et al.*, 1982). It can also be used as part of an adaptive sampling strategy where sampling density is determined by activity in the picture.

11.3 Statistical coding

The practice in statistical coding methods is to exploit any non-uniform probability of occurrence of output 'symbols' generated by a data

Table 11.1 Variable length coding (VLC) example (Huffman)

| | Reduction process | | | |
Source symbols	Stage 1 PDF (original)	→	Stage 2	→ Stage 3
00	0.48		0.48	0.52
01	0.25		0.27	0.48
10	0.16		0.25	
11	0.11			

| | Splitting process | | | |
Variable length output	Stage 3 code PDF	←	Stage 2 code PDF	← Stage 1 code PDF
1	1 0.48		1 0.48	0 0.52
01	01 0.25		00 0.27	1 0.48
000	000 0.16		01 0.25	
001	001 0.11			

source, by allocating short codewords to the symbols that occur most often, longer words to less likely outputs, and so on, which of course results in a lower transmission rate. The simplest example of this in everyday experience is the Morse code.

The measure of average 'information' in a sequence is given by its statistical entropy:

$$H = - \sum_i p_i \log_2(p_i)$$

where p_i is the probability of occurrence of symbol i (Shannon, 1948). Thus, in a system that generates eight possible outputs, and where these are equally likely, the entropy is: $-[8 \times 1/8 \times (-3)] = 3$ bits, which accords with expectation. Any non-uniformity in the probabilities reduces the total information carried by the sequence, until at the other extreme when a system generates just one symbol continuously, $H = -1 \times \log_2(1) = 0$.

Huffman coding (Huffman, 1952) is a systematic technique for allocating bits in a non-uniform way that is able to exploit probabilistic non-uniformity. It can achieve rates which approach the theoretical entropy measure of a source. Table 11.1 illustrates the procedure for a simple example; the incoming data have four possible values which in fixed rate coding obviously requires 2 bits/sample. The coding requires two stages. In the first, the individual probabilities are ranked in decreasing order. At each stage of the iteration, the two smallest probabilities are combined, and the results again rank ordered. This continues until only two entries remain in the probability column.

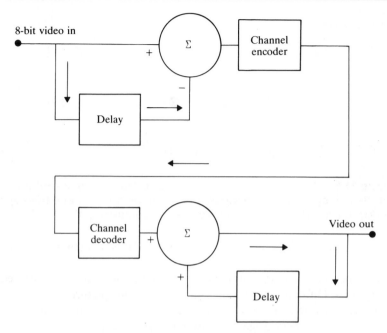

Figure 11.4   Statistical coding system (reversible).

In the second stage (splitting) process, the final two probabilities from the first stage are allocated codes 0 and 1 in step 1. In steps 2 and 3 the probabilities obtained by summing in stage 1 are split, and additional codes added to describe them. The process continues until the original probability density function (PDF) is obtained. The codewords allocated to this list become the final variable length code (VLC) for the data source. In this example the average variable-length bit rate is:

$$1 \times 0.48 + 2 \times 0.25 + 3 \times 0.16 + 3 \times 0.11 = 1.79 \text{ bits/symbol}$$

The calculated entropy for this example is 1.29, which is less than the Huffman code generates; this slight inefficiency is because the Huffman coder is forced to use integral numbers of bits per output codeword. However, there is still an improvement over the 2 bits/symbol for the raw data.

If we examine the PDF of the sample values of a typical digitized image, there is no particular structure, and what structure there is varies from picture to picture. Indeed we expect the averaged PDFs of a large number of pictures to be virtually uniform and hence the entropy is equal or close to the number of bits per sample generated by the quantizer.

The situation is radically different for the *changes* between adjacent sample values. Because any picture that contains useful information is correlated (if it was not, the samples would be white noise!), the

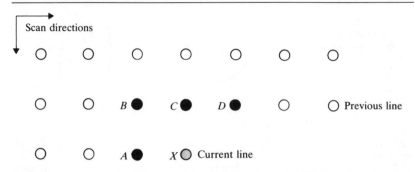

Figure 11.5 Potential predictors (A–D) for element X. In a real-time (interlaced) system, the previous line would be on the same field and therefore two physical lines above the line containing X.

differences are likely to have a non-uniform PDF which tends to peak at zero.

A simple scheme to exploit local statistical dependencies is illustrated in Fig. 11.4. Differences between sample values one picture element apart are generated. If the source data are in 8-bit form, the differences need 9 bits since their range lies between -255 and $+255$. The 9-bit values are passed to a channel processor, such as a Huffman coder, which allocates codewords as discussed above, in a way dependent on the source statistics (Huffman, 1952). At the receiver, the actual differences are recovered and fed to a summing loop, which regenerates the original sample values, without error.

11.3.1 Prediction

The single element delay in the last example can be thought of as a 'predictor', and what is sent down the channel then becomes the prediction error. Its performance is generally good, but is poor in situations where the picture contains a lot of vertical structure which generates horizontal contrast steps. Is it not possible to generalize the idea of a prediction, in the hope that the element of surprise can be reduced? One approach is to derive the prediction from a number of previously available samples spatially close to the one that is about to be coded. Figure 11.5 shows an array of candidate samples, A–D, which might be included in an estimator for element X. In the decoder the same prediction process is carried out, based on previously received samples.

11.3.2 Predictor performance

Some results are presented in Table 11.2, which relates to a 256 × 256 pel region of a single frame from the well-known moving test sequence 'Split Screen'. A number of predictors were tested, with experimental

Figure 11.6   Top: original image. Lower left: error using previous element prediction. Lower right: error using predictor 6 from Table 11.2.

adjustment of the weights given to each sample. The performance is given in terms of prediction error entropy. Figure 11.6 illustrates the original image, and prediction errors for two predictors: simple previous element (number 2 in Table 11.2) and that with the lowest entropy, number 6. Both the error images have been offset by $+128$ to enable positive and negative excursions to be seen. Note that these results refer to *one picture only* and depend heavily on the amount of contrast detail. Also note that in a real-time system with 2 : 1 vertical interlace the previous line predictor would normally be on the same field and hence spatially more distant than the previous element, which means that its performance would be inferior.

Predictor number 1 is the null case, which gives the entropy of the original image. The figure of around 7 bits for an 8-bit source is typical, and confirms that statistical coding of the raw PCM samples is not worth while. There is a large reduction to figures around 3 bits/sample as soon as *any* predictor is introduced, but the difference between the best of the single predictors (number 3) and the best multiple-sample predictor that was tested (6) is small at 0.368 bit. Number 6 was selected as the optimum after a series of trials where the contribution from the previous line was gradually increased—an approach based on the better performance of previous line prediction compared with previous element.

Table 11.2 Two-dimensional predictors: relative performance

Number	Predictor	Entropy (bits/pel)	Comment
1	0 0 0 0 X	7.142	no predictor: entropy of original 8-bit image
2	0 0 0 1 X	3.293	previous element (left)
3	0 1 0 0 X	2.946	previous element (above)
4	1 0 0 0 X	3.707	diagonal previous element (above, left)
5	0 1 0 1 X	2.721	diagonal mean, equal horizontal and vertical weights
6	0 5 0 1 X	2.578	diagonal mean, increased weight to vertical
7	0 2 1 1 X	2.590	additional contribution from previous line

That the simplest predictors are generally the most effective can be explained in two ways: the local correlation in a picture is indeed local, and bringing in additional components very quickly makes the prediction less accurate as irrelevant data are included. Alternatively, the predictor can be regarded as a filter, whose aim is to re-create the image *without error* from displaced local weighted averages of itself. This process must always fail, since success would violate causality, but more practically, because as the weighting mask grows in extent, its output becomes an increasingly smoothed and *less* accurate version of the source.

In a further test, using a proprietary variable length coding (VLC) program 'Pack' (Motorola, 1987), a file containing just the prediction errors was reduced to 21 909 bytes, compared with 65 694 for the original 256 × 256 pel image, a reversible compression to about one-third of the original data. Both files contain overhead information.

This lossless compression method is not usually considered practical for real-time use, because the possible range of prediction errors is ±255 from an 8-bit source. Although errors of this magnitude occur very rarely, when they do a VLC designed on the Huffman principle requires very long codewords (hundreds of bits) to represent them. This complicates any buffering task and makes recovery from the effects of transmission errors, which can have catastrophic effects on picture quality, difficult. However, the method is particularly suitable for single-image storage and recovery on an archiving system, where data integrity can be guaranteed, coding and decoding times are not critical, and where the exact values of the original samples must be available.

11.4 Differential PCM

Differential PCM (DPCM) was invented in 1952 by Cutler (1952) and has proved particularly successful as a basic data reduction method for digital television. From an 8-bit source it can generate good picture quality with 4 bits/sample, and acceptable quality with 3 bits. Because the output codewords still have non-uniform probability of occurrence, further statistical coding is possible and practical for real-time use, because the input data set is so small.

DPCM is another predictive method, but uses an alternative strategy to exploit the peaked nature of the prediction error PDF, a strategy related to companding where the number of quantum levels that the error is actually allowed to assume is severely restricted. The allocation of available levels is done either in relation to the PDF itself, with a criterion for success based on mean squared error, or better, entirely from subjective quality considerations. The major difference between DPCM and purely statistical coding is the deliberate introduction of error into the decoded picture as a consequence of the quantization process. Also because of the quantizer, there is a need to duplicate the action of the decoder at the encoder, so that the encoder makes its prediction purely on the (flawed) information available to the decoder. Figure 11.7 shows the structure of a DPCM encoding system. A prediction is subtracted from the incoming signal in the usual way, but the error component that results is passed to a non-linear quantizer, typically implemented as a look-up table, and also to a look-up table that generates the channel codewords. For an N-level quantizer, the output codewords have $\log_2 N$ bits. The quantized errors are added to the prediction to generate the local copy of the decoded picture, which is circulated for future use. The decoder consists of just the prediction generator and an adder, and takes its input from another look-up table which regenerates the numerical values of the quantized errors.

The negative feedback structure of the encoder means that the prediction always attempts to track the input, whatever perturbations arise from the input signal or because of the quantizer. Figure 11.8 shows an example of the behaviour of the local output for an input transition from zero to 63 with a four-level quantizer having representative levels at ± 3 and ± 19. It is assumed that the initial prediction is also zero. The illustration shows two of the standard defects that DPCM introduces: slope overload and oscillation. Slope

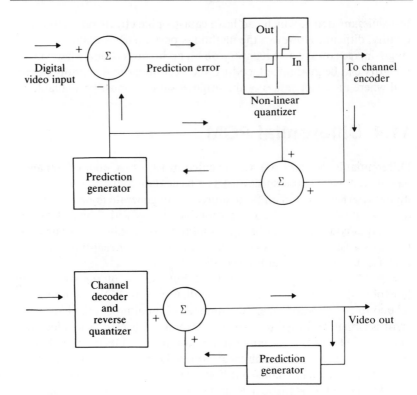

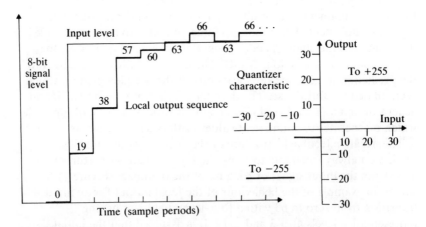

Figure 11.7 Differential PCM coding system (non-reversible).

Figure 11.8 DPCM output behaviour for input transition 0–63, with quantizer shown.

overload is the inability of the output to track a high-amplitude input transition; it is a phenomenon more commonly associated with delta modulation, but can occur in DPCM if the largest representative quantum level is much less than the largest possible input transition. The low-level oscillation is caused by the feedback connection and the absence of a zero level from the quantizer, and appears as a low-level granular interference pattern on encoded pictures. A third form of distortion known as 'edge busyness' also occurs; it is caused by the presence of low-level noise on the input signal, and the tendency of the coder to encode the same, or adjacent, contrast steps with a different sequence of representative levels. Thus, a vertical edge in a simple previous-element system appears slightly ragged and in a real-time system has moving noise associated with it.

A major factor in the success of DPCM is the way the distortions it introduces are of a kind that are masked by the human visual system. Slope overload and edge busyness are confined to sharp transitions, just where the eye is less sensitive than normal to associated luminance perturbations.

11.4.1 Quantizer design

The most striking feature when one experiments with the design of a DPCM quantizer is how insensitive the picture quality is to very large adjustments in the representative and transition levels. Almost any sensible distribution of levels that favours small errors at the expense of large ones works, but there is a degree of picture dependence: a scene with a lot of high-contrast fine detail requires a quantizer with larger outer levels, to minimize slope overload, than one consisting mostly of smooth contrasts, which needs a very small innermost level to limit granular noise. Alternatively, a quantizer with an odd number of levels can be used, the centre one being zero. This introduces a 'dead band' into the characteristic and suppresses oscillation; however, there is also a tendency to suppress very low contrast detail in the picture. Figure 11.9 shows two versions of a the same picture encoded with 2-bit (four-level) previous-element prediction DPCM, with deliberately maladjusted quantizers, one to exaggerate slope overload, the other granular noise.

11.4.2 Error performance

As with most data compression schemes, the removal of redundancy increases the significance of each bit that is transmitted, and hence the seriousness of its loss to the decoder. In previous-element or line-prediction DPCM the decoder is a directional digital integrator and a channel error results in an incorrect choice of quantized prediction error which persists as a constant offset and appears as a streak on the

(a)

Figure 11.9(a)   Two bits per sample DPCM coding with exaggerated slope overload.

picture. This effect is less severe with some, but not all, 2-D predictors, when it manifests itself as a decaying 'comet tail' radiating from the location of the error. The effects of errors (those that remain after any channel error recovery process) can be reduced by including a 'leak' factor in the integrators at the decoder and encoder. This is most easily achieved by scaling the output of the predictor by some factor, k, between 0 and 1, but usually close to 1 (Nicol, 1976).

Suppose k is 0.9 and the integrator starts at level 128. Then if the system is fed with a sequence of zeros from the channel the output sequence is (rounded to integers): 128, 115, 103, 93, 84, ..., which is an exponential decay to zero. Of course, the leak has an adverse effect on the performance of the system since it introduces its own prediction error component; the choice of k has to be a trade-off between inherent and channel-generated interference.

Another simple practice to limit the persistence of error effects is to perform a periodic reset or 'forced update' of the system by inserting an

(b)

Figure 11.9(b) Two bits per sample DPCM coding with granular noise and 'edge busyness'. In both parts (a) and (b) the image layout is as follows: upper left, original; upper right, decoded; lower left, prediction; lower right, coding error.

absolute sample value in PCM form. In the case of previous-element prediction DPCM, this might take the form of an implied initialization to zero at the start of each line, at both encoder and decoder.

11.5 Transform coding

Transform coding is generally an open-loop process in which the picture is handled in a semi-parallel manner in blocks of elements, compared with the closed-loop, continuous-sequence processing of DPCM. It operates by generating a set of output data for each block in which the individual values are no longer correlated with one another and in which most of the 'energy' of the original block is contained in a small proportion of the output samples.

The best-known transform in general application is that of Fourier, and it is worth restating what the process is actually doing to a discrete input sequence: the analysis stage (the forward transform) is identifying the amplitudes and phases of the sinusoidal components, which when added together in the synthesis stage (the reverse transform) reconstruct the original sequence. The transformed and original versions of the sequence of course contain exactly the same amount of information. The advantage of the transformed representation arises from the nature of the input data; suppose at one extreme the picture we transmit contains a single spatial sinusoid. This results in one non-zero component (or two, at positive and negative frequencies, which are complex conjugates for real input data and therefore knowledge of only one is needed). There is as yet no saving in transmission cost, as the receiver still needs to be told that all the other coefficients are zero in order to carry out the reconstruction. Suppose now it is *known in advance* that the picture contains only one sinusoid; now there is a large saving, since the receiver only needs to know *which* component it is each time, and its amplitude. The other extreme is a picture consisting of white noise. Now all components are present, on average at equal amplitude.

The situation with real pictures is somewhere between the extremes. As with DPCM, any picture carrying useful information is correlated, which corresponds in the transform domain to a fall-off in energy at high frequencies. The implication is that energy in the transform domain tends always to be concentrated in the same subset of components, usually those representing low frequencies. This is where the potential for data compression in transform coding lies, either by coefficient omission, quantization, or both.

In mathematical terms, the analysis or first stage of the encoding process is a linear transformation that converts a set of highly correlated pels with uniform probability density functions into a new set of less correlated coefficients with non-uniform PDFs. The number of bits required to represent the coefficients and hence the channel data rate depends on the information content and the subjective contributions of each of the transform coefficients to the reconstructed picture.

The success of transform coding in reducing the data rate is due to the fact that image energy in the transform domain is concentrated in relatively few coefficients and insignificant samples in this domain can be discarded. This depends on the type of transformation matrix; the compression efficiency of a particular transform is measured in terms of its 'energy compaction' property, which involves rank ordering of transform coefficients in order of decreasing statistical significance.

11.5.1 Principles of transform coding

In the transform coding system of Fig. 11.10, a set of pels $\{x_n\}$, $n = 0$, $1, \ldots, N - 1$, are subjected to a $N \times N$ transformation matrix $\mathbf{A}$, resulting in a set of N transform coefficients $\{y_k\}$, $k = 0, 1, \ldots, N - 1$.

Figure 11.10 Block diagram of a transform coding system.

Next the N coefficients are individually quantized to provide the data reduction and transmitted through the channel. At the receiver the quantized coefficients $\{y_k\} = Q\{y_k\}$ are retransformed via the transformation matrix **B** to yield $\{x'_n\}$ an approximation of $\{x_n\}$. The object is to ensure that $\{x'_n\}$ resembles $\{x_n\}$ as closely as possible within a minimum bit rate.

In this process the bit sequence $\{x_n\}$ may be either N pels along the horizontal or vertical directions of the picture or an array $U \times V$ of pels within the picture, where $N = UV$. In the first case the transformation is one-dimensional of block length N, and the transform coefficients are related to the input pels by $\mathbf{Y} = \mathbf{A} \cdot \mathbf{X}$.

The second case is a 2-D transform of block size U by V. Usually 2-D transformation matrices are separable and the UV transform coefficients are derived from two 1-D transforms of lengths U and V. For television applications this is done by first performing V times the 1-D transform of U pels in the line scan direction. This results in UV 1-D transform coefficients. The final and true 2-D transform coefficients are then derived from a further U 1-D transforms of the sets of V 1-D transform coefficients. This is illustrated in the following Hadamard transform example for the case $U = 4$ and $V = 2$.

Let **X** be an input block of pels, where

$$\mathbf{X} = \begin{bmatrix} 160 & 180 & 200 & 150 \\ 66 & 100 & 110 & 80 \end{bmatrix}$$

The Hadamard transformation matrices of lengths 4 and 2 are

$$\mathbf{A4} = \frac{1}{4}\begin{bmatrix} 1 & 1 & 1 & 1 \\ 1 & 1 & -1 & -1 \\ 1 & -1 & -1 & 1 \\ 1 & -1 & 1 & -1 \end{bmatrix} \qquad \mathbf{A2} = \frac{1}{2}\begin{bmatrix} 1 & 1 \\ 1 & -1 \end{bmatrix}$$

The transformation of the pels in the rows of matrix **X** by matrix **A4** is

$$\mathbf{Y} = \mathbf{X} \cdot \mathbf{A4} = \begin{bmatrix} 172 & -2 & -17 & 7 \\ 89 & -6 & -16 & -1 \end{bmatrix}$$

The final stage is to transform the columns of **Y** by matrix **A2**, which generates

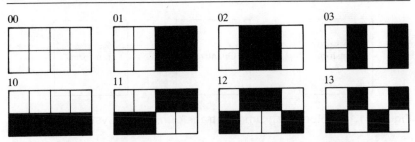

Figure 11.11 Hadamard 4 × 2 transform basis pictures; each small square represents a picture element with white + 1 and black − 1.

$$\mathbf{C} = \mathbf{A2 \cdot Y} = \begin{bmatrix} 130 & -4 & -16 & 3 \\ 41 & 1 & 0 & 4 \end{bmatrix}$$

These matrix operations are equivalent to overlaying the original block of pels by the set of eight *basis pictures* illustrated in Fig. 11.11, multiplying each pel value by the basis picture value, + 1 or − 1, and summing the results. The transform coefficients thus represent the amount of each basis picture that needs to be included in an overall summation to *reconstruct* the original block of pels, as illustrated in Fig. 11.12. For example, to calculate the second pel from the left on the top row requires the following summation: $(130 - 4 + 16 - 3 + 41 + 1 + 0 - 4) = 177$. The error from the original value of 180 is because the coefficients have been rounded to integers.

Note that the distribution of large coefficient values reflects the spatial structure of the original block. The coefficient value 130 describing basis picture 00 corresponds to the average amplitude over the block; since these are all positive, a large number is expected. All elements in the top row of the block are larger than those in the bottom row, which might represent a horizontal edge in the picture. The coefficient that describes a basis picture of this kind—one containing a horizontal edge, number 10—is correspondingly large in magnitude at 41. Another structural feature of the block is that the pels in the central columns are larger than those in the edge columns; this time the basis picture is number 02 and its value is relatively large at − 16.

For efficient bandwidth compression the transformation matrix **A** has to have the following properties:

- *Decorrelation*: to generate less correlated or uncorrelated transform coefficients for greater or greatest efficiencies respectively.

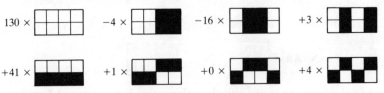

Figure 11.12 Reconstruction from weighted basis pictures.

- *Linearity*: to allow a one-to-one mapping between the pel and transform domains and hence $\mathbf{B} = \mathbf{A}^{-1}$. This also implies that the matrices must be singular.
- *Orthogonality*: the energy in both domains should be the same, and therefore no energy is either lost or carried redundantly.

11.5.2 Transform coding methods

Karhunen–Loève transform

The only unitary transform whose transformation matrix fulfils the above requirements is the Karhunen–Loève transform (KLT). The elements of the KLT transformation matrix are obtained by diagonalizing the covariance matrix of the image data, which results in completely uncorrelated transform coefficients. The bandwidth compression possibility of this transform arises in the usual way from the fact that if the image is highly correlated most transform coefficients are small and can be deleted without introducing serious distortion to the reconstructed picture.

Since the variances of the KLT transform coefficients tend to decrease in value monotonically with increasing order, in comparison with other transforms it has the best energy compaction property and is an optimum transform. In spite of the optimality of this transform, it has no applications as a practical data compression method. This is primarily because of the very high computational complexity in the four stages of calculation: the original correlation matrix; the diagonalization; the elements of the KLT matrix, and finally the value of each transform coefficient. Secondly, since image statistics are rarely stationary, for each new block of the picture a new inverse transformation matrix has to be transmitted to the receiver, which makes it impractical. The KLT is, however, used as a reference to evaluate the relative performance of other transforms.

Fortunately, it is possible to avoid these difficulties by using transforms that may not be optimum. These suboptimal transforms use a fixed set of basis vectors that do not need to be recalculated; moreover, they can have properties that speed up the calculation of the transform coefficients. Surprisingly, the compression efficiencies of these transforms turn out to be not significantly different from that of the KLT, and examples follow of such suboptimum transforms that have been successfully used in image coding.

Discrete Fourier transform

The discrete Fourier transform (DFT) is one of the suboptimum transforms that possess defined basis functions with the elements of the form $e^{-j2\pi nk/N}$ with n and $k = 0,1 \ldots N-1$. N is the matrix length, k is the frequency or sequency index of the basis vectors, and n is the pel

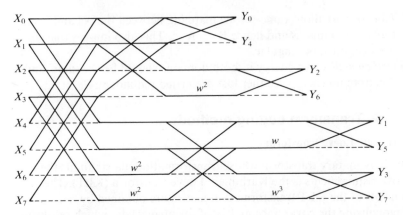

Figure 11.13 An FFT algorithm for $N = 8$, $w = e^{j\pi/4}$. Solid lines mean addition, dotted lines subtraction.

index. It has the advantage that the transform coefficients can be efficiently calculated using the fast Fourier transform (FFT) technique as shown in Fig. 11.13 for $N = 8$.

Since the elements of the DFT matrix are complex numbers, it appears that $2N$ real numbers are needed to define the N complex transform coefficients. In fact this is not so, since because the input samples are real, the transform coefficients have conjugate symmetry and only half the components need to be transmitted, while the other half can be reconstructed at the receiver. The transmitted values are derived via two submatrices, each being the real and imaginary parts of the complex DFT matrix. These matrices are usually sparse, which means that varying numbers of pels are not involved in the calculation of particular transmitted components. Those that are involved come from a spatially extended region, and are thus inherently less correlated than if they were adjacent. This is one explanation of the poor performance of the DFT compared with other transforms (Ghanbari, 1979).

Hadamard transform

Another suboptimum transform that also possesses a fast transformation algorithm is the Hadamard transform (HT). The elements of the mutually orthogonal basis vectors of this transform are either $+1$ or -1, which results in very low computational complexity in the calculation of the transform coefficients. The transform coefficients can be calculated using a fast transformation algorithm similar to that of the FFT flowchart in Fig. 11.13, but containing no physical multiplications.

The Haar and Slant transforms are other examples of suboptimum transforms with known basis functions that also possess fast

Table 11.3 Variances of DCT coefficients for 8 × 8 blocks from 'Split Screen'

	3202	983	455	260	115	46	20
2628	818	256	116	71	40	18	10
864	320	110	48	35	18	6	6
198	116	50	20	16	6	4	1
97	42	17	9	5	2	1	0
32	20	11	4	2	1	0	0
9	7	3	2	1	1	0	0
4	3	1	1	0	0	0	0

transformation algorithms (Ahmed and Rao, 1975). However, their performances are not substantially different from that of the HT, whereas their computational complexities are higher. In image coding where computational complexity is of prime importance, the Hadamard transform is preferred.

Discrete cosine transform

Finally we come to what is known to be the most efficient suboptimum transform, the discrete cosine transform (DCT). The elements of the kth basis vector of this transform for matrix length N are the real values $\cos [k\pi(2n + 1)/2N]$. It has the advantage over all other suboptimum transforms in that its basis vectors resemble closely the basis vectors of the KLT for smoothly varying video inputs. It also possesses a fast transformation algorithm (Chen *et al.*, 1977; Ghanbari and Pearson, 1982), which has meant that in the past decade it has become almost universal in image data compression applications requiring transform coding.

11.5.3 Quantization

Among the transform coefficients, the one which represents the average value of the block of pels in the block is called the DC coefficient. This coefficient carries the greatest share of the energy in the transform domain, with nearly uniform PDF and is hence uncoded. The remaining transform coefficients, which all represent basis functions with zero mean, are called AC coefficients. They have non-uniform PDFs, and can thus be quantized for bandwidth compression. Table 11.3 shows actual coefficient variances obtained from one frame of the 'Split Screen' sequence, using 8 × 8 blocks and the DCT. As can be seen, the variances, which are measures of energy, decrease as the frequency order of the coefficients increases.

The quantization of the AC coefficients is non-uniform and is matched to their statistical characteristics. The number of bits assigned

Table 11.4 Bit assignment table for the variances of Table 11.3

10	6	5	4	4	3	2	2
6	5	4	3	3	2	2	1
5	4	3	3	3	2	1	1
4	3	3	2	2	1	1	0
3	2	2	1	1	0	0	0
2	2	1	1	0	0	0	0
2	1	0	0	0	0	0	0
1	0	0	0	0	0	0	0

to the quantizer for each AC coefficient should be such that the quantization distortion is almost evenly distributed among the coefficients. This is equivalent to assigning bits to the coefficients proportional to the logarithm of their standard deviations (square root of variance) (Ghanbari, 1979). Table 11.4 shows a typical bit assignment corresponding to the variance matrix of Table 11.3. The average bit rate with this assignment is 1.8 bits/pel, compared to the original input of 8 bits/pel.

Figure 11.14(a) shows the quality of the coded image with this bit rate. At a lower bit rate of 0.6 bits/pel, the quality deteriorates, giving

(a)

Figure 11.14(a) Discrete cosine transform coding, 8 × 8 blocks: 1.8 bits/pel, allocation according to Table 11.4.

(b)

Figure 11.14(b) Discrete cosine transform coding, 8 × 8 blocks: 0.6 bits/pel using a restricted version of Table 11.4 to enhance the visibility of block structure artefacts.

reduced resolution and block-structure visibility in the detailed areas as shown in Fig. 11.14(b). The blocks become visible because the exact nature of the distortion in adjacent blocks varies. Because the boundaries are straight lines and highly structured, the discontinuities are particularly noticeable to the human observer.

11.6 Sub-band coding

Sub-band coding (SBC) was introduced by Crochiere *et al.* in 1976, and has since proved to be a simple and powerful technique for speech and image compression. The basic principle is the partitioning of the signal spectrum into several frequency bands, then coding and transmitting each band separately. This is particularly suited to image coding because, firstly, natural images tend to have a non-uniform frequency spectrum, with most of the energy concentrated in the lower-frequency bands. Secondly, psychovisual phenomena are involved through the varying tolerance to noise of the human vision system; noise visibility tends to fall off at both high and low spatial frequencies. This enables the designer to adjust the compression distortion according to

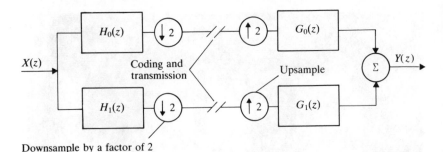

Figure 11.15 Sub-band decomposition and recovery with two bands.

perceptual criteria. Thirdly, since images are processed in their entirety, and not in artificial blocks, there is no block structure distortion in the output, as occurs in the transform and vector quantization methods (Sec. 11.7). The other inherent deficiency of block coding, residual interblock correlation, is also absent.

In SBC the band splitting is done by passing the image data through a bank of band-pass analysis filters. Since the bandwidth of each filtered version of the image is reduced, they can now in theory each be downsampled at a lower rate, according to Nyquist criteria, giving a series of reduced size sub-band pictures. The sub-band pictures are then coded, quantized and transmitted. Finally, the received sub-band pictures are restored to their original sizes and passed through a bank of 'synthesis filters', where they are interpolated and added to reconstruct the image.

In the absence of quantization error, it is required that the reconstructed picture should be an exact replica of the input picture. This can only be achieved if the spatial frequency responses of the analysis filters 'tile' the spectrum without overlapping, which requires infinitely sharp transition regions and cannot be realized practically. Instead, the analysis filter responses have finite transition regions and do overlap, which means that the downsampling/upsampling processes introduce aliasing distortion into the reconstructed picture.

In order to eliminate the aliasing distortion, it is possible to choose analysis and synthesis filters such that aliased components in the transition regions cancel. To see how such a relation can make alias-free SBC possible, consider a two-band system, as shown in Fig. 11.15. In this diagram, filters $H_0(z)$ and $H_1(z)$ represent the z-transform transfer functions of the respective low-pass and high-pass analysis filters. Filters $G_0(z)$ and $G_1(z)$ are the corresponding synthesis filters, and the down- and upsampling factors are 2. Downsampling by 2 is carried out by discarding alternate samples, the remainder being compressed into half the distance occupied by the original sequence. This is equivalent to compressing the source image by a factor of 2, which doubles all frequency components present. The frequency domain effect of

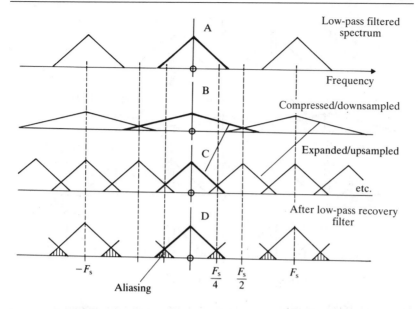

Figure 11.16(a)   Low-pass sub-band generation and recovery.

downsampling/compression is a thus a doubling of the width of all components in the sampled spectrum. Upsampling is the complement: it is achieved by inserting a zero-valued sample between each input sample, and is equivalent to a temporal or spatial expansion of the input sequence. In the frequency domain the effect is as usual the reverse and all components are compressed towards zero frequency.

The problem with these actions is the impossibility of constructing ideal, sharp-cut analysis filters. We illustrate this in Fig. 11.16(a). Spectrum A shows the original sampled signal which has been imperfectly low-pass filtered so that some energy remains above $F_s/4$, the cutoff of the *ideal* filter for the task. Downsampling compresses the signal and expands the spectrum to give B, while C is the picture after expansion or upsampling. As well as those at multiples of F_s, this process generates additional spectral components at odd multiples of $F_s/2$. These cause aliasing when the final sub-band recovery takes place, as at D.

In the high-pass case, Fig. 11.16(b), the same phenomena occur, so that on recovery there is aliased energy in the region of $F_s/4$. The final output image is generated by adding the low-pass and high-pass sub-bands regenerated by the upsamplers and associated filters. The aliased energy would normally be expected to cause interference; however, if the phases of the aliased components from the high- and low-pass sub-bands can be made to differ by π, then cancellation occurs and the recovered signal is alias-free.

How this can be arranged is best analysed by reference to

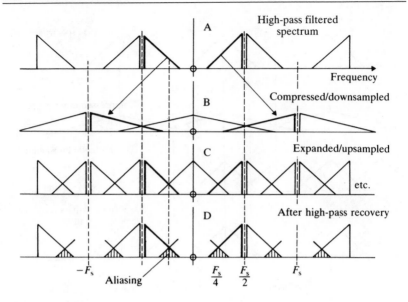

Figure 11.16(b)   High-pass sub-band generation and recovery.

z-transforms. Referring to Fig. 11.15, after the synthesis filters, the reconstructed output in z-transform notation can be written as:

$$Y(z) = G_0(z)\, Y_0(z)\ +\ G_1(z)\, Y_1(z) \tag{11.1}$$

where $Y_0(z)$ and $Y_1(z)$ are inputs to the synthesis filters after upsampling. Assuming there are no quantization and transmission errors, the reconstructed samples are given by

$$Y_0(z)\ =\ 1/2\,[H_0(z)\, X(z)\ +\ H_0(-z)\, X(-z)] \tag{11.2a}$$

$$Y_1(z)\ =\ 1/2\,[H_1(z)\, X(z)\ +\ H_1(-z)\, X(-z)] \tag{11.2b}$$

where the aliasing components from the upsampling of the lower and higher bands are given by $H_0(-z)\,X(-z)$ and $H_1(-z)\,X(-z)$ respectively (Vaidyanathan, 1987). By substituting Eqs (11.2) into (11.1), we get

$$\begin{aligned}Y(z)\ =\ &1/2\,[H_0(z)\, G_0(z)\ +\ H_1(z)\, G_1(z)]\, X(z)\\ &+\ 1/2\,[H_0(-z)\, G_0(z)\ +\ H_1(-z)\, G_1(z)]\, X(-z)\end{aligned} \tag{11.3}$$

The first term in Eq. (11.3) is the desired reconstructed signal, while the second term is aliased components. The aliased components can be eliminated regardless of the amount of overlap in the analysis filters by defining the synthesis filters as

$$G_0(z)\ =\ H_1(-z) \tag{11.4a}$$

$$G_1(z)\ =\ -H_0(-z) \tag{11.4b}$$

Given the synthesis filters as in Eqs (11.4), the alias-free reconstructed signal now becomes

$$Y(z) = 1/2 [H_0(z) H_1(-z) - H_0(-z) H_1(z)] X(z) \qquad (11.5)$$

If we define $P(z) = H_0(z) H_1(-z)$, then Eq. (11.5) can be written as

$$Y(z) = 1/2 [P(z) - P(-z)] X(z) \qquad (11.6)$$

Now the reconstructed signal can be a perfect, but delayed, replica of the input signal, the delay m elements, if

$$P(z) - P(-z) = 2z^{-m} \qquad (11.7)$$

Thus the z-transform input/output signals are given by

$$Y(z) = z^{-m} X(z) \qquad (11.8)$$

In Eq. (11.7), $P(z)$ is called the product filter and m is the delay introduced by the filter banks. As Eq. (11.8) shows, the reconstructed pel sequence $\{y(n)\}$ is an exact replica of the delayed input sequence $\{x(n - m)\}$.

The design of analysis/synthesis filters is therefore based on factorization of a product filter $P(z)$ into linear phase components $H_0(z)$ and $H_1(-z)$. With the constraint of Eq. (11.7) on $P(z)$, the product filter must have an odd number of coefficients. Le Gall and Tabatabai (1988) have used a product filter $P(z)$ of the kind

$$P(z) = 1/16 (-1 + 9z^{-2} + 16z^{-3} + 9z^{-4} - z^{-6}) \qquad (11.9)$$

and by factorizing have obtained several solutions for each pair of analysis and synthesis filters

$$\begin{aligned} H_0(z) &= 1/4 (-1 + 3z^{-1} + 3z^{-2} - z^{-3}) \\ H_1(-z) &= 1/4 (1 + 3z^{-1} + 3z^{-2} + z^{-3}) \end{aligned} \qquad (11.10a)$$

or

$$\begin{aligned} H_0(z) &= 1/4 (1 + 3z^{-1} + 3z^{-2} + z^{-3}) \\ H_1(-z) &= 1/4 (-1 + 3z^{-1} + 3z^{-2} - z^{-3}) \end{aligned} \qquad (11.10b)$$

or

$$\begin{aligned} H_0(z) &= 1/8 (-1 + 2z^{-1} + 6z^{-2} + 2z^{-3} - z^{-4}) \\ H_1(-z) &= 1/2 (1 + 2z^{-1} + z^{-2}) \end{aligned} \qquad (11.10c)$$

The synthesis filters $G_0(z)$ and $G_1(z)$ are then derived using Eq. (11.4). Each of the above equation pairs gives the result $P(z) - P(-z) = 2z^{-3}$, which implies that the reconstruction is perfect with a delay of three sample periods.

Figure 11.17 shows a two-band split and recombination of the zone plate, using horizontal high- and low-pass filters as defined by Eq. (11.10c). Upper left is the original; upper right is the recovered low-pass image; lower left is the recovered high-pass image (with 128 added to the 8-bit signal amplitudes to make negative values visible) while lower

Figure 11.17 Two-sub-band decomposition and reconstruction of the zone plate. Upper left, original; upper right, low-pass sub-band (L); lower left, high-pass sub-band (H); lower right, reconstruction (H + L). Image H has been offset by + 128 levels for the photograph.

right is the sum of the sub-bands. Both sub-bands have aliasing on high horizontal frequencies, which shows as faint replications of the zone plate pattern, but these disappear through phase cancellation in the sum image as predicted by the design equations. As explained in Chap. 7, the faint alias patterns that are present in the original *and* reconstructed images are inherent features of the television scanning and sampling processes.

Higher-order systems

Multidimensional and multiband sub-band coding can be developed from the two-band low-pass and high-pass analysis/synthesis filter structure of Fig. 11.15. For example, SBC of a 2-D image can be performed by carrying out a 1-D decomposition along the lines of the image and then down each column. SBC of this type for seven bands is illustrated in Fig. 11.18.

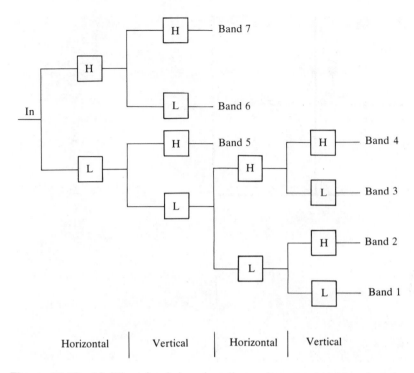

Figure 11.18 Multiband sub-band coding using repeated two-band splits.

Figure 11.19 shows all seven subimages generated by the coder in Fig. 11.18 for 'Split Screen', with low-pass and high-pass analysis filters again of the type defined by Eq. (11.10c). The original image (not shown) was 352 pels by 288 lines. Bands 1–4, at two levels of subdivision, are 88 × 72 while bands 5–7 are 176 × 144. All but band 1 have been amplified by a factor of 4 and offset by + 128 to enhance visibility of the low-level detail they contain. The scope for bandwidth compression arises mainly from the low energy levels that appear in the high-pass sub-bands. Any suitable coding technique from those discussed already can be applied.

11.7 Vector quantization

The bit rate reductions that the coding methods discussed so far achieve are obtained by scalar quantization of prediction errors, transform coefficients, and sub-band images. A further compression technique is to quantize directly $M \times N$ blocks of samples, treating them as a vector with $M \times N$ dimensions. The trivial case of one dimension corresponds to scalar quantization, and we have already seen that a good approximation to the amplitude probability distribution of raw PCM

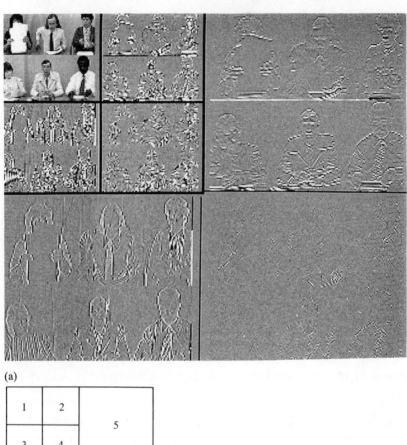

(a)

1	2	5
3	4	
6		7

(b)

Figure 11.19 (a) The seven subimages generated by the coder of Fig. 11.18. (b) Layout of individual sub-bands.

samples is a constant, so there is no advantage in attempting a statistical code, or non-linear quantization of raw digital video. However, making the usual assumptions about local correlation in visual images the situation is very different for groups of pels.

If we plot in a 2-D space the points corresponding to pairs of adjacent elements $\{x_0, x_1\}$ a distribution like that in Fig. 11.20 is obtained, with a strong clustering about the diagonal where $x_0 = x_1$. Figure 11.20 was generated by sampling at random 256 such pairs from a frame of

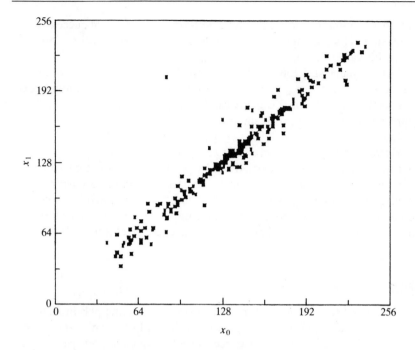

Figure 11.20 Joint distribution of 256 pairs of horizontally adjacent elements from 'Split Screen'.

the 'Split Screen' sequence. The correlation coefficient between x_0 and x_1 is 0.97.

It is interesting to compare the utilization of the 2-D space with what might be expected from a system where the pel values are uncorrelated.

Joint distribution of random sample pairs

Assuming a uniform random distribution between 0 and 255, we construct a 2-D histogram in x_0, x_1 space. The probability of a location in the histogram being incremented in any one trial is $p = 256^{-2}$. This is a binomial process, and the mean value of the number of occurrences at each location in x_0, x_1 space is $\mu = N \times 256^{-2}$, where N is the number of pel pairs in the trial. The probability of getting exactly M 'hits' in any one location after N trials is closely approximated for such small p by a Poisson frequency distribution

$$f(M) = \frac{e^{-\mu}}{M!}\mu^M$$

The probability, p_{oc}, that a location in the x_0, x_1 histogram contains one or more after N trials is obtained from the probability of it containing zero: $p_{oc} = [1 - f(0)]$. To find the mean and variance of the number of occupied locations, we consider scanning the space in full; this is another binomial process, this time with probability p_{oc} of success at each step. Thus the mean number of locations occupied will be $256^2 \times p_{oc}$, with variance $256^2 \times p_{oc} (1 - p_{oc})$.

For an image size 256×256 there are $N = 32\,768$ pairs of elements, hence $\mu = 1/2$ and $p_{oc} = (1 - e^{-1/2}) = 0.3934$. The mean number of occupied locations for this many random input pairs is thus approximately $25\,786$, with standard deviation 125.

In a test on occupancy of x_0, x_1 space for the $32\,768$ horizontally adjacent element pairs from a 256^2 array of samples from the 'Split Screen' frame which was carried out by plotting a full joint distribution, we found that only 7185 different combinations actually occurred, equivalent to about 28 per cent of the figure to be expected for random data. The entropy measure on the same data set which includes the effect of non-uniform probability of occurrence, gives a figure of 10.7 bits per pair, or 5.35 bits/pel.

Higher dimensionality

We extended the process to three dimensions, by taking pels in $22\,016$ horizontally adjacent triplets, again from the 'Split Screen' frame, this time a 258×256 region. It was necessary to reduce the bits per sample from 8 to 6 to enable direct measurements to be taken, so with this amplitude resolution there are 2^{18} or $262\,144$ possible combinations. The result was 4669 different occupied locations (compared with a mean of $21\,116$ occupied locations for $22\,016$ random triplets), giving an occupancy ratio of 22 per cent of the random figure. The entropy measure was 11.45 bits per triplet, or 3.15 bits per 6-bit pel, which corresponds to 4.2 bits per 8-bit pel. Table 11.5 and Fig. 11.21 summarize these results, including an additional set for four element vectors which consist of sets of four adjacent pels in a square pattern on the sampling lattice.

Table 11.5 Effect of vector dimension on occupancy ratio and entropy, starting from the same areas on a frame of 'Split Screen'

Dimension	Occupancy (% of random)	Entropy (bits/pel)
1	~100	7.14 (from Table 11.2)
2	28	5.35
3	22	4.20
4	20	3.52

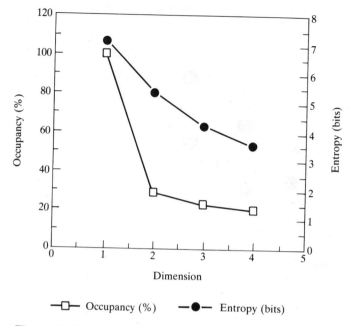

Figure 11.21   Occupancy and entropy in graphical form.

Representative vectors

The examples discussed so far have been used to show that there is statistical redundancy in images when groups of elements are treated as vectors, caused by the presence of local correlation. If local correlation is high, all the pels in the block will tend to have similar values and the points representing each vector will cluster along the diagonal in the hyperspace. In practical implementations of vector quantization (VQ) the real savings arise through the assignment of a set of representative vectors to the picture information, in such a way that a distortion measure, objective but preferably subjective, is minimized. Figure 11.22 illustrates this principle for the 2-D case.

The function of the vector quantizer is very easy to understand in principle. Given that there is a set of representative vectors that form the codebook, each vector to be encoded is allocated a codeword that describes the 'nearest' representative vector. At the receiver, this vector is displayed. The quantizer design process can be done iteratively (Gray, 1984), although this procedure is not guaranteed to produce an optimum choice:

1   Provide a training set and choose an initial set of representative vectors.

2   Allocate each training vector to its 'nearest' representative vector,

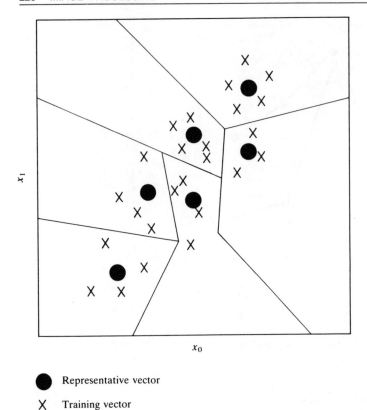

● Representative vector

X Training vector

Figure 11.22 Two-dimensional vector quantization. The lines indicate the regions associated with each representative vector.

using a suitable distortion measure. If the total distortion is acceptable, then stop.

3 For each representative vector **V**, replace it by a vector positioned at the centroid of the subset of the training vectors that were mapped into **V** during step 2. Go to step 2.

In practice, several attempts might be made to choose the codebook, each starting with a different initial 'guess'. A number of methods have been devised for making first approximations. One involves a 'splitting' process, where the first vector is just the centroid of the training set, effectively giving a vector quantizer that encodes with zero bits per vector. Another vector is generated, either close to or distant from the first, and the optimization rule above applied; we now have one bit per vector. This can be repeated indefinitely until the codebook is of the desired size (Linde *et al.*, 1980).

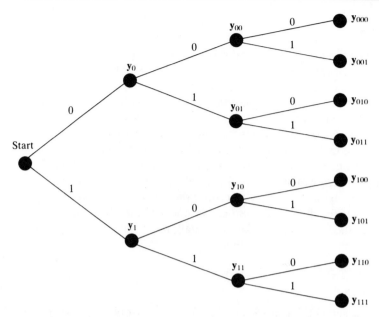

Figure 11.23 Three bits per sample VQ implemented as a binary search. $y_0, y_1, \ldots, y_{111}$ are representative vectors.

Encoding and decoding

The decoder for simple VQ can be implemented as a look-up table. Assuming the receiver is aware of the representative vectors in advance (they may be specific to and accompany the picture information in an image archive), then each incoming codeword is used as an index into the table which generates the representative vector at once. The main complexity is at the encoding stage, especially for high dimensionalities. With small vectors (up to 4 pels) look-up tables are just feasible: based on the representative vectors, all possible incoming combinations are tested, possibly using the search algorithm discussed below, and assigned to the 'closest' in the space.

Since the number of locations in the hypervolume for 8-bit image samples grows rapidly as 256^N for vector size N, then some kind of online search procedure has to be used to find the best representative for each incoming block of samples. One possibility is a binary tree search illustrated in Fig. 11.23 (cf. Gray, 1984), which progresses through a series of intermediate stages choosing at each between two alternatives. This is a natural extension from the splitting rule, which automatically generates 'acceptable' quantizers at each level of precision. Thus for any vector to the left of the diagram it is certain that all subsequent vectors on its branch are at least as good, and probably better, at representing the input vector.

Performance

VQ has been tested on speech and images, and can give excellent results at fractional bit rates per sample. A number of modifications to the simple idea exist, e.g. multistep VQ, where a later stage encodes the residual error produced by a coarse earlier stage. At the receiver, the final output is the sum of the outputs of all the intermediate stage decoders. There are also systems that encode the vectors in terms of mean and residual components: the average value of a block is subtracted from every pel and the differences (now containing only a.c. components) vector quantized in the usual way. The mean is encoded separately, probably with high precision; the rationale behind this process is that the d.c. component carries most of the information, especially if the block size is relatively small, much as happens with the d.c. coefficient in transform coding.

Developments

Although direct VQ of (say) 8 × 8 blocks of pels would be expected to give high compression efficiency, the training and search phases for such a high dimensionality are not practical. VQ can be exploited effectively, however, in combination with other compression methods, e.g. the vector analogue of DPCM. It can also be used in transform coding to compress further the coefficient sets from each transformed block. We have tested this idea in the laboratory for VQ of the most active 15 coefficients from a size 8 × 8 cosine transformer. In a particular case, the transform coder alone takes the data rate to 2 bits/pel, while the VQ stage further reduces it to 0.125 bit. A further example is the VQ of sets of sub-band coefficients in an interframe hybrid scheme (Ahmad-Fadzil and Dennis, 1989) (see Sec. 11.8).

11.8 Interframe coding

We have seen that television pels are nearly always highly correlated in the spatial domain. Unsurprisingly this property extends to the temporal dimension as well. The degree of spatial correlation depends on the amount of picture detail, while temporal correlation depends on the amount of motion. These correlations can be partially, or totally, removed by applying the coding techniques described in Secs 11.3–11.7, in the desired domain. Generally, when the coding is performed in the 2-D spatial domain, it is called 'intraframe' (within-frame) coding, while exploitation of the temporal domain is called 'interframe' (frame-to-frame) coding. In practice, a combination of both coding techniques is used for the highest possible compression efficiency.

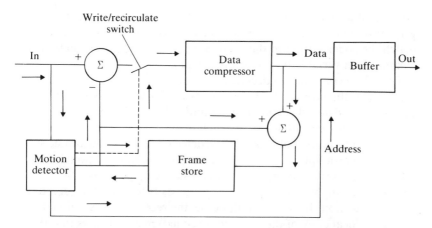

Figure 11.24 Block diagram of a conditional replenishment coder.

For example, consider simple element prediction DPCM. The best predictor for the current pel in the stationary parts of the picture is the same pel in the previous frame, whereas in the moving parts of the picture such a prediction is no longer sensible. In this case a good single predictor can be an adjacent pel in the *present* frame, as moving parts of the picture usually tend to have low resolution, mainly due to camera integration. A simple adaptive system would be able to select the best predictor based on the amount of motion, previous frame or previous element.

11.8.1 Conditional replenishment (CR)

Conditional replenishment (CR) is a coding technique suitable for picture sources with moderate degrees of motion, such as occur in videoconferencing. The original CR technique was devised by Mounts in 1969, and has undergone extensive development since then.

Basically, in a CR coder, only moving parts of a picture are coded and transmitted. Incoming data to the receiver updates (replenishes) a local frame store, which holds and displays at standard rates a copy of the picture. Unchanged parts of the scene are simply repeated. The division of the source image into moving and stationary areas is done by a movement detector. The movement detector compares the present value of an incoming pel (or a region of pels for block coders) with that in the previous frame, and when a change greater than a threshold occurs a pel or block is declared as moving.

A general form of a CR encoder is shown in Fig. 11.24. When movement has been detected, the input signal could be fed in PCM form direct to the channel, but this is rarely done as considerable further data compression is possible using one or more of the intraframe schemes discussed already. Because motion from frame to frame can vary from none at all to that caused by a complete scene change, the data generation rate is highly non-uniform. This requires an elastic buffer to match the coder output to the fixed rate provided by a channel (but see Chapt. 13 on variable bit rate transmission).

The CR encoder has to decode and maintain a copy of the picture available to the receiver, and use *this* copy in its motion detector rather than a frame-delayed version of the input. Closing the loop in this way creates a negative feedback path which tends to eliminate accumulated errors introduced by both the motion detector and any intraframe stage. As a counterexample, consider the situation where the motion detector uses the previous incoming frame, and a slow change of overall video level is occurring whose slope between frames is too small to exceed the motion detection threshold. In this case, the receiver is never updated. Using the local copy of the received (decoded) image ensures that the difference is eventually large enough to be detected.

The positions or addresses of the changed pels detected by the movement detector, along with the new pel amplitudes, however coded, are combined and fed to an elastic buffer for transmission to the receiver.

To prevent the elastic buffer from overflowing, a measure of its fill can be fed back to the coder. Typically, as the buffer fills, the feedback lowers the incoming data rate into the buffer. This can be done in a variety of ways to achieve a progressive effect: increasing the movement detector threshold level; subsampling of moving parts of the picture; coarse quantization of data samples, or a combination of all methods. In severe cases, when the data rate is much higher than the channel rate, the complete omission of a frame may even be required. Such methods transmit moving areas with progressively lower resolution and quality as motion increases. The effect of increasing threshold level causes areas of low detail and low-level noise within a moving object to be missed by the movement detector. This results in a noticeable static pattern in and following moving areas, known and very well described as the 'dirty window' effect.

11.8.2 Motion-compensated interframe coding

In the conditional replenishment coder of the previous section, moving parts of the picture are coded for further data compression. Moving pels exhibit some degree of intraframe correlation (between themselves) and with the corresponding pels in the previous frame. The amount of intraframe correlation depends on the spatial detail of the moving object, while interframe correlation depends on the amount of motion.

Objects moving at very low speeds tend to have higher temporal than spatial correlation. As the speed increases, temporal correlation decreases. However, if the direction and speed of the motion can be estimated, then it is possible to compensate for it. Coders that make use of a displacement measure between the current 'island' of moving pels

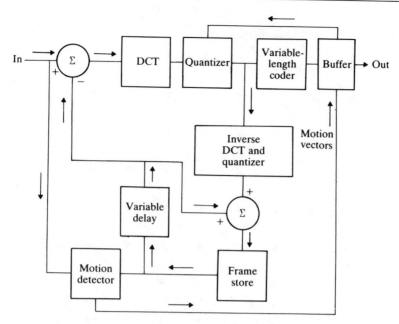

Figure 11.25   Block diagram of a hybrid DPCM/DCT coder.

and the same island in the previous frame are called motion-compensated coders.

In a motion-compensated coding technique and for the case where the motion is simply translational, there is no difference between the actual and predicted values of the moving pels, apart from random noise. This drastically reduces the entropy of these pel differences. However, if the motion is not a simple shift, but includes rotation, it is still possible to track the motion, but the entropy of the compensated prediction errors is increased.

In the event that motion is not completely compensated, the short-term bit rate may be greater than if compensation was not attempted, because the motion vectors have to be transmitted and increase the overhead information. However, experience shows that efficient motion compensation can result in a reduction factor of 1.5–2 (Koga *et al.*, 1981).

Hybrid coding

Combining a variety of data reduction techniques results in a so-called hybrid coding method. Figure 11.25 shows a block diagram of a motion compensated hybrid DPCM/DCT interframe coder taken from a laboratory simulation of a working design. This technique is very efficient and can successfully compress videoconference-type signals to rates in the region of 64 kbits/s.

In Fig. 11.25 the variable delay is the amount of delay required to

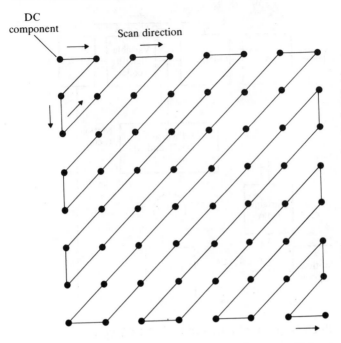

DC component

Scan direction

Figure 11.26 Zigzag scanning of transform coefficients.

compensate for motion. Once the motion is detected, the differences between the current block of pels and those in the motion-compensated block are transform coded. Since the input pel differences are inherently small, the transform coefficients themselves have low entropies. Note that the DC coefficient out of the transform coder is the average of the pel differences, which is also small.

The quantizer in Fig. 11.25 actually consists of a set of quantizers, one for each coefficient. In adaptive coding, the DCT coefficients can either use a variety of quantizers, or they can be scanned in a zigzag fashion as in Fig. 11.26, where only the first N significant coefficients are quantized, with the remainder set to zero (Ghanbari, 1989).

The end point of the scan, indicating the last transmitted coefficient, has to be transmitted as overhead information. The control feedback from the smoothing buffer to the coder makes sure that the generated date rate never exceeds the channel rate. In the case of buffer overflow, in a similar way to the general CR coders, the movement detector threshold, zigzag threshold, and quantizer characteristics are all changed.

11.8.3 H.261 standard video codec

Study Group XV of the CCITT has recommended an interframe coder for low bit rate transmission of visual telephony signals at multiples of

Table 11.6 Part of a block coefficient set

83	12	21	7	−10	7
−10	35	11	5	−31	
−5	17	12	−18		
18	−24	−3			
5	17				
6					

64 kbits/s, known as model H.261 (CCITT, 1989). This coder basically is similar to that given in Fig. 11.25, but with some special characteristics. A version of this codec known as Reference Model 8, one of an expanding series (CCITT, 1989) has the following characteristics: first, the quantizer is uniform and its step size is dynamically selected as a function of the state of the buffer. Second, the variable length coder is 2-D, in the way that it codes pairs of linked 'events'. The first event is the length of any zero run preceding the value of a coefficient greater than the selection threshold: if a value is greater than this threshold, it is transmitted. The second event is the quantization index—the ratio of quantized coefficient to the quantizer step size, rounded to the nearest integer.

In order to increase the lengths of zero runs, the coefficients are zigzag scanned in the same way as Fig. 11.26, and during the scanning if a coefficient value is less than the selection threshold, then the threshold is incremented, otherwise it is reset to the quantizer step size. The increase of the selection threshold is continued up to a maximum value of 3/2 times the quantizer step size.

As an example, Table 11.6 shows part of the coefficient set for a block. Assuming a quantizer step size of 16, the procedure to generate the 2-D events is shown in Table 11.7. These events are subjected to 2-D variable length coding.

Table 11.7 Two-dimensional events after zigzag scanning and variable thresholding

Raw coefficients	83	12	−10		−5	35	21	7	11	17	18	5	−24	12	5		−10	7	−31
Threshold	16	16	17		18	19	16	16	17	18	19	20	21	16	17		18	19	20
New coefficients	83	0	0		0	35	21	0	0	0	0	0	−24	0	0		0	0	−31
Quantized values	88	0	0		0	40	24	0	0	0	0	0	−24	0	0		0	0	−24
Index	5	0	0		0	2	1	0	0	0	0	0	−1	0	0		0	0	−1

Events to be transmitted: (run, level) (0,5) (3,2) (0,1) (5,−1) (4,−1)

11.9 Summary

Data compression for the transmission of television pictures has a long history of engineering effort in researching ideas and possible methods, but a very short one in practical application. However, the process has given designers valuable insights into the handling of multidimensional signals. In this chapter we have shown how the break from the simple interpretation of the sampling requirements for video signals—'twice the analogue bandwidth'—has enabled simple modifications to sampling structures so that an apparently severely undersampled picture can be reproduced with a minimum of degradation.

The major feature of picture signals that represent real scenes is that they come from sources containing physical structure that can be exploited in order to reduce the data rate that needs to be sent in order to describe the scene. While Chap. 12 on model-based coding describes methods that do this in a highly sophisticated object-oriented manner, here we have been more concerned with basic statistical and psychovisual phenomena. For example, DPCM is a coding method that exploits both local statistical correlation and the inability of the human visual system to perceive small degradations (coding errors) near high-contrast boundaries. In transform coding, which is normally done by dividing the image into small blocks, and coding each individually, the saving arises firstly through the matching of the basis functions to the image content and secondly through the inability of the eye to perceive errors at high spatial frequencies. If the basis functions naturally match image content, like the sinusoids in the DCT, then it is guaranteed that most of the information about the picture is carried by a small subset of them. Thus, although the transform domain representation of an image block contains exactly the same information as the original, it differs in the visual significance of its set of coefficients. Whereas all the original picture samples have the *same* significance, only the high-amplitude subset of the transform basis functions need to be transmitted; the remainder can often be omitted altogether or represented with low accuracy. The major defect of block-based transform coding is the tendency of the block boundaries to become visible at very high compression factors, particularly when the coding is such as to reduce the data to less than one bit per picture element.

Sub-band compression is similar to transform coding, but overcomes the blocking problem by handling the picture as a single entity at all stages. It couples frequency domain decomposition with subsampling (contraction) and upsampling (expansion) to provide a coding method comparable in performance with transform coding. Although the idea of sub-band coding is another old one, it has only recently been made practical by the invention of a very simple digital filter structure. The new filters enable error-free reconstruction of images from their sub-bands and the automatic cancellation of the aliasing introduced by the subsampling processes.

Vector quantization is another very simple idea. Instead of treating samples as single entities—be they in the spatial, sub-band, or transform domains—they are considered in groups or vectors. The savings arise through the tendency of the vectors nearly always to be concentrated in particular regions of the hyperspace they represent. We illustrated this phenomenon with statistics from a simple spatial example, which showed that the potential compression efficiency increases with the dimensionality of the vectors. The implementation of VQ is relatively difficult, however. The quantization process requires the subdivision of the hyperspace into regions, each associated with a representative vector. Whereas scalar quantization can be done instantaneously with a look-up table, this is not practical once the vector has a dimensionality greater than 4. Instead, a search procedure has to be used. The real power of VQ has proved to be in combination with other coding schemes which have carried out some initial reduction of dimensionality.

Coding techniques that exploit temporal correlation—the tendency of one frame of a sequence to be similar to the next—offer the greatest potential for data reduction. However, this can only be fully realized by combining such features as motion compensation with one or more of the spatial methods already discussed to create 'hybrid' systems. An advanced example of this tendency is the hybrid DPCM/DCT interframe motion-compensated reference model H.261 for visual telephony.

References

Ahmad-Fadzil M. H. and Dennis T. J. (1989) 'Video subband coding using short-kernel filter banks and VQ with an improved motion compensation technique', *Abstracts of the Second International Workshop on 64 kbit/s Coding of Video Signals*, paper 2.3, University of Hannover.

Ahmed N. and Rao K. R. (1975) *Orthogonal Transforms for Signal Processing*, Springer-Verlag, Berlin.

CCITT (1989) *Reference Model 8*, CCITT SG XV (Specialist Group on Coding for Visual Telephony) COST 211 bis, Paris.

Chen W., Smith C. H. and Fralick S. C. (1977) 'A fast computational algorithm for the discrete cosine transform', *IEEE Transactions on Communications*, vol. COM-25, no. 9, pp. 1004–9.

Chiariglione L., Nicol R. C. and Schaefer P. (1982) 'The development of the European videoteleconference codec', *GLOBCOM Proc.*, vol. D4, pp. 3.1–3.5.

Crochiere R. E., Weber S. A. and Flanagan J. L. (1976) 'Digital coding of speech in sub-bands', *Bell System Technical Journal*, vol. 55, pp. 1069–85.

Cutler C. C. (1952) 'Differential quantisation of communication signals', US Patent 2 605 361.

Ghanbari M. (1979) 'Real-time transform coding of broadcast standard television pictures', PhD thesis, University of Essex.

Ghanbari M. (1989) 'Two-layer coding of video signals for VBR networks', *IEEE Journal on Selected Areas in Communications*, vol. SAC-7, no. 5, pp. 771–81.

Ghanbari M. and Pearson D. E. (1982) 'Fast cosine transform implementation for television signals', *Proceedings of the IEE*, vol. 129, pt. F, no. 1, pp. 59–68.

Gray R. M. (1984) 'Vector quantisation', *IEEE ASSP Magazine*, pp. 4–29, April.

Huffman D. A. (1952) 'A method for the construction of minimum redundancy codes', *Proceedings of the IRE*, vol. 40, pp. 1098–110.

Koga T., Hirano A. Iijima Y. and Ishigura T. (1981) 'Motion-compensated interframe coding for video conferencing', *National Telecommunications Conference Proceedings*, G5 3.1–3.5

Le Gall D. and Tabatabai A. (1988) 'Sub-band coding of digital images using symmetric short kernel and arithmetic coding techniques', *Proc. International Conference ASSP*, pp. 761–4.

Linde Y., Buzo A. and Gray R. M. (1980) 'An algorithm for vector quantiser design', *IEEE Transactions on Communications*, vol. COM-28, pp. 84–95.

Motorola (1987) *System V/68, User's Reference Manual*, Sec. 1.

Mounts F. W. (1969) 'Video encoding systems with conditional element replenishment', *Bell System Technical Journal*, vol. 48, no. 7, pp. 2545–54.

Nicol R. C. (1976) 'Television data compression for a digital telecommunications network', Ph.D. thesis, University College, University of London.

Shannon C. E. (1948) 'The mathematical theory of communication', *Bell System Technical Journal*, vol. 27, pp. 349–423.

Vaidyanathan P. P. (1987) 'Quadrature mirror filter banks, M-band extensions and perfect-reconstruction techniques', *IEEE ASSP Magazine*, pp. 4–20, July.

12 Model-based image coding

BILL WELSH

12.1 Introduction

When images are coded digitally for storage or transmission, it is desirable to keep the quantity of data generated as low as possible as the cost of storage or transmission is related to this quantity. Several of the established techniques for achieving this compression have been described in the previous chapter. Many coding schemes being developed today, however, aim at a very high compression and this necessitates some degradation of the images.

A great deal of effort is being expended worldwide to develop videophone and videoconference systems that will operate over a 64 kbits/s channel. This is because all modern digital telephone exchanges are based on 64 kbits/s switching as it is the rate required to transmit speech digitally with the same bandwidth as on the analogue telephone network. The requirement for transmission of video at such a low bit rate stretches current algorithms to their limits. Current algorithms exhibit poor performance when there is significant motion in the scene. They may require several frames to be dropped or the spatial resolution to be reduced in order to achieve the compression needed.

The idea of model-based or analysis–synthesis image coding has arisen because there is a possibility of exploiting much more of the redundancy in a sequence of images than is exploited at present. The term 'model-based' refers to the utilization of models of the objects in the scene. As a simple example, consider a scene containing a cube moving around on a plain coloured background. The information needed to generate a moving sequence at the receiver would be a description of the contents of the scene followed by a description of the motion of the object. Of course, the feasibility of extracting redundancy in this way depends on the complexity of the objects and the background. It is fairly straightforward to produce computer-animated sequences of cubes but videoconferencing requires the modelling of people, which is not so easy.

A question that must be considered before proceeding further concerns the fidelity of the image displayed. A measure of fidelity used by some authors is the normalised mean-square error (NMSE) between the received image and the original at the transmission end. With some types of coding there is a relation between this measure and the subjective quality of the image; an image with a high NMSE may appear blurred or contain annoying artefacts. However, it can be argued that if the coded pictures are intended for videoconference or videophone purposes, the important information required is the identity of the subjects, their facial expressions, and their approximate body movements. As an example, consider a moving sequence in which a subject raises her arm and lowers it again. The requirement for a successful coding scheme would be to display a moving sequence of the woman raising and lowering her arm. If the precise speed, angle, and height of the arm displayed were not exactly that which occurred in reality, it would probably not matter as far as the viewer was concerned and he would not notice any defect in the image. However, the NMSE between corresponding frames of the original and the displayed sequence might be very high. In a model-based system, the model of the person displayed has to be animated using instructions that have been generated after analysis of the source scene. Inaccuracies in position may not be crucial.

12.2 Applications of model-based coding

12.2.1 How can model-based coding be used?

In practice, there are two ways to use model-based image coding. The first way is to improve existing videophone and videoconferencing systems operating at 64 kbits/s. In this case, the intention is to allocate more bits for the coding of areas of subjective importance in the image at the expense of less important areas. In normal videoconferencing, the faces of the subjects would be regarded as of prime importance, the background of least importance. It is especially important to maintain the maximum temporal resolution around the mouth area in order to keep lip synchronization. Another possibility for using model-based methods in 64 kbits/s coding is in the formation of a better prediction frame in a motion-compensating codec.

The second way of using model-based coding is in systems where the image displayed at the receiver is wholly or partly synthetic. Most of the work done so far has been in this area and the rest of the chapter will therefore concentrate on this.

12.2.2 Model-based coding for improvement of quality at 64 kbits/s

Recently work has been done on a coding scheme that combines model-based methods with conventional coding techniques (Musmann et al., 1989). Most conventional coding schemes divide the image into square blocks of pixels and encode the luminance and chrominance of each block independently. The new coding method subdivides the image into moving objects and encodes each object by three sets of parameters defining the motion, shape, and colour information of the object. The parameter sets are used to construct a synthetic image at both transmitter and receiver. The transmitter compares this reconstructed image with the true image of the scene and transmits the differences between the two images. In this sense, the scheme closely resembles a conventional hybrid predictive coder. However, the differences are encoded and transmitted only if they exceed a predetermined threshold as well as some other criteria. This is allowed because a certain amount of geometrical distortion of the images can be tolerated before it becomes noticeable to a human observer. The geometrical distortions are less annoying than quantization error distortions when the modelling of the objects is sufficiently exact.

It is claimed that, even though shape information has to be transmitted, this is more than compensated for by the reduction in the data required for transmitting the differences. Therefore, an improvement in subjective quality should be obtained using the new scheme compared with a conventional hybrid coder.

12.2.3 An analysis–synthesis approach for a videophone system

Parke (1982) wrote a paper concerning a method of facial animation in which he suggested a use for his system in low bit rate videotelephony. The facial animation was based on a computer model of a head. A common way of representing objects in 3-D computer graphics is by a net of interconnected polygons. It is easy to make the computer draw such a 'wire frame' because each side of every polygon projects to the screen as a straight line. The model is stored in the computer as a set of linked lists or linked arrays, as has been described in Chap. 6. There would be a set of arrays giving the x, y, and z coordinates of each polygon vertex in object space: $X[V]$, $Y[V]$, $Z[V]$ where V is the vertex address. There would also be a pair of 2-D arrays, one of which could be called $LINV[L][E]$, which gives the addresses of the vertices at the end of a line L, E being either 0 or 1 depending on which end of the line is being considered. The other array called $LINL[P][S]$ gives the line address for each side S of a polygon P. The wire frame is drawn on the screen by iterating through all the values of L in $LINV[L][E]$ which gives the vertex addresses and, in turn, yields the coordinates of the vertices using the arrays $X[V]$, $Y[V]$, and $Z[V]$. The side of the polygon must be projected on to the screen and this may involve a perspective projection. This gives the screen coordinates of the ends of the line and the most basic graphics facility on a computer will have a routine to draw a line between two points. An example is shown in Fig. 12.1.

In order to make the models appear more realistic, the polygon net

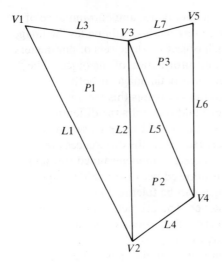

Figure 12.1   A section of a wire-frame model showing how the vertices, lines, and polygons may be numbered. Coordinates of vertex 5 are $X[5]$, $Y[5]$, $Z[5]$ indexed by vertex addresses. Addresses of vertices at ends of line 6 are given by LINV[6][0] and LINV[6][1]. Addresses of each side of polygon 3 are given by LINP[3][0], LINP[3][1], and LINP[3][2].

can be shaded. The shading is made to depend on the presence of imaginary light sources in the model world and the assumption of reflectance properties of the model surfaces as shown in Fig. 12.2. If the planar surfaces of the polygons in the wire frame are each given a uniform shading, the faceted appearance becomes apparent. A smooth shading technique such as Gouraud or Phong shading (Chap. 6) can be used to improve realism. In these techniques the shading in each polygon is effectively interpolated between the shading values at the vertices as shown in Fig. 12.3. This gives the impression of a smoothly rounded surface (Newman and Sproull, 1981).

In the case of Parke's model, Phong shading was added to improve the appearance. The face can be made to move in a global way by applying a set of rotations and translations to all the vertices as a whole. In addition, the vertices of certain polygons can be translated locally in order to change the facial expression. Two American psychologists have worked out a system of categorizing facial expressions in terms of about fifty independent facial actions (Ekman and Friesen, 1977). They call this the Facial Action Coding System (FACS). These actions were translated by Parke into a set of vectors that could be applied to the vertices. An example of one of these so-called action units is given in Fig. 12.4.

Parke suggested that if the face model could be made to approximate

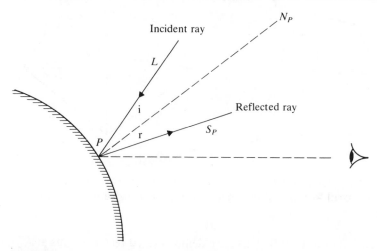

Figure 12.2 The shading of point P depends on the directions of light sources, the viewpoint, and the normal to the surface at P (N_P).

that of a real person, then a moving image of that person's face could be generated by determining the motion of the face and using this information to animate the model. By this means, a form of videotelephony could be established that would require extremely little information to be transmitted. Simulations at the British Telecom

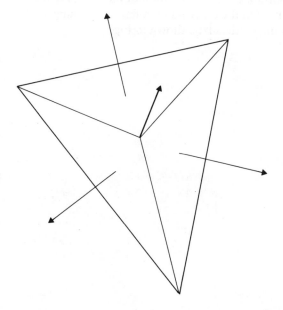

Figure 12.3 Normal vectors at a vertex are determined by averaging normals of neighbouring faces. Gouraud shading is achieved by interpolating the shading between the vertex normals.

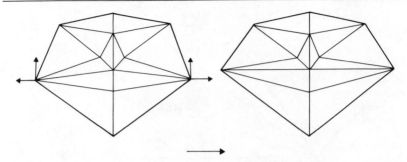

Figure 12.4 Vectors are applied to the two indicated vertices to produce the 'sharp lip puller' action unit on a wire-frame model of a mouth.

Research Laboratories (BTRL) have demonstrated results of this at only 200 bits/s.

Forchheimer and Fahlander (1983) produced a specification for a low bit rate coding system based on an analysis–synthesis method. They built hardware to generate moving images of a polygon net in real time with facial movements based on the FACS system. The net model they use, called CANDIDE, was kept to a size of only 100 triangles in order to make real-time operation feasible. The triangles are distributed so that a large number of small ones are located in areas of high curvature and in areas that are important for the generation of facial expressions such as the eyes and mouth. On the other hand, a few large triangles are used in flat areas such as the forehead, as shown in Fig. 12.5.

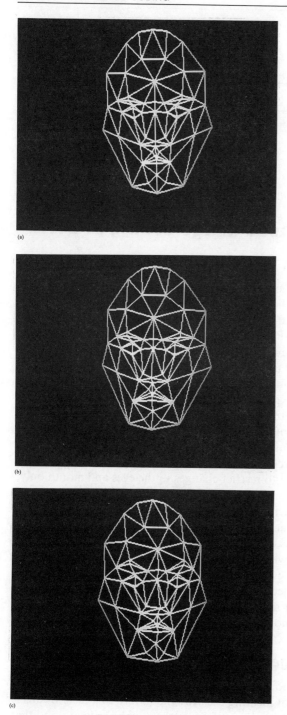

Figure 12.5 (a) 'Lip purse', (b) 'lip corner depression' and (c) 'eyebrow raise' action units on the CANDIDE wire-frame model.

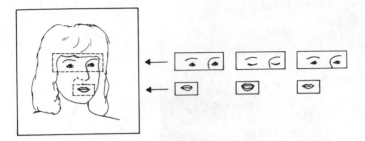

Figure 12.6 The use of templates of mouths and eyes to create a variety of facial expressions.

12.3 Model-based image coding at BTRL

12.3.1 Introduction

The initial approach to model-based image coding was to concentrate on the analysis part of the problem that had been neglected by other workers. We also wanted to ascertain the subjective effect of synthetic facial expressions using image data from real faces. It did not seem a feasible proposition to model faces with sufficient realism for videotelephony without using some element of real image data. A method was developed in which a range of facial expressions are generated by a montage process. Sub-images containing various facial features are pasted together to form a complete face. The current method uses templates of eyes and mouths and a single full face image. Using 10 eye and 10 mouth templates and a single full face, a total of 100 different facial expressions can be produced. Figure 12.6 shows the principle. It was decided to restrict changes to the eyes and mouth only, at this stage, as it is generally accepted that these are the most important areas concerned with facial expression.

The main problems tackled were to locate the eyes and mouth in a face, to derive templates of eye and mouth areas from a head-and-shoulders moving sequence, and to select the eye and mouth templates that are the best match for the eye and mouth areas in the sequence. The main objective was to construct a moving sequence in which the movement of the eyes and mouth was a convincing approximation of the movement in the original.

12.3.2 Facial image analysis

A facial recognition algorithm developed by Nagao (1972) was employed for the task of locating the eyes and mouth in a face. In this method, a large cross-shaped mask is convolved with the image and the output thresholded to produce a binary image. The mask is shown in Fig. 12.7 and an original plus processed image in Figs 12.8(a) and

			1	1	1			
			1	1	1			
			1	1	1			
1	1	1	−4	−4	−4	1	1	1
1	1	1	−4	−4	−4	1	1	1
1	1	1	−4	−4	−4	1	1	1
			1	1	1			
			1	1	1			
			1	1	1			

Figure 12.7 The Nagao mask.

12.8(b). The effect of the mask is to low-pass filter the image and apply a Laplacian operator. Thresholding the output is equivalent to isolating negative peaks in the luminance function and produces the subjective effect of a good artist's sketch of a face. This result agrees well with the findings of Pearson and Robinson (1985) who refer to the line elements in such images as luminance valleys. The pixels that belong to a luminance valley will, in the description of the algorithm, be referred to as valley pixels.

The next stage of the algorithm requires a window to be scanned vertically down the image from top to bottom. The width of the window is the full width of the image and is eight lines high. The valley pixels in each column of the window are summed and the values stored in an array. The window is moved down the image by four lines at a time so that the window is overlapped by its previous position. The values in the array correspond to vertically oriented valleys in the image. As the window is moved down the image, an attempt is made to locate the positions of two vertical valleys that might correspond to the sides of the head or face. If two likely candidates are found, the area between them is searched for symmetrical activity corresponding to the eyes. Locating the eyes enables the axis of the face to be found; a narrow window is then placed centrally on the image extending from the eye line to the bottom of the frame. The valley pixels are summed along each row of this window, making it a sensitive indicator of the horizontal valleys marking the bottom of the nose, the lips, and the chin. The mouth can then be located by a rule-based process. It is possible that a wrong identification of a feature can occur at some stage of the process. The original algorithm of Nagao incorporated backtracking so that if this occurred, the process could be restarted

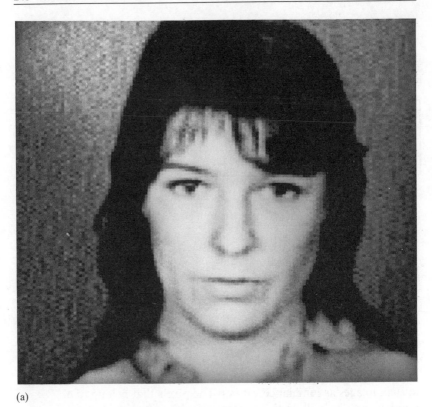

(a)

Figure 12.8(a) Original image 'Julie'.

from a previous stage and a new candidate selected. Nagao used a large sample of over 700 faces and claims that the inclusion of backtracking improves the performance significantly. However, although he claims a 90 per cent success rate for subjects displayed full face with no glasses or beard, the performance falls considerably for other cases. The algorithm, in its present form, only works when the head is vertical.

12.3.3 Feature tracking

The requirement to produce templates of the eye and mouth areas and assemble them into codebooks means that the features have to be tracked very accurately as the head moves. When the image to be displayed is constructed, the eyes and mouth have to be taken from the codebooks. The codebooks must therefore be developed so that the features are always located in the same place in the area covered by the codebook entry. If this were not the case then a noticeable jump might occur in the position of the feature between two frames. We found that a jump in the position of the eyes by only one pixel (in a 128×128 image) was visually disturbing. A similar jump in the position of a

(b)

Figure 12.8(b)   Image 'Julie' processed by a Laplacian operator and thresholded to give a binary image.

mouth is not so disturbing, probably because the mouth is a more flexible object and the concept of position, in its case, is more difficult to determine. Initially, we tried to use Nagao's algorithm to locate the features in each frame of the sequence but the positions obtained were too coarse. Therefore, after the features were located in the first frame of the sequence, they were subsequently tracked from frame to frame using a method based on template matching (Fig. 12.8(c))

12.3.4 Feature codebook generation

The method used to form the codebooks is as follows. Unlike the tracking stage, the comparisons between mouths at this stage are made using the full luminance data of the image. The mouth in the first frame is made the first entry in the codebook. The mouth in the second frame is compared with this first entry in the codebook by calculating the sum of the absolute differences of the corresponding pixel values. If this value is greater than some arbitrary threshold the mouth shape is considered to be sufficiently different to merit its inclusion into the

(c)

Figure 12.8(c) Image 'Julie' processed as in (b) and with tracking boxes around the eyebrows and mouth.

codebook. This procedure is continued for each frame of the sequence, and each time the current mouth is compared with all the mouths in the codebook. The threshold set when creating the codebook determines how many mouths will be put into it. A large threshold produces few mouths but a sequence coded using the resultant codebook has rather jerky mouth movements.

How many mouths should there be in the codebook? There is evidence that there are only about 13 visually distinct mouth shapes associated with vowel and consonant phonemes (Berger, 1972). This number must be increased to account for different facial expressions as well as for intermediate positions between the mouth fully open and the mouth closed. The moving sequences used in our own work were about 5 s in length (128 frames) and the threshold was usually set to put about 20 mouths into the codebook. The sequences used to produce the codebooks were then coded using the same codebooks, although it would be a better test to code another sequence of the subject used to produce the codebook. A synthetic sequence is created by using one full face from the original sequence and the best match from the codebook for the mouth in every frame. The best match mouth is overlaid on the full face in the correct position, the border of the mouth area being blended into the face using a cross-fading technique. The results were an adequate representation of the original as far as the mouth movements were concerned. Of course there was no head movement at this stage (Fig. 12.9).

The most noticeable defect in the coded sequence is the quantization effect due to the small number of mouths in the codebook. One mouth shape tends to be selected for a number of frames and then there is a sudden jump to a different mouth shape, which is then maintained for a few frames. In order to get over this problem, it is necessary to increase the number of mouths. Since the present method requires an exhaustive search of the codebook the time required increases in proportion.

Up until now no mention has been made as to how the above techniques could be used in a real coding scheme. One possibility is that the codebooks would be derived offline by the person using the system and either stored in the transmitter or introduced into it using a data

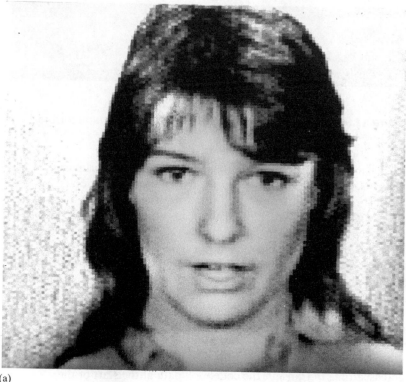

(a)

Figure 12.9(a) Synthetic face of 'Julie' with relaxed mouth from codebook of mouths

(b)

Figure 12.9(b) Synthetic face of 'Julie' with mouth shape for the 'ee' phoneme.

card. The video data would be stored in a compressed form using conventional compression techniques. When communication is established with another user, the data is transmitted down the line to the other user's receiver. If the connection is made over the ordinary analogue phone line, there is some delay until all the data is received. After this stage, visual communication can begin. The codebook is searched for the best match to the mouth in the current frame and the code for this entry transmitted. The code requires a very small number of bits depending on the number of mouths in the codebook. For a codebook with 64 entries, only 6 bits are required to code each mouth and a 25 frame/s sequence only requires 150 bits/s to code the mouth movements. The codebook can be doubled for an increase of only one bit per frame but this is at the expense of increased search time and increased time to transmit the codebook data at the start of the conversation. The latter problem could be ameliorated to some extent if the data for the people most often conversed with were stored in a personal receiver.

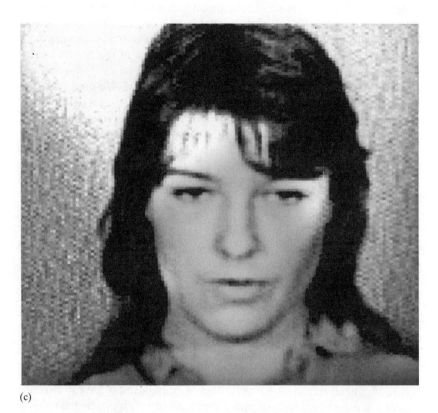

(c)

Figure 12.9(c) Synthetic face of 'Julie' with half-closed eyes entry from codebook of eyes.

12.3.5 Introducing head movements

It is obviously unsatisfactory to display a static head with moving eyes and mouth. Head movements that match the head movements of the subject at the transmission end must be introduced, but this must be done without having to transmit new video data at each frame. A 3-D head model is created using a polygon net as used to model solid objects in computer graphics. Image data from a real face is then projected on to the surface of the model using a technique called texture mapping. The net is rotated and the image values stored on its surface back-projected into the output frame. The effect of viewing the face from a different angle is produced.

Duffy and Yau (1988) use a depth map of a person's face obtained by laser scanning. From this depth map, a polygon net is created by using an automatic triangulation procedure. An image of the face of the subject from whom the depth map was obtained is projected on to the surface of the net. A technique called Phong shading is used to create the effect of fixed light sources in the model world. A quite realistic appearance is created when the model is rotated (Yau and Duffy, 1988).

It was found that, to a certain extent, it is not critical if the depth values of the net are not strictly the same as those of the person whose face is being modelled. A general head model can be used, the outline of which is conformed to match the face of the person. We used the CANDIDE model mentioned in Sec. 12.2.3 which has only 100 triangles. The incorrect depth profile only becomes apparent if the model is rotated beyond 45° from the forward-facing position. The model needs to be improved by adding more triangles but CANDIDE will be used as the basis for it. Aizawa *et al.* (1987) use a general head model that is conformed both from the full face point of view and also from the profile. It also has about 400 triangles, resulting in fairly smooth outlines.

As the CANDIDE model contains only 100 triangles, it is more amenable for implementation in real time. A fast shading algorithm was developed which would be suitable for implementation in hardware. Shading a 3-D object requires hidden surface removal, but the standard hidden surface removal algorithms were developed to cope with complex scenes containing many occlusions (Newman and Sproull, 1979). In the case of the head model most occlusions occur at one side of the head when the head turns in that direction. These occlusions correspond to a triangle turning over, an event that is easily detected. This leads to an algorithm being developed to cope with the specific case of a head model. A list is formed of triangles that have not turned over after the net is rotated and are potentially visible. The triangles are shaded in order of decreasing depth from the viewpoint and this takes care of occlusions that are not due to the previous case. An instance of this is the part of the face hidden by the nose as the head turns. This latter case occurs much less commonly than the former in objects such as the face. The slight reduction in efficiency due to having to shade the same part of the image twice is compensated for by the simplicity of the algorithm.

12.3.6 Conforming the net

The shape of the net must be conformed to match the shape of the face being used. At present, this is achieved by selecting nine key points on the face and repositioning these. An algorithm has been developed that automatically moves all the other vertices accordingly. A graphical technique is used that allows a representation of the net to be moved over the facial image being used. The net is first positioned so that the nose vertex lies over the tip of the nose on the image. It is then scaled to match approximately the size of the face. The nine key points are selected by moving a cursor to the appropriate position on the image. These points consist of the top of the head and the chin, the eye and

(a)

(b)

Figure 12.10 Synthetic face of 'Dominique' with (a) 'lip purse', (b) 'lip corner depressor'. (*Continued.*)

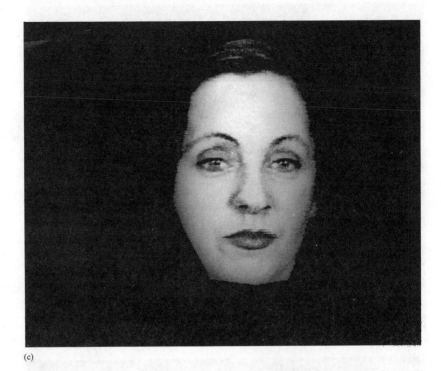

(c)

Figure 12.10(c) Synthetic face of 'Dominique' with 'eyebrow raise' action units.

side of mouth on one side of the face, and five extra points around the outline of the face on the same side. All other vertices on that side of the face are repositioned by means of a cubic transformation; the vertices on the other side of the face are moved on the assumption that the face is symmetrical. Using the FACS of Ekman and Friesen, fairly realistic facial expressions are obtained, as shown in Fig. 12.10.

12.4 Future work

12.4.1 Image synthesis

Production of facial expressions using FACS has a number of advantages over the method of using codebooks. The production of codebooks requires very accurate tracking of the features so that the feature in question remains in a fixed position in the codebook entry. If this condition is not met, there is a disturbing jitter in the position of the feature when the synthesized image is displayed. If the codebooks were built up offline, the head could be restrained in some way while this took place, but this is not really desirable. However the codebooks are derived, the data needs to be transmitted to the receiver at the beginning of the conversation and this could take an appreciable time. The production of facial expressions by manipulating the net does not require any further image data to be transmitted apart from a single full face image. Some means of recognizing the facial expression of the subject at the transmission end is required, but there should not be a need for very accurate tracking of the features. Further work needs to be done in order to produce convincing mouth movements; extra image layers showing the interior of the mouth would be sited behind the main full face image.

A more difficult problem concerns the modelling of the hair. It is obviously unsatisfactory to attempt to model every strand as the amount of processing required would be prohibitive. It would also be quite pointless to do this as the viewer would not appreciate such accuracy; what is required is to capture the overall appearance of the subject's hair. A possible way forward would be to use some generative process akin to the fractal process used to create natural landscapes in computer graphics. The basic 'unit' of hair could be considered to be a cluster of hairs (a strand) in which the individual hairs are visually inseparable. A generalized cylinder with a constant cross-section could be used as a model for a strand. A set of strands would be attached to the surface of the head in such a way that the overall shape and colour of the hair matches that of the subject. A randomizing function could be used to allow a strand to break up into 'substrands' and this process could continue down to single hairs depending on the processing power available at the receiver. By this method, it may be possible to avoid the unrealism of making the hair look like a solid object.

12.4.2 Feature extraction

The most difficult problems to solve concern the reliable extraction of information from facial images. Despite many years of research there is no reliable way of automatically making measurements on facial images for the purpose of facial recognition. The method of Nagao mentioned above is not sufficiently flexible or robust, and other model-based methods for recognition of people have since been developed. David Hogg of Sussex University has developed an algorithm for locating a walking human being in a moving sequence (Hogg, 1984). The model used in the method is constructed from a number of cylinders in the shape of a person. The first two frames of a sequence are differenced in order to locate moving edges. The model is scaled and positioned to match its edges optimally with the moving edges in the scene. The next frame is examined to determine how the model can be moved so that it remains aligned as well as possible with the edges of the moving person. The motion of the cylinders is constrained so that they only execute natural walking movements. The algorithm has been shown to track a walking person successfully, although it is susceptible to noise and clutter in the image.

A version of the algorithm could be used for tracking the head and facial features in a model-based coding system. The main problem lies in processing the image so that features are extracted which can be matched successfully with the model used. The low-level vision process requires moving from an array of luminance values to an array containing indicators of actual object features. The original array of luminance values is highly dependent on the lighting conditions in the scene.

A method developed by Sexton and Dennis (1988) has been used to find the best arrangement of features in a facial image corresponding to the eyes, nose, and mouth. In common with Nagao's algorithm, a backtrack search is used. Initially, a feature is selected as a candidate for an eye by virtue of its position in the frame. A search is made within some angular range for a region that could possibly correspond to the other eye. If a match is found, the search continues for the next feature. If a match is not found, the procedure backtracks so that another match is searched for at the previous stage. If such a match is found, the procedure continues to search for the next feature. After a match is found for the last feature, the initial feature selected is searched for within the prescribed error margin. This accounts for the possibility that spurious matches may have been made at one extreme of the error margin.

12.4.3 Using neural networks

Recently there has been a surge of interest in the use of artificial neural systems for solving some of the problems that have eluded conventional artificial intelligence methods. The use of rule-based systems for automatic facial recognition may not be ultimately successful. Although most faces have the same general structure, there are great variations between specific features and overall shape. Neural networks have the ability to learn from examples and this indicates the attractive possibility that, after training on a large set of faces, the net may be able to generalize sufficiently to recognize a new face.

The WISARD system developed by Wilkie, Stonham, and Aleksander is quite successful at distinguishing between faces and can even distinguish between different expressions on the same face (Aleksander and Burnett, 1983). This is quite a remarkable ability as WISARD is a very basic form of neural net. A more physiologically plausible system is that of Grossberg and Mingolla (1987) which is put forward as a model of low-level human vision. Conventional algorithms for low-level vision can usually be divided into two classes. The edges can be extracted in order to locate boundaries, which then define regions; otherwise regions can be located by segmentation, which then defines boundaries. Neither of these approaches is really suitable for faces as the edges are rather soft and broken, and there are few clear cut regions. The Grossberg–Mingolla model effectively combines both approaches in parallel to derive a good representation of the shape of objects in the form of 'boundary webs' and might be capable of dealing with facial images.

12.5 Summary

Model-based image coding has emerged as a research area within image processing in the last few years. Results obtained so far have shown that there is potential for transmission of moving head-and-shoulder images at bit rates around 1 kbit/s. Several workers have shown interesting results producing synthetic head animations, but facial feature extraction is lagging considerably behind the synthesis work. Much interest has grown up recently in the use of neural networks for automatic vision. Certainly, better automatic vision procedures are necessary if the work is to come to fruition.

This new area requires the integration of state-of-the-art techniques in computer graphics and animation, computer vision and telecommunications hardware. As well as its importance for future visual telecommunications it will also stretch each of the above-mentioned disciplines to the limit and, hopefully, produce results that will be of benefit to each of these areas in general.

References

Aizawa K., Harashima H. and Saito T. (1987) 'Model-based synthetic image coding—Construction of a 3-D model of a person's face', *Picture Coding Symposium (PCS '87)*, Stockholm, paper 3–11.

Aleksander I. and Burnett P. (1983) *Reinventing Man: Robot Becomes Reality*, Kogan Page, London.

Berger K. W. (1972) *Speechreading: Principles and Methods*, National Education Press, Baltimore, MD, pp. 73–107.

Duffy N. D. and Yau J. F. S. (1988) 'Facial image reconstruction and manipulation from measurements obtained using a structured lighting technique', *Pattern Recognition Letters*, vol. 7, pp. 239–43.

Ekman P. and Friesen W. V. (1977) *Manual for the Facial Action Coding System*, Consulting Psychologists Press, Palo Alto, Calif.

Forchheimer R. and Fahlander O. (1983) 'Low bit rate coding through animation', *Abstracts of the Picture Coding Symposium (PCS '83)*, pp. 113–14.

Grossberg S. and Mingolla E. (1987) 'Neural dynamics of surface perception: boundary webs and shape-from-shading', *Computer Vision, Graphics and Image Processing*, vol. 37, pp. 116–65.

Hogg D. C. (1984) 'Interpreting images of a known moving object', PhD thesis, University of Sussex.

Musmann H. G., Hötter M. and Ostermann J. (1989) 'Object-oriented analysis–synthesis coding of moving images', *Image Communication*, vol. 1, no. 2, pp. 117–138.

Nagao M. (1972) 'Picture Recognition and Data Structure', in *Graphic Languages*, Rosenfeld N. (ed), North Holland, Amsterdam, pp. 48–69.

Newman W. M. and Sproull R. F. (1979) *Principles of Interactive Computer Graphics*, McGraw-Hill, New York.

Parke F. I. (1982) 'Parameterised models for facial animation', *IEEE Computer Graphics and Applications*, vol. OGA-12 pp. 61–68.

Pearson D. E. and Robinson J. A. (1985) 'Visual communication at very low data rates', *Proceedings of the IEEE*, vol. 73, pp. 795–812.

Sexton G. G. and Dennis T. J. (1988) 'Primary feature identification in facial images', *International Workshop of 64 kbit/s Coding of Moving Video*, Hannover, paper 8–2.

Yau J. F. S. and Duffy N. D. (1988) 'A texture-mapping approach to 3-D facial image synthesis', *6th Annual EUROGRAPHICS (UK) Conference*, University of Sussex, pp. 129–134.

13 Packet video

MOHAMMED GHANBARI

13.1 Introduction

Most of the work on the digital coding of moving images (Chap. 11) has assumed that the network accepts bits at a fixed rate. Video source coders are therefore required to limit the generated data rate to be below the channel capacity of the network. This is usually done by controlling the amount of generated data at the expense of introducing some distortion.

The relation between the introduced distortion, D, and the minimum achievable bit rate, R, is given by the rate distortion function $R(D)$ (Berger, 1971). For moving images with various degrees of motion and spatial resolution, a family of rate distortion functions can be drawn, as shown in Fig. 13.1. If, in this figure, the channel is bounded to a constant bit rate, the received pictures incur a variable distortion, as shown by line AB. On the other hand, constant-quality pictures can be received if the allocated channel bandwidth can vary according to the bit rate requirement of the source (line CD). This is a new aspect in telecommunications and recent developments in network architectures have made it possible to realize such a goal (Hughes and Atkins, 1979). A packet network is a common form of network capable of accepting bits at a variable rate and the new field has become known as *packet video*.

In this chapter, various aspects of transmitting video signals through variable bit rate (VBR) channels are examined. These include examining the bit rate variability of coded video signals, their transmission through VBR channels, and tackling the problems arising from VBR transmission. The advantages of such a procedure over conventional fixed bit rate (FBR) transmission are outlined.

13.2 Nature of bit rate variability in digitally coded images

Images are not inherently variable in their bit rate. In studio PCM television, for example, the bit rate is a fixed 216 Mbits/s. Variability may arise from the choice of a particular data compression technique. Techniques such as DPCM, transform coding, sub-band coding and

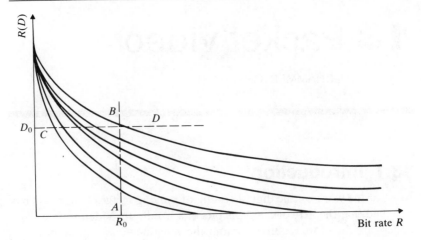

Figure 13.1 Rate distortion functions.

vector quantization tend to produce a fixed bit rate, but if they are made adaptive or are followed by a variable word-length coder (VLC), the rate becomes moderately variable, due to spatial and temporal variations in scene content.

A coding technique that produces a very variable bit rate is conditional replenishment (CR). Here the rate is a function of unpredictable frame-to-frame changes, which are largely due to movement, but may also occur because of scene or illumination changes. The primary sources of bit rate variation in this coding technique are local spatial variations, local movement and large-area movement in the scene (Ghanbari and Pearson, 1989). Bit rate variations due to local spatial/temporal changes can be adequately smoothed by a small buffer for transmission over fixed-rate channels, but those due to large area movement can only be smoothed if buffers of a size corresponding to perhaps tens of seconds are used, which introduces unacceptable delay.

A typical bit-rate variation of television signals coded by the CR technique using DPCM in the moving areas is shown in Fig. 13.2. For this figure the source material was obtained off-air from one of the four UK broadcast channels (ITV) for almost 72 h. For almost every 6 min of actual programme, 48 consecutive television frames (nearly 2 s) have been processed (Ghanbari and Pearson, 1988). The instantaneous variations in the bit rate are then smoothed by a buffer of 48 frames. This has been done partly in order to be able to present all the recorded information in one page, but for two additional reasons.

Firstly, it is not just the instantaneous peaks that are of interest to network performance engineers, but also how often they are sustained for relatively long periods, as is indicated by (i) the high peak value of the 48-frame mean and (ii) the fact that the 1-frame mean is greater than 4.2 times the long term mean for 0.1 per cent of the time.

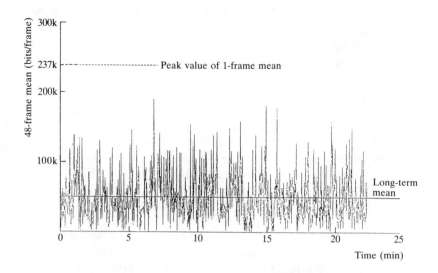

Figure 13.2   Instantaneous bit rate of conditional replenishment coded television signals (from Ghanbari and Pearson, 1988).

Secondly, although buffering can be used to smooth instantaneous peaks in the coded data before input to the network, large buffers as big as 48 frames still leave significant residual variations in bit rate. Thus a buffer that holds nearly 2 s of the signal is not sufficient to smooth bit rate variations in broadcast television. This emphasizes the need for transmitting coded video signals through VBR channels.

13.3 Transmission of VBR video signals

The main characteristic of the existing circuit-switched network is that the bit rate offered by the channel is fixed. For video sources with a relatively high activity index (peak to mean bit rate ratio), this requires that the channel has to accommodate the peak bit rate of the signal, if no picture degradation is desired. However, this is uneconomical and the current method of transmitting video signals is to lower the peak data rate, either at the expense of introducing some distortions, or smoothing the data rate by an elastic buffer.

As has been explained in Sec. 13.2, only a portion of the rate variations can be smoothed by a reasonable buffer. There are occasions where high data rates are sustained for a long period so that smoothing is no longer possible (Fig. 13.2) . In these cases instead of smoothing the data rate by increasing buffer sizes, the generated data rate is controlled. This is done by monitoring the rate of fullness of a reasonably sized buffer via a feedback loop, and then trying to reduce the generated data rate as the buffer fills up. Data reduction is done either by increasing the movement detector threshold, coarse quantization of sampled data, coarse quantization of sample intervals (subsampling), or in severe cases by frame skipping. These conditions introduce visible distortions which are undesirable, especially for low bit rate video application. For example, in 64 kbits/s videotelephony, the frame rate has to be decreased to perhaps 1 frame/s if violent motion arises, which causes very objectionable distortion.

If the network can absorb all or most of the rate variability, then there is no need to control the data rate, or to use any elastic buffer. With no rate control feedback to the coder the picture quality is therefore likely to be more constant as a function of time. Elimination of the smoothing buffer reduces the round trip delay, which is desirable in two-way videoconferencing. These features—constant picture quality and less delay—are attractive aspects of the new network architectures which allow transmission of video data in a VBR form.

VBR transmission of video signals through these networks is realized by dynamically varying the amount of transmitted information per unit time T. Since there is no fixed route connecting a video source to its destination, the video data have to be packed in groups and stamped with destination addresses. These packets can then be identified at the destination by the labelled addresses.

Besides achieving a better subjective picture quality in a VBR system than an FBR one, the average transmission bandwidth can be significantly reduced. For example, consider a multiplexed VBR network where each video source generates a varying number of packets, depending on its activity during time T. Assuming that high activity sources do not entirely coincide with each other, then a high packet rate from one source may be compensated for by a low packet rate from another. If the number of sources sharing the transmission channel is large, then the channel rate is less variable, despite the variable packet rate of individual sources. The average channel rate for VBR transmission is then almost the mean packet rate, whereas for FBR transmission with the same picture quality it is the peak bit rate. This is a very significant advantage of VBR over FBR transmission.

For video sources with activity index defined as the peak to mean bit rate ratio, the bandwidth compression advantage of a VBR over an FBR channel can be equal to the activity index multiplied by U, where U is the utilization factor. U dictates how efficiently the multiplexed VBR channel can be used (Hughes and Atkins, 1979). It is very much dependent on the type of multiplexing technique used and is roughly equal to 0.5 and 0.8 respectively for synchronous and asynchronous multiplexing, which are described below (see also Sec. 13.6).

13.3.1 Synchronous transmission links

Frame-synchronous time division multiplex (TDM) links are those in which the multiplexed signals are subjected to the discipline of a regular frame structure. (The frame here should be distinguished from the frame of video signals; the same word is unfortunately used for both in common practice.) Each frame is divided into a fixed number of time-slots that may be used in various ways. In a conventional TDM system, each source channel is allocated a particular time-slot for the duration of the call, an arrangement that is referred to as 'circuit switching'. One possibility, used when the source channels are idle for a significant fraction of the time, is to allocate a time-slot only when the source channel is active. This is the basis of digital speech interpolation (DSI) systems (Wu, 1984), used on transoceanic cables and satellite links. As a further development, each source channel may be allocated a number of slots in the frame according to the instantaneous requirements of the source channel, an arrangement that provides an effective means of multiplexing signals from conditional replenishment video coders.

In these latter systems, there is a possibility that the instantaneous demands from the source channels exceed the number of time-slots in the frame. This results in a condition known as 'freeze-out', and the loading must be kept down to a value that leads to an acceptably low probability of freeze-out. Furthermore, additional signalling is required to indicate the relationship between the time-slot and the source channels, and this constitutes a further overhead on the system. It can, in some circumstances, be reduced by signalling the difference in channel allocation but the signalling must be well guarded against transmission errors, since the knock-on effect of a signalling error could cause severe disruption to the communication channels.

13.3.2 Asynchronous transmission links

If there is no regular structure on the multiplex link, the system is usually referred to as asynchronous transfer mode (ATM) or 'packet switched'. The output of each source is assembled into packets and sent on the multiplex link as soon as it becomes free. If a packet cannot be sent immediately, it is stored until it can be sent. Thus loss of information in a synchronous system is replaced by delay. In practice, an asynchronous system suffers loss if the buffer store overflows or, in the case of a real-time system, if the delay exceeds the maximum time acceptable to the user.

Each packet must carry an address, which constitutes a transmission overhead. The address need not contain the full information needed to route the packet through to its destination. If a virtual circuit is set up at the beginning of a call, subsequent packets need only carry a reference to that call and the necessary routing information is obtained from look-up tables at each switching node.

13.3.3 Prioritization

One of the advantages of a VBR system over an FBR one is the higher flexibility of the former in handling mixed services. In particular, VBR systems have a high tolerance to the inevitable uncertainties in the forecast of traffic mix. This is particularly important for video services of different standards, such as HDTV, broadcast television, videoconferencing, very low bit rate television, and so on.

The other advantage of the VBR systems relating to mixed services is the possibility of assigning high priority to delay-sensitive services such as video and speech signals. In this case, when the traffic load is high, transmission of delay-tolerant services (e.g. data) is temporarily abandoned and the extra bandwidth is made available to delay-sensitive services.

The philosophy of prioritization can be extended between the delay-sensitive services themselves, or even within a particular service. In the former case it prevents the problem of one service destroying the continuity of the other. For example, the high peak bit rates of coded video signals have severe adverse effects on the continuity of speech signals, unless provision is made to protect the integrity of individual calls under a range of network conditions. Conversely, the presence of a large number of voice calls (which are more in number than video calls) on the network may lead to excessive degradation of a video call.

In the second case, packets from a particular source are prioritized with respect to each other, in the same way that packets relating to different services are prioritized. This method can improve the quality of teleservice under overload conditions. For example, in a sub-band coding method (see Chap. 11), each band can be transmitted with a different level of priority, and the effect of channel overloading can be confined to loss of high-frequency bands, which has a very marginal effect on the quality of the received picture, rather than losing part of the picture (Karlsson and Vetterli, 1989).

13.4 Error and delay in VBR networks

An ideal network should convey video information from a coder to the decoder without any error, but may introduce a short, constant delay. However, in a multiuser network this situation is rare; the received information is sometimes erroneous and the delay is in general variable. Since video signals are continuous in time, the delay variation as well as errors cause some perceived distortions. Network engineers have to keep these spurious effects to an acceptable limit.

13.4.1 Channel errors

Digital networks are not immune to errors. Some networks, such as satellite and terrestrial radio links, are more error prone than others.

For video applications, the amount of permissible error depends on the type of data compression technique used in coding video signals. For example, highly compressed video data, such as those of a motion-compensated interframe conditional replenishment coder, are far more sensitive to errors than those from a simple open-loop coder.

For packet video networks the effect of channel errors may cause additional problems. Errors in the header of a packet can lead to lost packets in video services, as retransmission of corrupted packets would be too late to be useful. Header errors may deliver the packet to a wrong destination. However, in practical networks, the probability of an erroneous header not being detected is negligible.

13.4.2 Delay variation

In a multiuser network delay variations experienced by a particular service are dependent on the coder, number of users, transmission media, channel capacity, switching technique, etc. This delay should be kept constant, which is usually done by introducing a buffer store at the receiver to pad out the delay variations.

Since video signals are delay sensitive and cannot be delayed beyond a certain limit, the maximum constant delay should be limited. The maximum delay limit for video signals depends on that of the audio ones, as the former delay is measured relative to the latter. According to a CCIR report (1987), the human vision delay tolerance with respect to speech should not exceed 20 ms if the sound is advanced with respect to picture, or 40 ms if the sound is delayed with respect to picture. However, in practice, due to video codec buffers (e.g. coding/decoding delay plus the smoothing buffer), it is unlikely that video can lead voice packets. Also, the extra video coding delay may just reach the 20 ms limit, leaving no permissible relative delay between these two services.

In a VBR network the total delay can be divided into a number of components—codec delay, transmission delay, switching delay.

Codec delay

The delay introduced by a video coder/decoder can vary from a pel in a DPCM codec to several television lines in the transform coding and sub-band codecs (sub-band coders with parallel pipelines and limited tap filters). For example, in a practical, highly efficient, conditional replenishment coder with hybrid DPCM/DCT in the moving parts of the picture, the major part of the delay is the transformation and motion estimation delays. The former is at least equal to the number of television lines, corresponding to the vertical size of the DCT matrix. With the fast transform algorithms, this delay may increase by a factor of 2.5 (Chen et al., 1976). The delay due to motion estimation is at least equal to the motion speed in the vertical direction, if motion estimation is performed by parallel pipelines. Other coding delays such as quantization, variable length coding and packetization are relatively small.

Besides coding/decoding delay, it is necessary to introduce an elastic buffer at the coder and necessarily at the decoder to smooth the bit rate variation. In Sec. 13.5 it is shown how smoothing the bit rate variations (lowering the burstiness of the video data or peak to mean ratio) can reduce the lost packet rate.

A good buffer size for non-interlaced videoconferencing applications in terms of delay time is of the order of one-ninth of the picture size (Ghanbari and Pearson, 1989). This is almost equal to 4 ms for pictures with common intermediate format (CIF) standard (Okubo, 1987). Thus for these pictures a motion-compensated CR coder using an 8×8 DCT in the moving areas can cause a total codec plus smoothing buffer delay of the order of $2(4 + 2.5) + 1 = 14$ ms, assuming that the transformation algorithm is fast and the motion speed is 8 pels/frame. However, this may be a minimum time delay introduced by those practical coders suitable for packet video applications. In practice, the larger transformation matrix and elastic buffer sizes and the complexity of motion estimation increase the coding delay up to the permissible delay limit of 20 ms with respect to the coding of speech signals, as the other sources of delay are common in both packet video and speech.

Transmission delay

The amount of transmission delay depends on the size and speed of a network and transmission media. For local area networks this delay can be very low, but in wide area networks containing a satellite link, it can be increased to over 240 ms. For these types of networks not much is left from the total delay budget for the other sources of delay.

Switching delay

The switching delay is at least equal to the time required to read the header of each packet to switch to the correct outlet. In high-speed networks, this delay is small, because the multiplex links usually operate at a much higher speed than a video coder at the inlet to the link.

In addition to switching delay, packets usually encounter queuing delay in network nodes. Packets arriving at irregular intervals pass through one or more switching stages and are then queued for transmission on the outlet. For a network with one multiplex link and exponential packet arrival rate (see Sec. 13.5), this delay can be evaluated using an M/D/1 queuing model.

13.5 Coding of video signals for ATM networks

As we have seen, a conditional replenishment coding technique is very suitable for VBR transmission but it is sensitive to transmission errors. Practical solutions have already been found to the problem of transmitting videoconference signals using this form of coding over noisy satellite channels, using special protection for the field and line synchronizing information (Carr *et al.*, 1982). We may imagine a generalization of this procedure whereby unequal error protection codes are used to provide progressively decreasing protection for field start codes, moving area cluster addresses and motion-adaptive codes used within the moving area, in an appropriate order. If this information can be packetized with different levels of priority, then, with increasing traffic, it may be possible to arrange for video circuits to degrade gracefully.

One method of generating video data with different levels of priority is the 'two-layer' coding technique (Ghanbari, 1989). In this method of coding a conditional-replenishment coder is composed of two stages or two layers. The first layer generates data that are transmitted with a high priority and should be accommodated in a guaranteed channel of an ATM network (no packet loss). The second layer, which codes the difference between the input and the output of the first layer, produces 'add-on' information to improve picture quality. This data is transmitted with a lower priority and may be discarded in the network if congestion arises. Figure 13.3 shows a block diagram of this two-layer coder and decoder.

An ATM network that can support two levels of priority is the Orwell ring. 'Orwell' is a flexible protocol and was primarily designed to carry integrated mixed speech and data services on a slotted ring (Falconer and Adams, 1985). By controlling access to the slots from the nodes, it has the potential to provide guaranteed bandwidth for speech sources.

To transmit a two-layer coded signal through a network like the Orwell ring, the output of the first layer (the 'guaranteed' packets) are treated as speech signals. Here, every new video call tests the ring for a guaranteed bandwidth before setting up a call, and is blocked if this bandwidth is not available. Once the video call has been set up, however, the connection within the allocated bandwidth is guaranteed for its duration. In this protocol the 'add-on' information or 'enhancement' packets can be treated like data services, with the exception that they are discarded from the queue if they suffer excessive delay prior to transmission.

Given that the network can guarantee packets produced by the first layer, the loss of packets from the second layer does not cause picture break-up or any objectionable distortions. For example, a two-layer

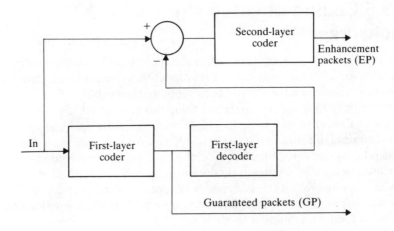

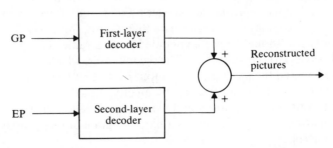

Figure 13.3   A block diagram of a two-layer coder/decoder.

codec with a motion-compensated hybrid DPCM/DCT in the base layer and DPCM in the second layer can be very resilient to packet losses from the second layer (Ghanbari, 1989). Figures 13.4 and 13.5 show the quality of coded pictures by this method for 10 and 100 per cent packet losses respectively from the second layer. For these pictures the portion of the guaranteed bandwidth is 20 per cent of the total bit rate. However, if the network cannot guarantee such a bandwidth, it is still possible to apply unequal error protection coding for the first-layer data, and possibly a less non-recursive form of coding for the second layer.

Recently there has been growing interest in two-layer coding. Within a short period, various methods have been devised for the realization of two-layer coders (IWPV, 1990). In particular, an adapted H.261 two-layer codec that can maintain compatibility between a two-layer ATM network and existing circuit-switched networks has been introduced (Ghanbari, 1990). A major advantage of this two-layer coder is its simplicity. The base layer uses an H.261 standard video codec and

Figure 13.4 Two-layer coded picture with 10 per cent packet loss rate in the non-guaranteed channel.

the second layer is simply a requantizer, which finely quantizes the quantization distortion of the base layer. To use this codec in a circuit-switched environment, the data from the second layer is discarded and the base layer data rate is increased. A hardware prototype of this coding method has been constructed (Ghanbari *et al.*, 1990). This provides the possibility of performing real-time comparisons between VBR and FBR systems.

13.6 Statistical analysis of coded video signals

The analysis and simulation of VBR multiplexed links is facilitated if simplified forms can be used to describe the characteristics of the coded video signals. One of the main characteristics of these signals is the bit rate profile. The bit rate profile is the probability density function of the instantaneous bit rate and varies with picture material and the type of coding system used. With the coding method mentioned in Sec. 13.2 (CR with DPCM coding in the moving areas of pictures), the relative occurrences of bit rate averaged over a frame are shown in Fig. 13.6.

Figure 13.5 Two-layer coded picture with 100 per cent packet loss rate in the non-guaranteed channel.

This figure shows that if the generated data is Huffman coded (as is usually the case), the shape of the bit rate profile tends to be nearly Gaussian, whereas the profile for non-Huffman coded data is approximately negative-exponential. If two-layer coding is used, the bit rate profile of the base layer is almost an impulse and that of the second layer is similar to the one given in Fig. 13.6, but with a different bit rate (Ghanbari, 1989).

Considering the close proximity of the two curves and the fact that the negative exponential function can be approximated by a staircase function, as shown in Fig. 13.7, the bit rate profile can be represented in a very simple form. In this case, if it is assumed that each television frame can give rise to a number of packets (or time slots) up to a maximum of Q_m and at least one packet is sent in each frame, then the probability of Q packets being generated in each frame is given by a truncated geometric distribution, i.e.

$$P(Q) = \frac{a^{Q-1}(1-a)}{1-a^{Q_m}} \qquad 1 \le Q \le Q_m \qquad (13.1)$$

The constant a is adjusted to provide an acceptable fit to the distribution in Fig. 13.7 (e.g. $a = 0.75$ in this figure).

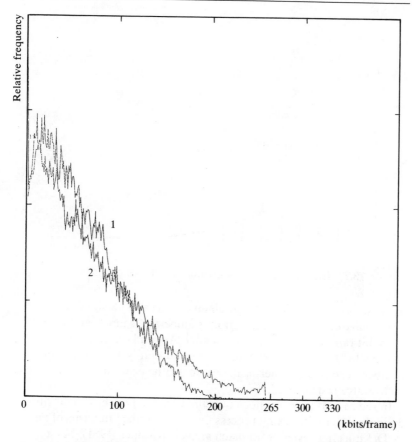

Figure 13.6 Bit rate profile of television signals. Graph '1': Huffman coded with mean bit rate = 58 kbits/frame. Graph '2': non-Huffman coded with mean bit rate = 68.5 kbits/frame.

The above simplification provides a basis for the analysis of a packet multiplexed system. In a synchronous system, a straightforward analysis (see Appendix) shows that the probability of freeze-out, i.e., of generating more packets than the available number of slots, S, in a multiplexed frame period, is given by a negative-binomial series:

$$P(Q > S) = \frac{1}{(1 - a^{Q_m})^C} \sum_{i=S+1}^{CQ_m} \binom{i + C - 1}{C - 1} a^{i-C} (1 - a)^C \quad (13.2)$$

where C is the number of source channels and a is defined as before (fitting a staircase curve).

If slot allocation signalling is ignored, the channel loading ρ is given by

$$\rho = \frac{Cm}{S} \quad (13.3)$$

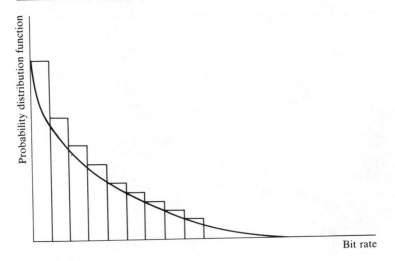

Figure 13.7   Simplified bit rate profile of video signals.

where m is the mean bit rate per channel. Figure 13.8 shows the probability of freeze-out for various numbers of sources and peak to mean bit rate ratios of a source channel. As can be seen for a given channel loading, ρ, the probability of freeze-out is decreased if the number of source channels is increased, or the peak to mean bit rate for each source is decreased.

In the case of asynchronous transmission, analysis has so far proved difficult. The multiplexing process may be described in terms of an M/D/1 queuing system with batch arrivals (Cooper, 1981), but a considerable extension to the theory would be required to derive an accurate expression for lost packets. Recourse has therefore been made to a simplified model. Assume that there are already C sources in the multiplexed channel, and the human vision system can tolerate delays of up to n television frames. In a steady-state condition, it can be said that an asynchronous system is similar to a synchronous system with $(n + 1)$ times the number of sources and $(n + 1)$ times the number of channel slots. Thus the probability of lost packets for an asynchronous system can be written as for a synchronous system but with the new parameters:

$$P(\text{lost}) = \frac{1}{(1 - a^{Q_m})^G} \sum_{i=H+1}^{GQ_m} \binom{i + G - 1}{G - 1} a^{i-G} (1 - a)^G \qquad (13.4)$$

where $H = (n + 1)S$, $G = (n + 1)C$, and n is the frame delay.

As for the synchronous system, increasing the number of channels and reducing the peak to mean bit rate ratios decreases the probability of lost packets. Also, increasing the tolerable queuing delay (n in Eq. 13.4) reduces the probability of packet loss.

In an asynchronous system a better result for the probability of lost

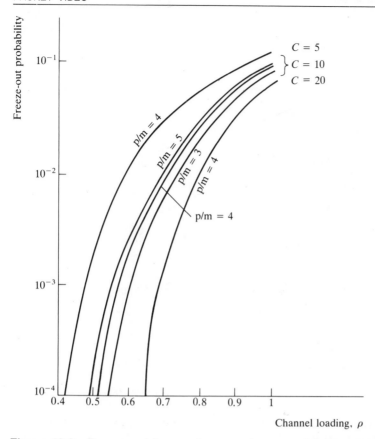

Figure 13.8 Freeze-out for synchronous frame multiplex systems. *C* is the number of channels and *p*/*m* the peak/mean bit-rate ratio.

packets can be obtained from simulations. Using the simplified bit rate profile model as a basis for simulations, the queuing delay distributions can be derived. In this case packets exceeding the capacity of the transmission channel are buffered and put in a queue for future transmission (rather than being lost as in the synchronous case). Thus as the load in the network increases, the queuing delay also increases. Figure 13.9 shows the queuing delay distributions for a 10-channel multiplex link. In the figure, increasing the channel loading factor increases the probability of queuing delay.

From Fig. 13.9, knowing the delay tolerance limit, the probability of lost packets can be calculated. Due to the delay tolerance, the probability of lost packets in an asynchronous system is usually less than that of the synchronous one, or for the same lost packet rate the transmission efficiency of the asynchronous system is higher than that of the synchronous one. This can be justified by comparing Figs 13.8 and 13.9. For example, for a 10-channel multiplex link, if the delay tolerance limit is set to one television frame period, then a channel

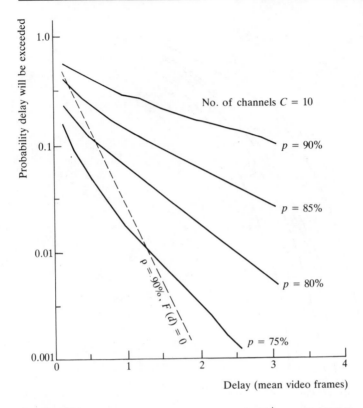

Figure 13.9 Delay in asynchronous transfer mode (ATM) systems. (From Ghanbari *et al.*, 1988)

loading of 0.8 for an asynchronous system gives the same error performance as that of a synchronous one with a loading factor of 0.5.

13.7 Interaction between video coding and VBR networks

In a circuit-switched network, the only network factor to be considered is the bit rate provided by a multiplexed channel. The coding technique and parameters can then be chosen to provide the best service to the user within the channel. When variable bit rate networks are considered, the situation becomes more complex. Both synchronous and asynchronous time multiplexing may be considered and the network parameters in each case have a strong influence on the performance of the teleservice. A range of coding techniques may be considered for use in such a system. The characteristics of the video signal, the coding technique, and the network characteristics then act together in a complex manner to affect the quality of service as experienced by the user (Ghanbari *et al.*, 1988).

As we have already seen, the effect of networks on video codecs is that the codecs should be designed to be tolerant of packet loss. This causes the design of video codecs for ATM networks to be substantially different from those for conventional fixed bit rate systems. Two-layer coding is one example of this interaction.

The other interaction between video coders and VBR networks is the effect of video signal statistics upon the network performance. Basically, VBR networks are designed according to the characteristics of video signals. As was explained in Sec. 13.6, the bit rate profile of video signals can determine certain parameters of the VBR network such as freeze-out (or delay), loading, etc. In particular it was shown that increasing the peak to mean bit rate ratio of video signals leads to higher packet loss rate in a multiplex link. The other interaction between the network and video coded signals is the effect of correlation between bit rates generated in successive frames. Periods of rapid movement are likely to persist for several frames and may overload the network.

The interframe correlation between the bit rates generated in a conditional replenishment coding technique, averaged over one television frame, is shown in Fig. 13.10 (Ghanbari et al., 1988). This is almost a negative exponential function, and can be better illustrated on a linear–log basis. In a synchronous system, there are no memory effects, so that interframe correlation does not affect the performance of the network. However, in an asynchronous system, the interframe correlation tends to increase the queuing delay and affect the link performance (Ghanbari et al., 1988). The performance of the link with zero interframe correlation (without correction) is shown by the broken line in Fig. 13.9.

13.8 Summary

The bit rates of interframe coded television signals exhibit a wide degree of variation. Variable bit rate (VBR) networks are therefore best suited for transmission of these signals. Compared with conventional fixed bit rate (FBR) systems, VBR transmission has the advantage of conveying video information at constant quality and can give a lower mean bit rate for the same subjective quality as FBR. This improvement is more significant with the asynchronous transfer mode (ATM) systems than with synchronous ones. The main drawback with VBR systems is the possibility of packet losses due to congestion on the network. This is minimized if prioritization is used in a multiservice system, where delay-sensitive services (e.g. video) are transmitted with a high priority and transmission of delay-tolerant ones (e.g. data) can even be temporarily abandoned if congestion arises. Prioritization within the components of a service makes the coding system very robust to packet

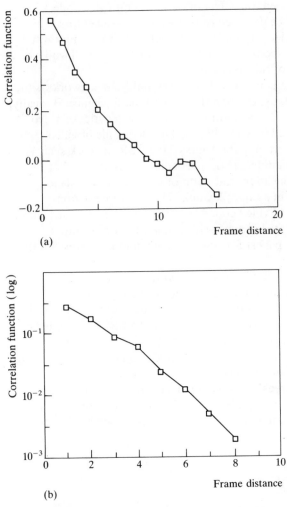

Figure 13.10   Correlation coefficient functions of bit rates generated in successive frames: (a) linear–linear scale, (b) log–linear scale.

losses. With the growing interest in two-layer coding, the technique has potential application as a means of video coding for ATM networks.

References

Berger T. (1971) *Rate Distortion Theory—A Mathematical Basis for Data Compression*, Prentice Hall, Englewood Cliffs, NJ.

Carr M. D., Temine J. P., Clapp C. S. K. and Jolivet J (1982) 'Practical problems of implementing a conditional replenishment video codec over an error prone channel', *Proc. IEE International Conference on Image Processing and its Applications*, University of York, p. 93.

CCIR (1987) Interim report 1081, November.

Chen W., Smith C. H. and Fralick S. C. (1976) 'A fast computational algorithm for the discrete cosine transform', *IEEE Transactions on Communications*, vol. COM-25, no. 9.

Cooper R. B. (1981) *Introduction to Queueing Theory*, North Holland, Amsterdam.

Falconer R. M. and Adams J. L. (1985) 'Orwell: a protocol for an integrated se vices local network', *British Telecom Technology Journal*, vol. 3, no. 4.

Ghar. oari M. (1989) 'Two-layer coding of video signals for VBR networks', *IEEE Journal on Selected Areas in Communications*, vol. SAC-7, no. 5, pp. 771–81.

Ghanbari M. (1990) 'An adaptive video codec for ATM networks', *Abstracts of the 3rd International Workshop on Packet Video*, Morristown, NJ.

Ghanbari M. and Pearson D. E. (1988) 'Variable bit rate transmission of television signals', *Electronics Letters*, vol. 24, no. 7, pp. 392–93.

Ghanbari M. and Pearson D. E. (1989) 'Components of bit rate variation in videoconference signals', *Electronics Letters*, vol. 25, no. 4, pp. 285–86.

Ghanbari M., Hughes C. J., Pearson D. E. and Xiong J. (1988) 'The Interaction between video encoding and variable bit rate networks', *Proc. Fifth IERE International Conference on Digital Processing of Signals in Communications*, Loughborough, pp. 125–31.

Ghanbari M., Beaumont D. O. and Morrison D. G. (1990) 'A hardware realisation of an adapted H.261 type codec for use on an ATM network', *Abstracts of the International Picture Coding Symposium*, Cambridge, Mass.

Hughes C. J. and Atkins J. W. (1979) 'Virtual circuit switching for multi-service operation', *Proc. International Switching Symposium (ISS '79)*, Paris, pp. 344–50.

IWPV (1990) *Abstracts of the 3rd International Workshop on Packet Video*, Morristown, NJ.

Karlsson G. and Vetterli M. (1989) 'Packet video and its integration into the network architecture', *IEEE Journal on Selected Areas in Communications*, vol. SAC-7, no. 5, pp. 739–51.

Okubo S. (1987) 'Work progress in special group on coding for visual telephony', *Abstracts of the International Picture Coding Symposium*, Stockholm, pp. 153–4.

Wu W. W. (1984) *Elements of Digital Satellite Communications*, Computer Science Press.

Appendix

Modelling a coded video source

In Fig. 13.7, step Q represents the probability of generating Q packets. Assume that each video source can give rise to at least one packet and a new packet is generated if all the preceding packets are already generated. If the probability of generating a new packet is a, then the probability of generating:

1 packet is	$P(1) = (1 - a)$
2 packets is	$P(2) = (1 - a)a$
Q packets is	$P(k) = (1 + a)a^{Q-1}$

This assumes that the source can generate an unlimited number of packets. However, if the maximum number of generated packets is limited to Q_m, then the probability of generating Q packets is

$$P(Q) = \frac{(1-a)\,a^{Q-1}}{(1-a^{Q_m})} \qquad Q \le Q_m \qquad (13A.1)$$

which is a truncated geometric distribution.

Synchronous multiplexing

For simplicity we assume C source channels have already seized a synchronous multiplexed link with a capacity of S slots frame^{-1}. Here the multiplexed frame period is taken to be equal to one television frame. Freeze-out then occurs if the number of generated packets from C sources exceeds S slots. Assuming that all the C sources are independent of each other and have a similar distribution to that given in Eq. (13A.1), the Cth joint probability density distribution is the C time convolution of one video source, P_1, with itself. This is equivalent to saying the probability generating function (PGF) of P_C is PGF of P_1 to the power C

$$E(Z^{CX}) = [E(Z^X)]^C$$

The PGF of one source with the probability density function in Eq. (13A.1) is given by

$$E(Z)^X = \frac{1-a}{a\,(1-a^{Q_m})\,(1-aZ)} \qquad (13A.2)$$

where Eq. (13A.1) can be derived from (13A.2) by

$$P(Q) = \frac{1}{Q!}\frac{\delta^{(Q)}}{\delta Z}\,E(Z^X) \qquad \text{for } Z = 0$$

Thus the PGF of multiplexed sources is

$$E(Z^{CX}) = \left[\frac{1-a}{a\,(1-a^{Q_m})\,(1-aZ)}\right]^C$$

and the probability of Q packets being generated in the multiplexed link is

$$P(Q) = \frac{1}{Q!}\frac{\delta^{(Q)}}{\delta Z}\,E(Z^{CX}) \qquad \text{for } Z = 0$$

which leads to

$$P(Q) = \frac{1}{(1-a^{Q_m})^C}\binom{Q+C-1}{C-1}\,a^{Q-C}\,(1-a)^C$$

where

$$\binom{Q+C-1}{C-1} = \frac{(Q+C-1)!}{Q!(C-1)!}$$

Freeze-out occurs when the number of generated packets exceeds the number of time slots S, i.e.

$$P(Q > S) = \sum_{i=S+1}^{CQ_m} \binom{i + C - 1}{C - 1} \left(\frac{1 - a}{1 - a^{Q_m}}\right)^C a^{i-C}$$

which is a truncated negative binomial distribution.

Asynchronous system

As for the synchronous system, we assume C sources have already seized the link, thus eliminating the effects of the queuing delay to seize the link. This gives a pessimistic result, and the actual values should be more promising. We also assume that the human visual system can tolerate delays up to n television frames. Thus after a delay of n frames, the total generated packets are the packets already generated from the C sources plus the delayed packets from n frames earlier. In the steady state condition this is similar to generating data from $(n + 1)C$ sources and sending them into $(n + 1)S$ slots. Since the delay limit is n frames, excess packets are regarded as lost packets. Therefore, using an expression similar to the synchronous system, but with the new parameters, the probability of lost packets is

$$P(\text{loss}) = \frac{1}{(1 - a^{Q_m})^G} \sum_{i=H+1}^{GQ_m} \binom{i + G - 1}{G - 1} a^{i-G} (1 - a)^G$$

where $G = (n + 1)C$, $H = (n + 1)S$, and n is the number of frame delays.

PART 4

Retrospective

Image processing can be a very absorbing subject. Its aficionados happily while away the small hours crouched over screens, while software speeds through multidimensional tasks of semi-astronomical size. Yet there is a danger, given this fascination, that the subject can become too technical and introspective; the human dimension can be lost in forests of algorithms and mountains of hardware.

This book therefore ends with a retrospective and critique by Charles Nightingale which, though humorous, raises many serious issues. Some of these have already been addressed by those working in the field. Others have not.

14 Image processing in visual telecommunications: a lighthearted critique

CHARLES NIGHTINGALE

14.1 Introduction

Many years ago, when selecting a science fiction novel from the shelves of a bookstall in south London the present writer was sufficiently struck by the frontispiece of one book to buy it without further delay. The picture was well executed and bore the caption: 'The young policewoman fired several times at the bestial Neptunian, but the shots had no effect, and she was led away with thousands of others to a life of degrading captivity.' Since then one's tastes have hopefully become a little more sophisticated, but the memory of this appetizing picture followed by an appallingly bad story has recurred at the prospect of writing this chapter. It first calls to mind the ease with which a very boring tract can be written even when the subject matter includes bestial Neptunians, and if memory is correct, a second appearance of the then-famous Mushroom Men from Mars. How much more difficult, then, is the task of injecting some signs of life into image processing, a subject that rarely concerns itself with anything more unusual than a tiny grey reproduction of a photograph of a perfectly normal young woman with a caption like: 'Bloggs transform at 1.76 bits pel'? Fortunately that science fiction book also reminds one that here was a picture which—to an immature mind at least—was worth considerably more than a thousand words—about fifty thousand was the probable length of the story. It seems to confirm that images play some special role in the human psyche that can never be replaced by words, and urges us to try to understand some aspects of the purpose of visual telecommunication that are seldom discussed in engineering circles.

The use of images in communication has been an important activity almost since the dawn of man. Some authorities believe that the drawings of contemporary animals that can be found on the walls of prehistoric cave dwellings were for passing on information about hunting from experienced to inexperienced hunters. Pictograms, based on pictures of familiar objects, were the progenitors of writing. Religious authorities used icons to bring the saints to the minds of the faithful. Mysterious symbols have assumed world-wide recognition and importance. Later newspapers and magazines found the use of pictures invaluable. The cinema became an international obsession and, interestingly, in its early stages pictures without sound were able to attract people from their firesides where they could listen to sound without pictures. Nowadays images are important everywhere. X-rays play a key role in diagnosis of many diseases. Blueprints, layouts and drawings are essential for the design of almost every artefact that we use. The advertising industry uses still and moving pictures in every shape and form. We collectively watch our television screens for astronomical numbers of hours. We use computer graphics to educate, inform, and entertain us. We have conferences with business associates using video. Our industries are peopled by robots that use vision to interpret the limited environments in which they work. And in the future we are expecting to see our colleagues, friends, and family members when we speak to them on the telephone. We hope to match fingerprints and faces by computer in security work. Looking further into the future, and making assumptions about the future advances of machine intelligence, we can suppose that we shall see machines that use vision in much the same way we do, communication systems that depend upon understanding as well as coding of pictures, and greatly enhanced methods of scene recognition and understanding.

The large number of applications for images mentioned above makes no reference to the media by which the images are transmitted and presented to the user. In many cases the media were not electronic. Cave walls, paint, ink, parchment, paper, photographic emulsions and film were the main media prior to the advent of cathode ray tubes, and the modes of transmission were as crude as asking the viewer to visit the site of the pictures, or at best the postal service. Furthermore, many of the applications above seem hardly to be visual communication at all. How is a system for matching a fingerprint a form of visual communication, for example? It is communication in the sense that information about an image—e.g. the fact that it matches an image already held in a database—is communicated to the user of a system—perhaps over a channel that could not easily have passed the image itself. This is a loose use of the word communication. Robot vision is even less obviously a form of communication—although since information about its environment is communicated to the robot via its vision system the word is not completely inapplicable. At the other extreme visual communication is sometimes taken to mean the use of data channels that are not capable of transporting bits at a much higher rate than 2 Mbits/s for two-way exchanges of moving pictures accompanied by speech. Broadcast television and visual communications are regarded as completely separate concepts. Of course this is a ridiculous distinction to make if common sense is to be taken into account, since broadcast television is a very powerful means of visual communication—even if it is only one way. The distinction is really made to recognize the very different financial and technological factors that influence the two forms of communication. In comparing the two forms, broadcasting is likely to use a very small number of channels, each of which has a large bandwidth. Videoconferencing and videotelephony are likely, in the near future, to use a very large number of channels, each of which has a small bandwidth. In broadcasting only a few transmitters will be required, whereas in videoconferencing and videotelephony every user requires a transmitter. A broadcasting transmitter may therefore be a much more expensive item than a receiver. A videotelephone transmitter should aim to be a no more expensive item than a receiver. In broadcasting only a one-way channel is required, whereas in videotelephony a two-way channel is required. It is also the case that for some broadcasting applications it is expected that any process applied to a sequence of images for transmission purpose may have to be applied several times, whereas usually for videotelephony it will only be applied once. All these differences mean that the distinction made between the two forms is very significant—even if the term visual communications actually incorporates both.

Another form of visual communication that often demands similar approaches to videotelephony is still-picture transmission over telephone networks. Here there may be asymmetry in that there may be fewer and thus possibly more expensive transmitters, but the requirement for low capacity channel working is the same as for videotelephony. In both cases, therefore, a great reduction in the amount of data in a PCM image or sequence of images is required if transmission is to be feasible. The requirement for a cheap transmitter may mean that even if a good method of obtaining such compression were known, it might not be possible to produce an equipment at a reasonable price. The necessary compromise is usually made by reducing both the quality of images and the speed at which they can be transmitted. For this reason the topics of image processing for videoconferencing, videotelephony, and photographic videotex systems are similar in nature and can usefully be treated together.

14.2 Purpose of low bit rate visual telecommunication

14.2.1 Relationship between engineering and images

In glancing through this book, or any other on image processing, one is struck by two things. Firstly, there are lots of pictures—of people, houses, and other things—something not found elsewhere in the serious worlds of engineering science, computer science, and telecommunications. Secondly, there are an awful lot of very intricate formulae and equations; double sums and double suffices gaily abound, with numerous appetizing references to works on probability and statistics, linear operations, and other strongly mathematical sources. This slightly paradoxical confluence of simple, easily understood pictures of people, places, and things, with complicated, less easily understood formulae is at the heart of image processing for visual telecommunications. An example of this contradiction made rather a deep impression on the writer when he first became involved in image processing some years ago. A group of about ten visual communications engineers were standing around a monitor that was attached to a moving picture simulation system which was thought to be mildly defective. Ten eager serious faces stared at the screen with intent concentration. On the screen a lissom young woman led a group of children in a rhythmic dance or exercise; one of her young charges was a first-rate comedienne. She aped her teacher's movements with exaggerated silliness, from just behind where she stood. The child's antics were so funny that the writer expected the engineers to burst out laughing as he was. But when he looked along the row of faces he saw not a flicker of amusement or a glimmer of a twinkle in any eye. Like Cortez of old he gazed upon the scene with a wild surmise. Were visual engineers totally lacking in humour? No. Their indifference to the content of the scene arose from a more obvious cause. They were not seeing the pictures. They were looking at a CRT projection of a digital waveform—and noting the missing pixel. Had the picture been a set of unintelligible sinusoids and similar oscilloscope figures, the scene would have been harmonious and no incongruity would have struck the onlooker. Had the audience been ordinary people laughing and relating to the girl's impertinence, no special thoughts would have troubled the writer. But the deep significance of the scene was there for any to see who would. What a visual engineer sees in a picture and what a layman or laywoman sees are completely different.

The ramifications of this observation are manifold. At first it may seem a frivolous distinction. The engineers were very properly concentrating on the job in hand—diagnosing the fault on the simulation system. The writer was letting his mind wander. But a further example may begin to reveal the significance of the point. A man frequently takes pictures of his wife and children with a disc camera, and on the basis of the pleasure she derives from the results he decides to upgrade his camera. He reads a few photographic magazines, is seduced by the marvels of precision engineering that adorn their pages and soon equips himself with an expensive reflex camera. Having a mild love-affair with the new camera he finds a backnumber of his magazine and sees that his lens is capable of resolving 90 lines per millimetre. He runs off a roll or two of film and excitedly shows the crisply printed portraits he took to his wife. 'They're marvellous', he says, 'you can see every hair on your head.' She sees the cruel sharpness of the rendering of the wrinkles round her eyes and promptly says 'How ghastly'. But they *are* better, he thinks. The lens is better, the shutter speed is more accurate, the whole camera is better engineered.

This sort of sad scene can, and does, take place at the more elevated levels of image processing for visual telecommunications. A codec designer is demonstrating his new eighty-thousand dollar codec to a customer. The customer does not think much of the pictures and says: 'This codec doesn't give as good a picture as the Samurai one does it?' The codec designer assures him that the pictures are in fact better. 'The MSE is 30 per cent lower, and anyway you can prove that this Bloggs transform is optimal for a Markov process. The Samurai only uses a DPCM based quadtree scheme.' What does it matter what the pictures look like to some fool of a layman even if he is the customer? The coding method can be shown to be better *mathematically*!

14.2.2 Purpose of videotelephony

The point made above is immediately applicable to examining the purpose of videotelephony. Because the initiation of a full video telephone service would be a costly business, its purpose is often questioned. When the question is asked by an engineer or scientist he or she expects to hear an answer in terms of what information is passing—because in most areas of telecommunications such an answer is easily forthcoming. The information might be speech, for example, which can contain all the kinds of things that both engineers and laypeople call information: the baby has croup; the boss has an appointment; there is a change to the venue of a meeting; the son or daughter requires a loan for the last seven weeks of term; the order has not come through. Speech needs no explanation. Data is even more readily acceptable to engineers. Lots of numbers, all exactly correct, giving information about everything under the sun; credit worthiness; financial transactions; stock-market reports; addresses. To the engineering mind these things are actually more like real information than speech. The answers that can be given for the extra information supplied by the pictures in a videophone are distressingly less concrete. One can see if the speaker is smiling—or scowling. Visual language and facial expression are quoted. If the image quality is sufficiently good to show drawings or documents, this seems to be an important bonus. When the extra equipment required for videotelephony is considered—camera, display, and complex codec—the cost is seen to be at least one order of magnitude more than that of a standard telephone. Videophone begins to seem a rather dubious enterprise—a service with only rather nebulous extra information for a large extra expense.

What then is the justification for all the effort world-wide to move towards the old science fiction cliché of a videophone? The answer does not lie in trying to identify, or worse, quantify, the information exchange. One must not fall into the trap of supposing that the only purpose of a communications device is to communicate information of a self-evident and measurable type.

Rather one should observe the behaviour of people. For example, when they speak face to face they tend to look at one another, even when protracted conversations take place. It is irritating to have a person turn away while one is speaking. For this reason such actions—if there is no good reason—are taken as negative and bad. The speaker is showing pointed lack of interest—or unable to look one in the eye: he or she is seen as rude or shifty. A strong human preference is being shown. People like to look at each other when they speak. It is not essential to know why or what information is passing. It is evident that they do. We can look further into this question. We cannot say what information is passing during many preferred actions of human beings. What information passes when a wind-surfer repeatedly falls into the water? Very little presumably, since he will be familiar with the sensations that accompany a sudden immersion in cold water. Yet he will lay out a substantial sum to enable him to participate in the activity.

Of course we should look at situations where two people seem to be necessary—we see tennis players, chess players, or even gypsy fortune-tellers happily engaged in bipartite activities in which it is at least dubious whether much information is being passed. Yet mutual pleasure is obtained. Nearer to the point one may notice, for example, that car enthusiasts may spend considerable periods of time discussing the merits of various types of car, and the immediate assumption is that information is being passed. A careful monitoring of the situation shows that this is rarely the case. Each piece of information is known to all the participants in the discussion: all know, for example, that the camshaft of such and such an engine is mounted over the cylinders as opposed to any other position. Yet pleasure is evidently obtained by repeating the fact a number of times—a kind of group reassurance that may be reinforced by actually imitating the sound produced by an engine of such a type. This observation is not restricted to car enthusiasts. Most of us have subjects we like to discuss with like-minded friends, where little information really passes from one to another. The point is that the conversation itself can produce pleasure without any passing of information. The same may apply to telephone conversations. Many quite long conversations that one may overhear between two relatives living in different countries can be very expensive, yet are seemingly summarizable by the phrase 'Oh nothing really'. Such a thing can appear amusing or even comical, and yet it is a perfectly reasonable use of the telephone. The sense of loss due to long separation is ameliorated by even a very banal and uninformative conversation. It is this function of the telephone that is strongly reinforced by images. The information passing is of an inexpressible nature; we cannot name it. Yet its presence can be deduced from the intent way a newsreader's face is regarded on the television. It is also evidenced by the production for television of numerous discussion programmes and even obscure philosophical dialogues. The visual aspect of the medium seems to play little part. A radio programme would seemingly supply all the information that a viewer might require; in some cases the unprepossessing nature of the participants might even seem to make sound only a preferable option. Yet it is doubtful if such programs would obtain a fraction of the attention they get if they were broadcast in sound only. As a final emphasis of the point one may see people passing around photographs of themselves and their children—all of whom may be of familiar and perfectly ordinary appearance to the viewers—with great pleasure, though it is difficult to know what information is passing.

From what has been said we must deduce that vision has a strong attraction for *Homo sapiens*. We assume that in the right form videophone and videoconferencing will be saleable products. For still picture transmission, and in particular photographic videotext, the information content is more evident. Finally, moving picture systems for surveillance have obvious information-passing aspects.

Summarizing, we can note the following fact. As well as information some sort of bond reinforcement passes between people when they speak which, because it is more or less impossible to measure, is not usefully regarded as information. This bond reinforcement is greatly enhanced by the use of images and is the main purpose of videotelephony.

14.2.3 Purpose of videoconference

Videoconferencing is easier to justify—the exigencies of business often involve meetings between people at distant locations. Travel can be expensive and if all the functions of a meeting are possible using electronic means, then money can be saved by the use of videoconferencing. The greater expense affordable by business customers allows the systems to use more bandwidth and more complex codecs. The higher-quality pictures allow documents to be shown—graphs, design layouts, or other important discussion items. Even here counterarguments are available. A good audioconferencing system with still pictures and visual aids would be perfectly adequate provided speaker identification were made easy. We are left trying to justify a visual image of a person or persons as a very expensive add-on. The arguments that applied to videotelephony are also applicable here, and perhaps with more concrete reasons. The appearance of colleagues is important in forming judgements. However much we may dislike the idea, superficial aspects of our business acquaintances are judged important. A row of serious-faced men in dark business suits with neatly cut hair slightly greying at the temples has a very different effect on a viewer and his or her subsequent behaviour than would a row of younger men with long unkempt hair, beards, corduroy trousers, and sandals. One may recognize a person as having been encountered when working with another company even when his name does not ring a bell. A big powerful-looking man may regain some of the imposing air he may enjoy in a face-to-face meeting that is lost when only his voice is heard. A remark made with a slight smile may pass a necessarily unpalatable fact without the antagonism that could be aroused in a normal audioconference. A particularly prepossessing person of either sex may find that they are able to impress their own point of view on others more easily when they are seen. These kinds of very non-engineering aspects of videoconferencing in business are largely unspoken, and for that reason little recognized, yet they exist and there are many more examples of how we use the opportunity of seeing and being seen.

14.2.4 Drawbacks to two-way visual telecommunication

The main and currently overriding drawback to visual telecommunication is its cost. Both capital outlay and running costs are high. A camera and monitor are essential pieces of apparatus and a high data rate is required. Attempts to reduce the data rate by compression algorithms may reduce the running costs but can increase the capital outlay, since codecs often cost tens of thousands of pounds. It is this drawback, and attempts to ameliorate it, that motivate most image processing applied to telecommunication. It may be thought that once this problem is solved, whether by the provision of cheaper transmission—by optical fibre networks, for example, or by the production of cheap efficient data compression—then visual telecommunication would become a profitable field. But there are also other, more subtle problems to overcome before we can say this.

Just as we identified positive but nebulous benefits that come from videotelephony, there are real but hard to pin down objections. When shown demonstrators or prototype videotelephones many people immediately react by saying that they would not like to own such a device. There are several possible reasons for this.

Visual communication has a very fundamental difference from

spoken communication. Most of us—but not all—have a very large measure of control over what we say to others. When asked the question 'Does this dress *make* me look fat?', common sense queries may occur to us. Does the speaker intend to convey the impression that if the dress were removed the plumpness alluded to would be any the less noticeable? Yet we will not ask this, but will probably answer 'Oh no, you look very slim in it.' If asked what we did in the war, we have the choice of describing a heroic but imaginary contribution to the Battle of Britain, or telling the less flattering truth that we were withdrawn from the fray at an early stage on account of a condition known officially as 'lack of moral fibre' but colloquially as blue funk. Few of us, on the other hand, have total control over our appearance. We may wish that we had a dashing, attractive look more appropriate to the age of twenty than our true age of fifty, but we cannot easily assume such an appearance. Attempts made to do so often give a farcical, clownish air. At this age we may be less attracted to the idea of a videophone, since with an audio-only system we may cloak our advancing decay in the mystery of the disembodied voice. Similarly a lady who spends a large portion of the day producing an unsigned painting on her face will not wish to engage in a two-way visual communication prior to or during the process. Such a woman will be very dubious about the merits of a videophone. Even if we cannot believe that most people would object on these somewhat vain grounds, we can see that many people are uneasy in front of a camera.

This double-edged aspect of two-way visual communication is a very real obstacle to people's appreciation of the merits of a videophone. In business, at least we expect to be reasonably dressed and presentable most of the time. In the domestic environment this may be far from the case—and this is a significant point against it. Further, many people do not immediately see that use of a switch or lens cap could ensure that vision is not transmitted until it is desired. Some even fear the presence of a camera, which they believe may be constantly monitoring them even when no telephone call is in progress. These considerations seem nebulous and perhaps far fetched when compared to the improvements in picture quality due to arithmetic coding of the core coder output bitstream, but they are very much more important in the real world.

14.2.5 Purpose of photographic videotex

Of the three examples of visual telecommunications at low bit rates, this application seems to have self-evident purpose. Still pictures are used in many situations, and having immediate access to a large database of pictures or the ability to transmit a picture from one location to another at short notice is a very useful thing. In medical circles the possibility of transmitting X-rays or other kinds of body-scan pictures to a specialist could assist in rapid diagnosis and increase the probability of cures. In police work, the ability quickly to compare photofit pictures or other identification aids helps in the speedy apprehension of criminals. Fingerprints too can be quickly transmitted from one location to another and to a central database if a good means of transmitting them electronically exists. Visual aids at audioconferences should include the facility to discuss documents, design layouts, or other pictures. Estate agents could quickly show prospective buyers houses in other parts of the country if they were linked by a photographic videotex system. These applications seem self-evident and obvious. Others are frequently quoted. Electronic mail-order catalogues are often cited as a potential application for still picture transmission. An examination of some simple parameters soon convinces one that this may be an illusion. A large mail-order company may send out a large (500 page) catalogue every month which may have half a dozen illustrations on each page. A person can look through a particular section of such a catalogue—twenty pictures of lawn-mowers, for example—in a couple of seconds. He may later look in more detail at one picture, but our very well developed capability of taking in *what is important to us* at a glance means that to compete successfully with such a catalogue a very efficient system indeed would be required, as seen below. As a quick comparison a 64 kbits/s uncoded transmission of 20 16 bit/pixel images of 576×720 pixels would take about 35 minutes. Of course, we can improve the comparison with a more advanced system in which compression algorithms are used, and from some points of view—speed of database update, for example—the electronic catalogue can be superior.

14.3 Aspects of image processing related to purpose

Having considered the purpose of several low bit rate visual communications systems it is now possible to consider how the various factors mentioned impinge upon the required image processing. It is seen in very clear form in the last example. No one in their right mind is going to be happy to wait 35 minutes beside a £2000 videotex terminal for information that can be obtained from a £5—or free—catalogue in about two seconds. The data must be compressed. The same applies for reasons of economy to moving-picture telecommunications.

We look, then, at the possible specifications for the three applications for low bit rate visual telecommunications that we have discussed above.

14.3.1 Videotelephone

We make certain assumptions about what is required for a commercially successful videotelephone. We have supposed that the purpose of the videophone is an image reinforcement of the intercommunication of two people. We consider that a capability of showing pictures or documents is desirable but not essential.

For this application we recognize that a widely available switched network is essential. There is no point in having a videophone unless a fair proportion of the calls made are to other videophone users. We also recognize that the target price must be within the range of other commonly available consumer products that might be used in the home or by lower and middle management in industry and commerce. Personal computers and videorecorders might be good examples of items whose price that of a videophone could not reasonably exceed for business and residential use, respectively. Similarly the equipment should be physically small—perhaps ultimately no larger than a large standard telephone. These plausible requirements immediately lead to some fairly concrete specifications. The network over which the videophone should operate should be either the Public Switched Telephone Network (PSTN) or the Integrated Services Digital Network (ISDN) since these are the only general switched networks that are or will become widely available in the near future. At present no reliable way of transmitting acceptable moving sequences over the PSTN is known. There are some early attempts at looking at artificial intelligence approaches to reducing the amount of data transmitted—model-based coding, for example—but in the immediate future it is to the ISDN that we look as a medium for videotelephony. The ISDN allows two channels of 64 kbits/s and we therefore expect that the video can occupy a complete channel of 64 kbits/s with the speech using the other, or the video could occupy say 48 kbits/s with the speech making up the other 16 kbits/s for a single channel. Because of the need for this great reduction of data it is normally assumed that it is better to reduce the number of samples in the spatial domain before any coding takes place.

In practice this is a good approach since it reduces the amount of data that must be processed by the codec, which means that a less powerful and presumably cheaper processing system may be used. Since it has already been supposed that a small physical equipment is desired, the lower resolution is not a drawback. The pictures will be shown on a small display and the reduction in processing should result in a smaller codec. The poorer resolution can also mask the effect of using a smaller, cheaper, and poorer-quality camera, so the requirements of cheapness, physical size and data reduction all point to using a lower-resolution picture. Reducing the processing requirement still further we may allow a frame rate that is below that of normal television, yet still acceptable to most people. For these reasons we might consider 180×144 pixels to be a good picture format. The exact numbers are related to a common intermediate format accepted internationally for coding that was originally designed to compromise between the NTSC (Japanese and American) and PAL (European) television display standards. The general resolution seems to be acceptable on displays that are about a quarter the physical size of an average television set—and which would be likely to be used for videotelephones. The number of frames per second is less easy to quantify since the rate could vary with the picture movement and complexity, but somewhere between 5 and 20 frames/s would be acceptable. Such a resolution is, of course, not much use for showing documents, but in accordance with our opinion of the purpose of videotelephony we consider this to be of secondary importance.

14.3.2 Videoconferencing

In considering videoconferencing we can build upon some of the ideas of the requirement for videotelephone with modifications for differences in the purpose. The main impetus for videoconferencing is the perception in commercial circles that in principle it should be cheaper in many cases to have a videoconference in place of a face-to-face meeting where travel would be involved. It is not difficult to see that if a piece of equipment were to be used most working days of the year to save regular travel, the price of the equipment could be high provided the operating costs were low. Codecs priced at more than £50 000 are not uncommon at the present time. It is also true that a switched network is not essential for the success of a videoconferencing service, since regularly used leased lines may be sufficient for its purpose. For successful videoconferencing we thus see that no large commitment to a widely distributed switched network is required, nor is volume production of highly optimized terminals necessary. It is not surprising in the light of the above that videoconferencing, as opposed to videotelephony, is already a commercial proposition in everyday use. Because of this, and the immediate requirement for efficient compression algorithms, it is the potential videoconferencing market that has motivated much of the low bit rate videocoding research and development in recent years.

14.3.3 Photographic videotex

We assume that the maximum resolution that an ordinary television display can deliver is one essential mode in this system. This would allow the use of volume production monitors, and deliver a picture quality with which customers are familiar. A higher resolution would mean more expensive cameras and displays, and would put greater strains on the coding to achieve practical results with the larger amount of data.

The required transmission time is more difficult to assess. If an important X-ray or layout were being transmitted a few minutes could be quite acceptable, since at least a day would normally be required for the postal service to deliver a hard copy. On the other hand, as has been stated earlier, it is hard to compete with a mail-order catalogue, especially from the point of view of browsing. The time taken to view a host of pictures in such a catalogue is minimal—and any single one is probably of better resolution than the photographic videotex equivalent. The catalogue can be read in an armchair or other more comfortable location, and can be lent to others who may not have a terminal. The estate agent application lies somewhere in between the two and can serve as a useful example. If 40 or 50 houses are to be viewed we must have a reasonable browsing mode where a minute or so allows a quick scan of all the properties. If a second is the maximum permissible time for a single transmission then we require that $720 \times 576 \times N/64\,000$ is less than 1 second where N is the number of bits per pixel. This gives N as being a maximum of about 0.17. In practice this is difficult to achieve with acceptable picture quality with any known coding scheme, and the mode for quick viewing has been internationally agreed as 0.25 bits/pixel. An intermediate mode of 0.75 bits/pixel for good-quality pictures has also been agreed and a final mode in which no visible degradation of the picture is permissible, at 2.25 bits/pixel. The transmission times for these modes are 1.4, 2.8 and 8.4 s respectively, provided the build-up is progressive (the data that encoded the lower modes is utilized in the encoding of the higher mode).

14.4 Coding methods and picture quality evaluation

The first part of this chapter was devoted to a discussion of aspects of the use of pictures that are often ignored or misunderstood. The problem of determining good methods of preprocessing and encoding images is very strongly rooted in this area. The difficulty of assessing the success or failure of an image-coding process dominates many aspects of image-coding work, but is by its nature almost intractable. We see similar problems in the field of sport. An athlete who specializes in sprinting, for example, has a constant exact measure of his or her ability. If training is going well, times improve. A figure-skater, on the other hand, must constantly worry about what the judges will think. Will a spectacular programme with one significant impairment like a bad landing on a jump be deemed inferior to a perfectly executed but mediocre routine? To most people the objective form of judgement exemplified by a race is far superior to subjective forms based on opinion. The engineering mind in particular craves a simple numerical measure of success to such an extent that almost any physical measurement is considered preferable to the uncertainties of subjective judgements. Of course many aspects of engineering are very easily quantified in this way. If a good engineer builds a bridge he can predict the maximum load that it can carry under the circumstances in which the bridge is expected to be used. The maximum load will be a very significant measure of the performance of the bridge. He does not need to run subjective tests as does an image coder. All people, with only a very few exceptions, are agreed that a bridge that collapses under the weight of those who use it is unacceptable. Most people are satisfied with a bridge that enables them to cross safely, and those who are not—environmentalists, artists, architects, and other habitual troublemakers—are not the engineer's concern and he can do his mathematical calculations in peace. Similarly, in the communication field a transmission system for a series of data can have a calculable error-rate. The engineer performs a calculation that enables him to say he expects his system to have an error rate of, say, less than 1 in 10 000. When built, the system performs in this way and is deemed satisfactory.

Unfortunately none of this applies to low bit rate image coding. Once images are introduced the objectivity is lost forever; yet so strong is the desire to quantify the merit of coding schemes that unsuitable measures are often introduced and used to monitor the performance of a developing method independently of any subjective opinion as to image quality. The very complexity of the compression algorithms at low bit rates ensures that radically different methods produce radically different artefacts in the pictures, which are almost impossible to compare, and which in any case may produce different responses in different people. The image coder is left wondering whether his pictures with a small number of strange artefacts in otherwise clear, sharp images will be deemed inferior to pictures that are generally soft, yet show no particular artefacts. He is in a very similar position to the figure-skater mentioned above.

14.4.1 Mathematical models

Mathematical models of images and measures of quality can easily be made up, and plausible arguments advanced in their support. But at bottom they are flawed, and predictably so. A favourite model of an image is a first-order Markov process. It is not difficult to show that most parts of most images conform rather closely to a first-order Markov process, yet this is not a good reason to model an image in this way. A simple way to convince oneself that a better model for images must be found is by examining a line drawing of, say, a famous politician on a plain background. From a mathematical point of view a line drawing is effectively modelled by a constant almost everywhere. If we, therefore, transmit a constant level for the picture the mathematical error will be very small. Yet the resulting picture—a blank frame—is subjectively unacceptable. The points at which a picture is not well modelled as a first-order Markov process are the edges—unpredictable discontinuities that again form a negligible set of points compared to the aggregate of pixels. Yet as we know, they are the most significant parts of images from a subjective point of view. Of course it can be argued that if the edges are coded with a sufficient number of bits, since they are a sparse set the totality of extra bits required may be small, and the remainder of the picture will be well modelled as a first-order Markov process. The many important coding schemes that employ transforms that are optimal for a first-order Markov process—like the DCT—normally exploit this principle, by allowing a few blocks to transmit a large number of bits while the majority only transmit a small number of bits.

14.4.2 Mathematical models of error

The mean-square error mathematical measurement of picture quality is a poor indicator of subjective effects on impairments. At higher bit rates it is sometimes indicative of the likely acceptability of a coded picture, but at low bit rates it is a very poor measure because it does not take account of the masking effects of high activity near edges, nor does it recognize the extra subjective significance of coherent errors like block structure, ghosting, or contouring. It is easy to show that a coded picture may be subjectively far superior to one with a lower MSE (Fig. 14.1). If we take the same case of a line drawing obtained by some edge detection and thinning process from a full 16 bits/pixel photographic original we obviously have a very large MSE.

The black and white pixel values of the line drawing will all take the extreme values of 0 or 255, and the MSE, MSE1 say, is the mean-square difference between these and the multilevel image pixels. If we then form the MSE between the original and a frame in which every pixel is set to the overall average of the original, say MSE2, it is evident that MSE2 will be a lot lower than MSE1 in almost every conceivable case—yet subjectively of course the line drawing is infinitely superior to the constant frame. This may be an extreme case, but it neatly demonstrates the inefficacy of a simple mathematical measure in modelling the subjective opinion of human beings.

14.4.3 Filtering and down sampling

Another contradiction between the basic instincts and the quagmire of picture quality arises in connection with the sampling and subsampling processes. Basic knowledge from his college days tells an engineer that, according to a principle established by Nyquist, a picture that contains frequencies that are higher than half the sampling frequency cannot be perfectly reconstructed after it has been sampled. Armed with this

(a)

(b)

Figure 14.1 In extreme cases the MSE beloved of objective measure enthusiasts can be a nonsensical assessment of the subjective acceptability of a picture. (a) shows a picture of former international sprinter Kathy Cook. (b) shows a Markov process.

(c)

Figure 14.1(c) A crudely edge-detected and thresholded version of (a). If the mean-square difference between (a) and (b) is measured, it is found to be lower than that between (a) and (c), yet no one in their senses would find (b) a more acceptable rendition of the original than (c).

information, and with the only justification that he wishes to remove the frequencies above the half-sampling frequency, he introduces a low-pass filter. If this were an ideal low-pass filter he could feel confident that he could reconstruct his picture perfectly. Of course it is evident after even a cursory examination that the reasons for introducing the filter are nonsensical. If his original picture contained frequencies above half the sampling frequency, then by the correct theory of sampling we know that the picture can never be perfectly reconstructed. If his low-pass filter were ideal, then he could perfectly reconstruct the output of the filter—but there is no reason to suppose that the output of the filter is a subjectively acceptable picture. The issue is confused by the fact that an ideal filter is anyway unobtainable. It is often supposed that the unpleasant ringing effects that appear in images that have been passed though high-order equiripple filters are due to the inaccuracy of the approximation to the ideal. Of course this is not the case: a brick-wall ideal filter can cause severe ringing. This ringing is then removed by allowing a good proportion of the forbidden frequencies to be transmitted and the previously sacrosanct dogma of 'The Nyquist Criterion' goes by the board without a word of explanation as to why the attainment of the ideal resulted only in misery and dishonour. Confused groups of engineers then happily indulge in sterile discussions as to the correct specifications of a presampling filter in which the previous rigorous mathematical approach has been quietly abandoned in favour of vague rules of thumb more appropriate to the determination of the effects of the Black Moon occurring in the House of Mars in a horoscope. Yet the use of very expensive video filters continues to be justified in the belief that an eternal physical principle is being exactly and mathematically adhered to. If any doubts are ever raised they are quickly quenched by the ritualistic intoning of the word 'aliasing' as if it were a self-evident mortal sin compared to the venial transgressions of blur or ringing. It is not easy to find any reports of subjective testing of the effects of aliasing, which is not surprising since it is regarded as having evil qualities that go far beyond the bounds of mere picture impairment.

Engineers who are confronted by these arguments often point to the beneficial effects that a presampling filter has on picture quality from the point of view of noise reduction—and this is a perfectly valid reason why a filter should be introduced. However, it should not be regarded as a justification for chanting the time-honoured Nyquist incantations: such a filter could well be introduced even if there were no intention to follow with a sampling process.

A brief reprise of this section could lead to the conclusion that the writer wishes to belittle the abilities and work of engineers. This is very far from the case. Most of the confused and rigid thinking of which the engineers are accused is engaged in by most of us, as we advance in our knowledge. The present writer is as confused, and probably more confused, than many of his engineer colleagues. Indeed it was engineers who originally began to challenge the frequency-oriented thinking that this section criticizes. In short, it is the very confusion in our thinking that tends to promote more fundamental examination of basic concepts, and, in turn, overturns the rigidity of thinking from which most of us suffer to some degree.

14.4.4 Subjective testing

Stripped of both a useful image model and a good objective measure of picture quality, image coders should be forced to conduct extensive subjective tests to check the efficiency of their coding techniques. The various coding schemes would be simulated on suitable pictures or sequences and any new scheme would be judged against other existing methods by a series of properly conducted subjective tests. For various reasons this is very far from the truth. A search of the literature reveals very few reports of subjective tests that compare different coding schemes. Even in the international standards arena very important decisions have been taken regarding the choice of coding schemes without any properly conducted subjective tests.

There are many reasons for this. Some are not very good. Coding engineers find it difficult to believe that their mathematical precepts require any confirmation by subjective tests. Numbers—whether mean-square errors or measurements of rate distortion—have a definite, unchallengeable feel about them. Subjects for tests appear not to understand what they are doing. They state their preferences from a position of complete ignorance and have no idea of the underlying importance of the frequency domain or the statistical model on which the coding scheme is based. We could derive amusement from taking this misunderstanding further by recollecting scenes in which highly numerate engineers gaze portentously at test cards and gleefully note the strange and sometimes beautiful appearances of aliasing on images which have no earthly resemblance to any useful picture that might ever be transmitted. Yet the reasons for the absence of subjective tests go deeper than this emotional preference of engineers for figures to subjective opinion. Subjective tests are expensive and difficult to mount. They cannot, therefore, be used regularly to monitor the progress of a developing coding scheme. During the time between the development of the coding scheme and the evaluation of the subjective test results, enhancements to the coding scheme may be developed that to some extent invalidate the results of the tests. And it is by no means certain even that what subjects say in subjective tests is a good guide to how they would react to every-day exposure to the same differently coded pictures if they were in competition.

How then, in practice, are decisions made about the picture quality produced by compression algorithms? At best, *ad hoc* tests, in which different coding schemes are applied to agreed test sequences and images, are conducted by groups of image coders in international forums. Reasonable precautions are taken to prevent bias and a vote is taken. No account is taken of the fact that experts in image coding are probably a very bad sample. At worst the usually calm objective world of scientific research is invaded by the same kind of self-interested dishonesty and outrageous conceit that is seen in the field of fine art. Coding schemes are presented and their better features given high weights and their worst features ignored. Preposterous assumptions are made about the efficiency of future enhancements and the data compression is announced as if these mythical enhancements had already been incorporated. Special crafting of the algorithm is done to optimize it for the particular source pictures coded, although in practice these adjustments would not be possible. Other deviations from the path of scientific objectivity also occur, but we draw a discreet veil over them.

All this suggests that if really appropriate models for images could be developed, along with objective measures that accord with the results that can be obtained with subjective tests, a lot more progress could be made more quickly. The objective measure could also be invaluable in the error criteria used to encode pictures by such methods as recursive binary nesting and vector quantization.

14.5 Coding schemes

The choice of coding scheme, in the light of what has been said above, is a very tricky business. In most cases—and certainly in videotelephony, videoconferencing, and photographic videotex—an international standard is required. In order to achieve a standard, agreement is necessary between many nations, and between individual companies and authorities in each nation. In some fields standards have been established by the universal acceptance of some proprietary method of operation in view of its prevalence. In the fields mentioned there has been international collaboration in studying all the possible methods of coding, with a view to choosing the best, to preclude the later emergence of a superior but non-standard method. In principle each partner in a collaboration produces simulated results for one or more possible coding schemes using agreed source material. The best method from many points of view is then adopted, and further work in optimizing the scheme is carried on in collaboration and later in building hardware testbeds. Of course, as with any situation in which prestige and financial advantage are at stake, more than mere technical considerations play a part. What has been said regarding the difficulty of measuring picture quality allows numerous claims and counter-claims from proponents of coding schemes. Even where unbiased and objective judgements are made there are difficulties. If one particular method of compression has been developed by a large number of workers over a long period, it is likely to show better picture quality than a superior new method that has had little development. And there is an equalizing factor at work that favours the more thoroughly optimized methods. If a poor core coding method is followed by a variable-length coder or arithmetic coder to remove the remaining redundancy, these secondary coders will have a lot more redundancy in the data presented to them: they will, therefore, work very efficiently and will go a long way to making up for the inefficiency of the primary coder. Indeed there is some truth in an often repeated saying in the world of image coding: 'Any coding scheme will match any other provided you fiddle about with it for long enough.'

A large number of coding schemes have been studied around the world over the last ten or so years, and their names alone would fill a page if all were listed. Amongst the better known transforms are discrete cosine transform, discrete sine transform (hardly worth dignifying with a special name one would have thought), adaptive DCT,

Haar transform, Slant transform, Haar–Slant transform, Hadamard transform (a Walsh transform with a more exciting name), high correlation transform, low correlation transform, annihilation transform, Karhunen–Loève transform (said to be optimal, but only with respect to dubious measures of quality) and human observer oriented transform, as well as generalized transforms in case one wished to avoid the vulnerability of too specific a description. Other schemes not involving transforms also abound: DPCM, adaptive DPCM, vector quantization, block truncation coding, recursive binary nesting, progressive coding scheme, pyramidal coding scheme, sub-band coding, two-component coding, arithmetic coding, fractal coding and many others. For moving pictures, in addition to these we have conditional replenishment, hybrid predictive DCT and motion compensation.

Most of these schemes have been introduced with optimistic announcements as to their superiority for obtaining high compression without impairing picture quality. The compression ratio is easily measured, while the picture quality assessment is, as we have seen, a difficult and controversial area.

Although picture quality plays an important role in selection of a coding scheme—whether for a standard or any purpose—other important factors come into consideration, chief of which is ease of implementation in hardware. This constraint is gradually easing as processing becomes cheaper, and complicated schemes, which would have been much too processor-intensive to consider, are now feasible. At the present time, as far as the applications discussed are concerned, we are more or less at the stage where any process that generates pictures of the right quality would be implementable in hardware. Cost still remains a restriction, but in the foreseeable future it is likely that the efficiency of the algorithms will be the determining factor in what methods are adopted. Indeed with the present rate of advancement there is a real possibility that any video algorithm will be implementable on a DSP chip, and most of the problems in realizing a moving picture codec will be in the production of software, reflecting a current trend in telecommunications. In the case of the photographic videotex application, for example, the emerging standard stipulates that the compressed picture data can be decoded using software on an unmodified PC, and this has been achieved on an IBM 80386 processor. In the case of the videotelephone many organizations are implementing the coding scheme using programmable DSPs—only in the larger, faster and more expensive videoconferencing codecs is special-purpose hardware still being produced. The picture quality of 64 kbits/s coding schemes is currently rather poor though, so research into improved methods of coding is still a vital area for a future generation of codecs.

As it turns out, schemes based on the discrete cosine transform have been largely favoured in the standards arena in the last couple of years. For videoconferencing a motion-compensated hybrid predictive DCT scheme is emerging as a world standard. A modified version of this will possibly be adopted for videotelephony, and an adaptive DCT scheme has been accepted as a standard for photographic videotex. There is no reason to suppose that any alternative standards will appear for photographic videotex since the data compression methods used there are very successful, and pictures coded as low as 0.75 bits/pixel are of good quality. It is quite possible that better compression methods for moving pictures may be discovered—especially at 64 kbits/s. For the really low data rates that could be used over the PSTN, one or two methods are emerging. Model-based coding has been demonstrated at various conferences, and hardware for transmitting very simple cartoon-like images at perhaps 9.6 kbits/s, enabling deaf people to communicate using sign language, is currently being developed.

14.6 Summary

We have examined the most significant aspects of image processing when it is applied to low bit rate telecommunication—a field often referred to as visual communication. We have looked chiefly at three forms of communication: videotelephony, videoconferencing and photographic videotex. We have noted that although image coding is a subject replete with mathematically based theories, complicated algorithms, and advanced technology, its objectives are strongly rooted in difficult-to-quantify human psychological factors. We have seen that for moving pictures the purpose of communication is less obvious than that of speech, yet equally real. For still pictures we have recognized that although the purpose may be easy to see, the technological difficulties of creating a viable competitor to existing services—such as postal shopping—are paradoxically greater in some cases than those of videotelephony or videoconferencing.

We have examined the relationship between the applications and the required algorithms and seen the likely picture formats that have been, or are likely to be adopted as world standards. We have noted that the judgement of picture quality is a very difficult area, and that it is by no means certain that the best schemes are always selected when decisions about picture quality are made.

Finally we have seen that although numerous coding schemes have been described in the literature, there is a general trend towards the discrete cosine transform in the standards arena.

Numerically biased readers eager for the cabalistic pleasures of formulae and algorithms, may experience some disappointment at reaching this point in the chapter without a crumb of comfort, but they may console themselves with the fact that at least they may now leave once and for all the disturbing and dubious world in which the human brain and the world of images meet. The more adventurous may recognize the very real problems associated with relating the technology of image coding to the human ends that are its ostensible purpose; they may be led to consider further the possibilities of developing true human-oriented error measures and image models or to making a more rigorous study of human attitudes to videotelephony.

Bibliography

Subjective testing

Allnatt J. (1983) *Transmitted Picture Assessment*, Wiley, New York.

Visual telecommunications

Kenyon N. D. (1985) 'Audiovisual telecommunications services—a unified approach', *British Telecom Technology Journal*, vol. 3, no. 2.

Data compression

Jain A. K. (1981) 'Image data compression—a review', *Proceedings of the IEEE*, vol. 69, no. 3.

Unusual transform method

Haralick R. M., Griswold N. C. and Paul C. A. (1976) 'An annihilation transform compression method for permuted images', Society of Photo-optical Instrumentation Engineers, *Advances in Image Transmission Techniques*, vol. 87.

Index

Date Due

MY - 6 '97			